Understanding the World Economy

Fourth edition

Tony Cleaver

Routledge
Taylor & Francis Group

LONDON AND NEW YORK

First published 2013
by Routledge
2 Park Square, Milton Park, Abingdon, Oxon OX14 4RN

Simultaneously published in the USA and Canada
by Routledge
711 Third Avenue, New York, NY 10017

*Routledge is an imprint of the Taylor & Francis Group, an informa
business*

British Library Cataloguing in Publication Data
A catalogue record for this book is available from the British Library

Library of Congress Cataloging in Publication Data
Cleaver, Tony, 1947-
    Understanding the world economy / by Tony Cleaver. — 4th ed.
        p. cm.
    Includes index.
    1. International trade.   2. Economic development.   3. Debts, External.
    4. Environmental economics.   5. Foreign exchange.   I. Title.
    HF1379.C55 2012
    337—dc23   2012016036

ISBN: 978-0-415-68130-8 (hbk)
ISBN: 978-0-415-68131-5 (pbk)
ISBN: 978-0-203-08444-1 (ebk)

Typeset in Times New Roman
by RefineCatch Limited, Bungay, Suffolk

For Billy, George, Andrew and Paul: that they may find fulfilment in the world economy

Contents

Illustrations

Figures

Tables

Boxes

Preface to the fourth edition

We are living through challenging times.

Since the last edition of this textbook, the world economy has been in upheaval. A major shift in global fortunes is taking place that has not only led to a redistribution of economic power relations between an unexpected set of winners and losers, but inevitably produced a rethink in all those economic theories that we thought governed world affairs.

This text therefore reflects the changes that we are coming to terms with: major sections have been rewritten, priorities have been re-ordered and new chapters have been added.

The current Great Recession, which followed on from what was called the 2008 credit crunch, is the biggest shock to the world economy since the 1930s. There are many important issues that contributed to it and which flow from it that need to be analysed if we wish to understand what is going on around us and where it might lead.

Those issues include:

- the history of spending, indebtedness and uncertainty in Western households and governments;
- the rise of the cheap-labour manufacturers of China and India that have accumulated large trade surpluses and, with them, growing economic power;
- the liberalisation, globalisation, boom and bust of the world's financial industry;
- the causes of widening income and wealth differentials between and within nations;
- the growth and volatility of prices of basic commodities, such as oil, minerals, foodstuffs and property;
- disagreement, disillusion and uncertainty as to where Europe is heading;
- environmental exploitation and climate change;
- social, political and economic unrest and the fracturing of community;
- and lastly, the rejuvenation of the academic debate between economists over the extent to which free markets can be allowed to operate without government intervention.

The Queen famously asked of the economics profession why nobody had foreseen the financial crash and the subsequent Great Recession– a question that many are still struggling to answer and one that has led to a lively difference of opinion, driving economics back to recycle old philosophical differences. Not so much 'Back to the Future'; more like Forward to the Past.

This text's central purpose remains the same as before – to provide an intelligible analysis of the major developments in the world economy – but the author is more aware than ever that in trying to provide an answer to the above question, it is impossible to avoid taking a position and expressing an opinion on hotly contested academic issues. The Introduction that follows explains more carefully why, in economics, objectivity and freedom from error and bias is so difficult to attain.

Earlier editions of this text started with an account of different economic systems and a lengthy investigation of the reasons for the collapse of the command model. That is history now. In its place, the focus of Chapter 1 is on the growth of markets; how world trade has evolved; and the current different experiences of emerging and mature economies. There is now only a passing reference to the demise of the old Soviet Union.

Chapter 2 contrasts the differences between those who believe that market systems are prone to fail, and thus require active government regulation, and those who assert that it is governments that are most likely to fail and who blame much of the world's recent economic woes on excessive intervention. Differences between micro- and macro-economics, and neo-classical and Keynesian theory are introduced and explained. These differences are further developed and debated in the analysis of unemployment and inflation in Chapter 3.

Issues in world commerce, outsourcing jobs overseas, and the theory and practice of trade policies follow in Chapter 4. This leads to a new chapter on the wisdom of specialising in the export of primary products – particularly relevant to the livelihood of low-income countries – and subsumes the analysis of oil economics of earlier editions.

The treatment of common markets, money and banking, currency union and financial crises all deserve their own chapters as before – though much has changed over the last few years and thus much rewriting has been necessary. Three major themes conclude the text: global inequality, with more contemporary data and theorising on the differences between the rich and poor nations; an entirely new chapter on terrorism and how far economics can explain and illuminate this worrying international phenomenon; and finally an emphasis on environmental economics and climate change, and how the very long-run destiny of the planet requires us to take some very urgent and short-run policy decisions if we are to safeguard the future world economy. A conclusion on what I see as the major challenges facing us all finishes the text.

In order to deepen understanding, there is a resort to a little more economic theory and the inclusion of some extra analytical diagrams, though most are included in boxes so that the reader can avoid these if he/she chooses to do so. One unique feature introduced in the first edition was the construction of summary diagrams at the end of each chapter. These have been retained but extensively redrawn since much of the text has been entirely rewritten.

I hope you enjoy the story I unfold of how the global economy works, or fails to work. I accept that this is, inevitably, a personal interpretation, and if you are sufficiently moved to passionately agree or disagree with my analysis and understanding of the forces at play in the world then that is all to the good. Objectivity in the social sciences is only possible as the outcome of lively debate. To understand the world economy is a fascinating and unending study which I encourage you to continue.

Tony Cleaver
Bogotá 2012

An introduction to knowledge, science and social science

Knowledge is an unending adventure at the edge of uncertainty.

Jacob Bronowski
(*The Ascent of Man*, BBC 1973)

It is alleged that Einstein gave up economics – it was too difficult.

Or rather, it is not that the difficulty lies with the subject . . . but more with the *subject matter* (that is, you, me and the rest of society). Our individual and collective behaviour is unpredictable and not easily captured by natural laws.

Of course that has not stopped economists generating lots of laws, theories and models about how people earn and dispose of their incomes. Economics is a social science that attempts to analyse how we arrange our affairs and predict what will happen to us as a result. The problem is that all too often the unpredictable happens.

The uncomfortable, and truthful, charge that the economics profession (bar one or two individuals) was unable to foresee the cataclysmic **black swan event** of the 2008 financial crash is a painful reminder of the limitations of our science. We are all very good at producing stories of why a number of things happened in the past and how various forces interacted to produce a given set of circumstances (this text is yet another in that series!), but it seems we are pretty incompetent at saying where current circumstances are going to lead us in the future. Hindsight is so much easier than foresight.

Interestingly, economists share that weakness with the followers of Charles Darwin.

The theory of evolution has been similarly criticised for coming up with beguiling stories to explain why existing flora and fauna look and behave as they do, but it is claimed that such narratives have little scientific, predictive value beyond that. *Homo sapiens* evolved to lose their tails and walk tall on two legs as they left the forest to venture forth on to the plains, but how evolution is going shape our particular appearance in the future is impossible to say. Why? Too many variables.

The evolution of our physique is determined by how our biology reacts over millennia to the slow-moving forces of change in the physical environment. Major biological innovations may arise and adapt relatively rapidly at times – but even for such a frenetic animal as humankind, such punctuated evolution still takes place over geological time frames.

In contrast, the evolution of our society and the welfare of every individual within it is determined by the choices people make all the time in the rapidly changing economic environment that we create around us. In a world where all sorts of information flows across the globe at the speed of light and myriad social experiences crowd in upon each of us every day, our economic institutions and fortunes can grow, change shape or die out extremely quickly, indeed in the space of hours in some cases.

Trying to make sense of it all and make accurate forecasts about what will pass even in the shortest time periods is not easy. Predicting the evolution of economic phenomena *is* difficult.

The evolution of economics

How the science of economics itself has evolved over time is the result of a singular natural selection. It has produced a beast that seems to have found it very difficult to navigate its way out of the native forest where the species first arose. It is this characteristic which makes it very different from the so-called 'natural' sciences of physics, chemistry, astronomy and others.

Robert A. Solo, in *The Philosophy of Science and Economics* (Armonk, New York: M. E. Sharpe, 1991), wrote:

> There is this paradoxical contrast of economics and physics. The nature of the physical world has not changed in all the time and space within the scope of human observation but during the past two centuries there have been numerous revolutionary transformations in physics. During the past two centuries there have been revolutionary changes in the character and organisations of society but no transformation of the economics paradigm. In the one case the reference universe remains the same but the word concerning it and our understanding of it through physics has been fundamentally transformed. In the other there have been fundamental transformations of the reference universe but the word concerning it and our understanding of it through establishment economics has for the past two centuries remained unchanged.

Solo gets it more or less right when he talks about the economics paradigm although, as I hope to demonstrate below, I cannot agree with his characterisation of physics.

In 1776 Adam Smith wrote what is generally credited as the very first book on economics. It was *An Inquiry into the Nature and Causes of the Wealth of Nations*, and a better title to sum up what economics is all about I cannot think of.

In this text he set out the first systematic analysis of how a modern **market economy** operates and, in introducing perhaps the most famous idea in all economics, he explains it thus:

> Every individual endeavours to employ his capital so that its produce may be of greatest value. He generally neither intends to promote the public interest,

nor knows how much he is promoting it. He intends only his own security, only his own gain. And he is in this led by an 'invisible hand' to promote an end which was no part of his intention. By pursuing his own interest he frequently promotes that of society more effectually than when he really intends to promote it.

The argument that society is best served by allowing individuals to conduct their own business without interference from any higher authority, that a market economy automatically organises itself and is self-equilibrating, is one that has been extensively developed over the years and is the dominant paradigm that Solo refers to above. The growth of western industrialised nations and the eclipse of the alternative of **central planning** as embodied in the old Soviet Union is cited as evidence of the superiority of the market model. We will examine critiques of this model throughout this text in chapters that follow, but the evolutionary supremacy of market systems of economic organisation cannot be doubted.

From the industrial revolution; from imperialism to fascism to communism; from two world wars and many regional ones; from a Great Depression to a Great Recession; and up to modern concerns of environmental degradation and climate change; through all that – the dominant view on the best way to organise the world economy has come back time and time again to the view that free trade and unfettered markets are best.

There are, however, undoubted problems with market systems and some are of immense significance as we shall later consider. As a result of such concerns, critics have periodically driven the free market animal back into the woods from which it wishes to emerge . . . but the problems of alternative forms of economic organisation have proved in the end to be even greater, indeed terminal. Thus the paradigm of market economics still reigns supreme.

Natural sciences, in comparison, appear to have made a steady progression from the earliest philosophers through distinguished contributors such as Galileo, Newton, Marie Curie, Einstein, up to the present day. The current theories of the make-up of the universe, and of the opposite, sub-atomic world, bear little relation to what was earlier held to be true. We no longer believe the world to be flat, or that light travels in straight lines. Thus modern researchers intent on pushing back the boundaries in physics, medicine or astronomy do not feel the need to refer back to the founding fathers of their disciplines to add authority to their arguments . . . which is not the same with modern economists who frequently invoke the names of Smith or Keynes (a towering influence, of which more later) to advance their views: more evidence of the circular evolution of this social science.

But a word of warning here: the very fact that all scientific theories have a history should make us aware of their fallibility. Philosophers have known for millennia, economists have known for the very much shorter period of two centuries, and even physicists (who should have known better) now understand, that none of our beliefs, none of the laws humankind has created, can ever be taken as certain. *All* knowledge is uncertain.

The philosopher and mathematician Bishop Berkeley famously argued that we cannot know anything outside the reach of our senses. All knowledge is based on perception. But our perception is necessarily subjective and uncertain. Hence all knowledge is uncertain.

The scientist, philosopher and media presenter Jacob Bronowski characterised knowledge and certainty as opposites – to be knowledgeable is to be uncertain; to be certain is to close your mind to knowledge (*The Ascent of Man*, London: BBC Books, 1973).

The notion that the physical world has not changed throughout all human history is thus false. What is out there is inseparable from us. It changes as we change. The laws that 'govern the universe' are in this way like the ones that govern our society. They are invented by us . . . and we keep changing them! True, the laws of physics are more reliable and have a shelf life longer than those of economics. But that is because atoms, stars and galaxies move in more predictable ways (we think) than humans.

To pursue this further: what observers actually see at the other end of the telescope, or microscope, or in the data surveyed, is merely what they *think* they see. As scientists, we attempt to measure what we think we see, looking for patterns from which we can then induce laws.

But what is a pattern? Only something that makes sense to us; which we can relate to previous experience. All science is subjective: what we see depends on who we are.

I'm told that quantum mechanics is pretty baffling, that it contradicts all previously known laws. Modern economic developments are similarly baffling for exactly the same reason. But whereas your body doesn't fall apart just because your sub-atomic components are not doing what previous theory predicted, the world economy *has* recently come frighteningly close to a catastrophic implosion because its individual components were similarly renegade.

Western economists, governments and central bankers thought they had the recipe to ensure sustained economic growth with neo-classical policies derived from Smith's 'invisible hand' . . . only for such certainty to collapse along with that of world trade and incomes in 2008.

Ouch! Economic theories, like them or not, have a very real impact on all our livelihoods. John Maynard Keynes, the radical who challenged classical theory, is responsible for the second most famous quote in economics:

> The ideas of economists and political philosophers, both when they are right and when they are wrong, are more powerful than is commonly understood. Indeed the world is ruled by little else. Practical men, who believe themselves to be quite exempt from any intellectual influence, are usually the slaves of some defunct economist.
>
> (*The General Theory of Employment,*
> *Interest and Money*, London: Macmillan, 1936)

Between these two giants of economic thinking – Smith and Keynes, and the neo-classical and Keynesian schools of thought that followed them – are played out the contrasting theories of economics that influence all our predictions and policy-making today . . . and incidentally keep turning the subject back to its beginnings as each generation has to decide for itself just precisely how far the market system can be allowed to operate free from any intervention.

Scientific method

Science advances by employing the tried and tested formula of **scientific method**. This is the time-honoured, systematic and rigorous procedure that must be satisfied if research findings are to have any acceptance among the scientific community. It involves the observation of phenomena, generalising of hypotheses, deduction of predictions and testing them for corroboration or falsification of theory. These are the essential steps in any scientific investigation and, if they can be replicated, they can lead to laws that build on all those from Archimedes to Einstein.

At every stage in this process, however, there are difficulties when we try to apply this methodology to the social, as distinct from the natural, sciences. Objective recording of data is more difficult, for example, when people are studying people. What one observer perceives from a given social phenomenon another will not. The cultural values the observer brings to the scene are inextricably bound up with his/her allegedly objective report.

Everyone has prejudices. We cannot avoid them since we make judgements every day based on our (inevitably limited) perception of others. It is thus impossible to be completely value-free.

In addition to the difficulty of defining and measuring certain phenomena in principle, this problem is compounded in practice by whatever technology we employ and the filter it inevitably imposes on the data produced. Even supposing there was agreement between countries on what constitutes unemployment, or how we might evaluate capital, the accuracy and reliability of data gathering can be questionable. Just counting the number of people is difficult enough in some places, let alone calculating what they do or produce.

What we observe to be happening in the world at large, therefore, is inevitably blinkered, right from the start. Our access to information is limited by technology and unreliable data, and even where our viewpoint is crystal clear our own perception is never uncluttered. What face do you first see in a crowd? Your own. All observation is to some degree subjective: you see what you best recognise.

Generating universal laws – the next stage in the scientific process – becomes more difficult the greater the complexity of the subject under the microscope. A fundamental difference between natural science and social science is the distinction between homogeneous and heterogeneous evidence that we have already touched upon. In natural science you deal with discrete data that are identical and behave the same way under similar circumstances (one hydrogen atom is the same as another). In social science our different units of data (people) are not alike. We can make relatively complex statements about the world in physics based on relatively few experiences and can hold these views with something close to certainty. We know, for example, when Halley's Comet will return for thousands of years into the future, thanks to remarkably few observations. We cannot make quite such confident claims about the world in biology (plants and animals constitute heterogeneous data also) and even less about humans. Who knows with any certainty when output and employment in Europe will return to pre-crisis levels?

There are numerous general laws in physics, that most respectable, forecastable of sciences. These are accepted by the scientific community and are of universal applicability throughout the cosmos as far as we can see. (Note that all such laws, as I have said, will have a 'sell-by' date. That is, there comes a time as our knowledge improves when they must be revised and replaced by a new scientific paradigm – Newtonian physics was surpassed by Einstein, for example – but the point is that in the meantime, given our limited vision, our laws of light, gravity, etc., are upheld everywhere we look, without exception.) They are general, universal axioms, infallible enough to send spaceships to the moon and back. Natural sciences based on more complex building blocks (e.g. organic chemistry) will have substantially fewer laws. In biology, there is only one: the theory of evolution – and that has limitations of scientific applicability. In economics, which has more scientific techniques of enquiry than any other of the humanities, there are none: all attempts at general laws are only statistical tendencies, where exceptions abound (though see the reference to Douglass North in Chapter 10). General laws in economics only apply if certain assumptions are maintained. (If workers ask for more wages, then assuming their motivation, efficiency and productivity do not change, businesses may employ fewer . . .)

Deducing specific predictions from general laws in social science is not too easy either. Or rather, predictions may be precise, but they cannot be used to falsify or corroborate hypotheses with a great deal of certainty since – unlike in laboratory experiments – other factors in society can never be held constant. (Did increased government spending stave off deepening recession or was it an irrelevant coincidence?)

This is a problem that laboratory science knows well enough (you may have done the experiment wrong!), but whereas the pure scientist can do the experiment again (although at a cost) and isolate the variables better next time, the social scientist has to take the world as he/she finds it, along with all its 'imperfections'. Unravelling what has been going on in society, and whether certain factors have had more or less influence than others on subsequent events, is thus extremely difficult to determine when all sorts of things are happening all the time. Some scholars have asserted that since falsification/corroboration of general laws in economics is impossible to achieve, so the whole attempt to apply Popperian scientific methodology is pointless. This seems somewhat extreme – we can rely on the scientific searchlight in some areas, if not all.

As a result of these difficulties, in comparison to the natural sciences, social scientists recognise the need for much larger and more representative samples, and much greater care in their interpretation, in order to make reasonable claims to knowledge. They are increasingly turning to more sophisticated computational techniques to assist them. Even then, there is an inevitable lack of precision: as the price of oil rises, people will generally buy less of it – a 'law' in economics with a great deal of statistical support – but exactly how much they will buy next time is more difficult to say. Contrast this statement with what can be asserted if the *temperature* of oil rises: chemical engineers in oil refineries can predict to a calculable degree exactly what will happen to it.

A final point of caution: humankind has an insatiable curiosity and a capacity to theorise in the search for causes. But the patterns of economic development that we observe and the models economists have devised to simulate them and predict what will happen are, in the end, based on irreducible uncertainties. To ignore this, to fanatically adhere to one particular paradigm or another, is foolhardy. Indeed it can be fatal where such certainty dictates the implementation of life-changing policies.

There are always some people who cannot accept not knowing why things happen and will rush into any causal explanations – usually those that confirm them in their existing prejudices – rather than admit to uncertainty. When such people are in the seat of power, the outcomes of their decisions will affect the lives and livelihoods of millions. All the more reason therefore to be cautious in our propagation of economic theories.

All societies somehow acquire institutions to govern them (with varying degrees of success), which is why economics can never escape the debate as to how they should operate. Are markets best left to regulate themselves or must we rely on the whim of governments and political influence? If the wealth and welfare of some nations outperform their neighbours, just why is that? Are there any lessons that policy-makers can learn and apply to benefit others?

At the end of the twentieth century, many free marketeers thought that their model had all the answers . . . only to be proved wrong with the biggest economic crisis since the 1930s. If anything, recent experience should have taught economists to be humble. It does us no good to pretend we know how best to organise our economic affairs when in fact all knowledge is based on ever-shifting foundations. It is too easy to leap to erroneous conclusions when surveying complex social phenomena. One of literature's most famous social scientists, Sherlock Holmes, knew what he was up against: 'It is a capital mistake, Watson, to theorise before one has sufficient data' (from *Scandal in Bohemia*). This is advice we should all take note of: suspending judgement is better than slipping into prejudice.

Key words

Black swan event Something contrary to experience and expectation; a complete surprise of momentous and long-lasting impact that was not computable beforehand, but in retrospect is rationalised and understood, and recriminations abound that it could have been predicted. Many historical turning points, wars, natural disasters, technological breakthroughs and unique artistic achievements are black swan events.

Central planning Instead of the movement of prices indicating where resources should be most profitably allocated, an organising committee of central planners may take over this function – moving society's assets to employments that they

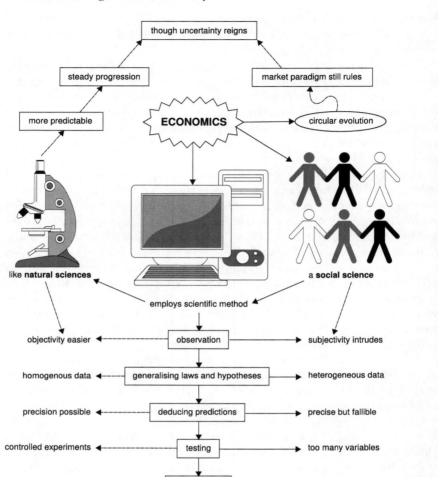

Figure 0.1 The themes of the introduction.

deem important; allocating final products to consumers not on the basis of who can pay most but by deciding who is most deserving. Central planning was characteristic of the command economies of the old Soviet Union, Eastern Europe and communist China until the market model superseded it. Planning is still important *within* nations: for example, the armed services, the police force, state education, Britain's National Health Service, all employ central planning, not prices, to allocate their resources.

Market economy A market economy is based on secure property rights, where traders can freely meet and exchange goods and services with minimal transactions costs, and where prices are agreed between many buyers and sellers – the impersonal forces of supply and demand. People sell their labour to private enterprise and use their incomes so earned to purchase whatever goods and services they desire. The price mechanism is the decentralised, invisible and automatic organising instrument of the economy – the movement of prices indicates to producers and consumers where they can best employ their resources.

Scientific method The progress of scientific advance began when people started to accept that things happened not because of the will of the Almighty but rather because of certain forces or laws accessible to humankind's understanding. Thus observations are made, raising a question as to why certain phenomena occur. A hypothesis is framed as a suggested reason; predictions are deduced and tested to see whether or not the hypothesis is robust. A scientific test attempts to isolate all variables and measure the effect of one input on the subject under study. If the subject reacts as predicted, the hypothesis is corroborated or supported (not necessarily proved true).

1   Going to market

As I was going to St Ives I met a man with seven wives,
Each wife had seven sacks, each sack had seven cats,
Each cat had seven kits: kits, cats, sacks and wives,
How many were going to St Ives?

There are several towns called St Ives in England. This traditional nursery rhyme and riddle is most probably based on the market town in Cambridgeshire. Despite appearances, only the narrator is going to St Ives, although he meets a man who is coming away with what seems like enormous wealth. But there is a cryptic message in this tale. 'Never buy a pig in a poke' is an old saying, 'poke' being a sack. That is, always check thoroughly what you think you have paid for. Unscrupulous traders would put a cat into a sack and pass it off as a piglet, so the buyer thinks he has bought an investment for his family until he opens it up and 'lets the cat out of the bag'.

Markets can create great wealth . . . but if not regulated properly they can be a means to exploit the unwary, subtract value and add despair.

Market systems have become the chosen form of economic organisation for most of the world now, in that a growing number of countries have introduced policies to increase the role and efficiency of markets within and across their borders. As a result, the world economy is undergoing momentous changes. Within the space of a generation, the way of life of billions of people across the globe has been transformed and the welfare of almost everyone else not directly involved has similarly been affected.

An increasing movement to, and freeing up of, market forms of economic organisation – and the benefits and costs this has brought with it – has therefore touched the livelihood of just about every person on the planet. The jettisoning of outdated systems of central planning, the spectacular economic growth of China and India, and the liberation of private enterprise from the restraints of central authority within developed and developing countries alike have brought billions of producers and consumers into direct contact with one another as the forces of globalisation have been released.

But just as emerging markets have been celebrating their economic freedoms, the richer industrial economies have been convulsed by the greatest financial crash and ensuing recession since the Great Depression era of the 1930s.

Market economic systems thus appear two-faced: offering increased hope for a better life for one half of the world, and the promise of debt, doubt and depression for the other half. And just for good measure, environmental degradation and climate change lie in wait for the future.

Organising world economic affairs does not appear too easy. This chapter looks in more detail at the nature of markets, their impressive adaptability, and how they may create, and sometimes destroy, wealth.

Markets and prices

Classical economic theory, which dates back to Adam Smith, emphasises the importance of entrepreneurs pursuing their own profits and thereby acting to serve consumers' interests. In any market place, it is argued, the seller of goods and services best helps him- or herself by aiming to please the customer. If each trader operates like this then, by the automatic movement of market prices, the overall economy adjusts itself to secure efficient outcomes for all – as though society was organised by an 'invisible hand'.

Impersonal prices are the essential allocating mechanism. There are two dimensions to this argument. On the demand side, there is **consumer sovereignty**. That is, if consumers increasingly desire to wear, say, denim jeans rather than woollen lounge suits, then the immediate effect of excess demand for the former will tend to push their prices up. Meanwhile unsold stocks of the latter will prompt price cuts. These price movements thus act as a signal to suppliers and retailers: they make more profits by switching from formal attire to an increase in production and delivery of the more popular casual wear. The effects will percolate all the way through the economy and overseas to the primary producers of cotton rather than wool. As demand and prices change, so wages and employment of resources will move similarly. Thus changes in consumer preferences on one side of the world may change employment and incomes on the other.

Price effects also work in the opposite direction. Consumers are really only half-sovereign. On the supply side there may be technological breakthroughs or shortages that impact on production costs. If existing oil supplies are running low and new discoveries are not keeping pace with demand, then the price of oil must rise. This signals a variety of changes for producers: renewed search for more oil and innovative technologies to help plumb previously uneconomic depths; also new investment in alternative energies which now become more profitable as businesses race to serve the unsatisfied demand. Additionally, there is enforced oil conservation on the part of consumers and more oil efficiency, if not actual replacement, by the manufacturers of engines and turbines and the providers of transport and energy services.

Changes in demand or supply conditions in the market place impact on prices. This communicates the need for adjustment to all related parties so that, in total, there are neither shortages nor unsold stocks of goods and services, and nor are there any unemployed or wastefully deployed resources.

So the theory goes. This automatic balancing of market systems is thus tremendously attractive on two counts. Firstly it is economically efficient. No scarce resources are wasted; no predominant consumer demand goes unserved. Secondly, especially for those who have laboured in the past under tyrannical regimes, it is liberating for all market participants. Consumers and producers are free to choose how to employ their efforts and how to spend their earnings. Any deal in the market place can only be struck between buyer and seller if both parties are satisfied with the outcome.

The same market system, it is argued, functions just as successfully for banking and financial services. Note that money, and promises to exchange money, can move much faster and transfer their allegiance far more quickly than land, labour or fixed capital. Excess demand or supply can therefore bring about a movement of financial resources very rapidly indeed to secure equilibrium between those who want to save surplus funds and those who want to borrow.

Why should governments interfere with such a process? At best it would be misguided since people know best what they want and it is not for some authority to try and 'improve' our choices; and at worst it would raise the suspicion that governments want to interfere with private markets in order to promote their own political ends or for corrupt self-enrichment.

The foundations for flexibility

The key to the success of market systems has been their flexibility and responsiveness to changing economic circumstances. Unlike centrally planned, **command economies** or some traditional cultures – where permission must usually be sought from a superior to experiment with new ways of consuming or producing things – decision-making in market economies is devolved down to the level of interested participants. Clearly some laws are necessary to prevent very anti-social activities, but in general the market leaves the individual alone (*laissez-faire*) to run his or her economic affairs within certain clearly defined limits.

Consider world economic growth. One of the puzzles of economic history is why agricultural and industrial revolutions occurred first in relatively small northwestern European nations rather than in the far more populous, well-organised and originally richer empires of East Asia. The record of Chinese technological prowess is dazzling – from the introduction of new crops and irrigation systems, to the invention of printing, the compass, gunpowder and ocean-going ships. In most cases these advances took place in the Orient centuries before similar practices were followed elsewhere in the world.

But the reason why these technologies did not bring the economic rewards in China that they later did in the UK, for example, was because the spread of ideas in this East Asian empire was subject to feudal control and was not led by market incentives. A number of social and economic factors came together in northwest Europe in the eighteenth century to lay the foundations of modern market organisation and so create an entrepreneurial and dynamic environment that was to generate exponential economic growth.

- Of prime importance are secure and widely dispersed property rights. People will only invest in an enterprise if they are assured they will have access to future returns, free from theft from others or confiscation by the state. Title to land and capital and to an individual's own labour must be established and protected by law before any employment and trade can flourish.
- A resort to science and experimentation comes next. The freedom to be intellectually curious and to challenge existing beliefs leads to the growth and application of knowledge. 'Learning by doing' permits technologies to improve and outputs to rise, provided that the incentive of rewards is guaranteed.
- Competition between rival producers to capture the custom of uncommitted consumers is vitally important as a stimulus to innovation, efficiency and keeping product costs down and quality up. If one business grows to take over all others and monopolise production then beware – the abuse of power to exploit the market will surely follow.
- Consumers will shop around and resources will transfer their employment – thereby guaranteeing flexibility – if information is readily available, transport costs are not prohibitive and thus markets are free to grow and integrate over time and space.

How did these most fundamental of market characteristics interplay in the course of economic history?

Excessive power must first be curtailed if the strong are not to dominate the weak and impair enterprise and innovation. The original Magna Carta, or great charter, was signed in England in 1215 between King John and representatives of the people to limit the authority of the monarchy, to ensure that none were above the law, and to protect all free men from arbitrary exercise of power. From that date on, the conduct of commerce began to grow. Although the movement of land, labour and capital was then tied by custom, religion and traditional employments, an entrepreneurial merchant class arose in Europe and plied its trade overland (Marco Polo first set off to China in 1271) and across the seas (Columbus famously sailed west in 1492).

Technological revolution

Competition between western merchants to secure trade advantage, with no supreme ruler determining which specific enterprise could or could not succeed, led eventually to breakthroughs in science, navigation, ship design and new forms of banking and finance. Contrast these developments with the over-centralisation of Chinese authority which treated technology as the gift of the emperor who alone could decide where it might be applied. For example, in 1432, despite a vast fleet and world-leading naval architecture at the time, the emperor of China decreed that ocean-going ships were to be outlawed, thus severely impairing his country's subsequent progress in trade, technology and economic growth (Jared Diamond, *Guns, Germs and Steel*, Norton, 1997).

In Europe, meanwhile, learning became established in universities and the spread of ideas could not be curtailed by state monopoly. Diffuse cultures, free movement and the lack of centralised control meant that any and all beliefs and practices could be challenged (see Box 1.1). This was also aided by the fractured physical and political geography of the European continent where, in the extreme, escape from repression in one country could quickly be achieved by moving across a nearby frontier, or setting sail like the Pilgrim Fathers.

A succession of enclosure acts which accelerated throughout seventeenth-century England concentrated landholdings in family farms, eliminated low-productivity open-field systems and facilitated a radical transformation of agricultural practices. With property rights delineated, now there were incentives to produce an agricultural surplus. New crops and selective breeding of livestock; mechanisation; management of fertilizer, irrigation and field rotation; all took place alongside the construction of canals and navigable waterways, and later roads and railways, that linked local to national markets and thence international exchange.

This was the era of agricultural and then industrial revolution. (See Figures 1.1 and 1.2.)

Box 1.1   Jethro Tull, eighteenth-century genius

Stable property rights, the resort to science rather than religion and the rewards of travel all came together in the example and influence of one man. Jethro Tull, born in 1674, went as a student to Oxford to study law. Whilst there, he also took to music and became an amateur organist, and it was his interest in this instrument's internal mechanics that was later to inspire him. Tull moved to London and became a barrister, although he never practised. Instead he took a tour of Europe where he visited vineyards in Italy and France before returning to the UK and his family's farm. An educated man, stimulated by what he had seen on the continent, he turned his mind to how best to improve cultivation at home – experimenting with various means of tilling the soil, applying fertilizer, watering and managing crops. He developed the first mechanised seed drill in 1701, applying the technology that regulated the passage of air into an organ pipe to the problem of regulating the input of seeds into his horse-drawn drills. Tull also wrote texts on the application of science to agriculture, and the brilliance of his ideas and his technological innovations are credited with helping to revolutionise the practice of farming, increasing outputs and stimulating related agricultural experimentation for more than a century.

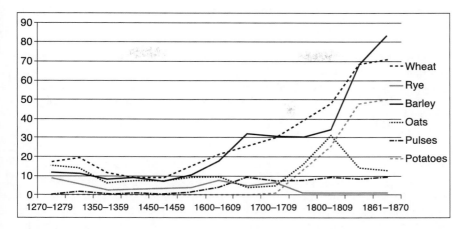

Figure 1.1 Growth in English arable output, net of seed and animal consumption: 10-year averages, in million bushels. Note that after a long gestation period, the take-off accelerates from 1700.

Source: *British Economic Growth, 1270–1870*, Broadberry *et al*, 2010.

Technologies developed in one employment could spill over to others. Cottage industries like weaving and pottery that originally occupied labourers on the farms in the slack season were now spun off into local towns and factories. Steam power used first for pumping water then drove industry and transport. Agriculture and industry became integrated in exponentially expanding markets. This process spread continuously outwards and onwards, sometimes fast, sometimes ·slow, linking markets, provoking innovation, promoting trade and increasing incomes in an ever-increasing virtuous circle.

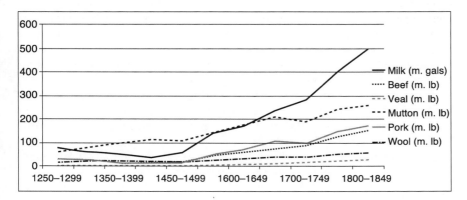

Figure 1.2 Output in English pastoral farming – a similar pattern to above.

Source: *British Economic Growth, 1270–1870*, Broadberry *et al*, 2010.

Writing in 1776, Adam Smith made a famous reference to workers in a pin factory where he observed:

> One man draws out the wire, another straights it, a third cuts it, a fourth points it, a fifth grinds it at the top for receiving the head; to make the head requires two or three distinct operations; to put it on, is a peculiar business, to whiten the pins is another; it is even a trade by itself to put them into the paper; and the important business of making a pin is, in this manner, divided into about eighteen distinct operations . . .

Smith estimated that somewhere between a *240 and 4800-fold increase in productivity* was made possible by dividing the labour in this pin factory. Specialisation, and the division of labour this affords, permits a great increase in outputs and a great reduction in the average cost of production. Thus the factory age and the era of mass production took off, heralding the modern era of self-sustaining economic growth.

Note the essential organising principle here. Smith emphasised that specialisation, and all the benefits this could bring, was limited by the *extent of the market*. There is no point in mass producing pins, or cars, or insurance services, or indeed any product, if you cannot sell them, if there is insufficient consumer demand. Similarly, just as final goods can only be sold if trade reaches out to distant consumers, so connected markets for labour, land and capital are equally needed to bring resources into employment and to tempt them away from low productivity enterprises and into more profitable ones.

North-western Europe saw the world's first concentration of modern industrial and economic power, and the reason for its success was because it developed the markets to mobilise its resources and sell its produce. As trade expands, it allows participants to get rich. (See Figure 1.3.)

Economic growth comes from employing increasing quantities of land, labour and capital inputs *and* by increasing the quality or productivity of each input. The application of labour and draught animals to the land is typically the first driver of growth until the limit of employable land is reached. This is known as the extensive margin. From then on, intensive use of given resources is required, and, necessity being the mother of invention, more and more efficient ways of combining existing resources is the way to boost productivity.

Where do technological revolutions come from? Borrowing ideas, trial and error, ingenious invention and experimentation are all involved, and it is the argument presented here that free markets, properly founded, are essential to secure such outcomes. Where customs are entrenched in tradition-bound societies, or where central authority is all-powerful in planned economies, then economic revolutions are discouraged or actively squashed.

Decline of the old Soviet Union

The twentieth-century experiences of the old Soviet Union and of China are instructive in this regard. In the case of the former, central planning had mobilised

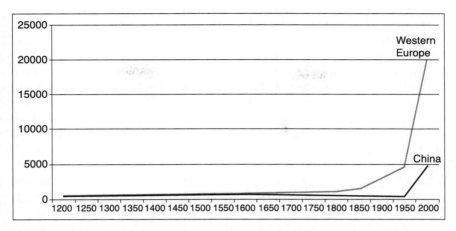

Figure 1.3 Income per person (GDP per capita measured in constant 1990 dollars) in Western Europe and China, 1200–2000. Note that these living standards in Europe begin to climb after 1750, whereas they actually declined in China until around 1950.

Source: Maddison.

capital and labour from old tsarist feudal employments, opened up the vast (and mineral-rich) hinterland and brought about rapid industrialisation up to the Second World War. But look at the contrast between combined factor inputs and productivity in Table 1.1. It shows that this vast, resource-rich nation followed an extensive growth path and that by the 1970s it had run up against the limits of this model. With the industrialised world's highest rates of capital investment and participation rates of the labour force, there was little potential left for increasing the *quantity* of inputs. Without improvements in productivity, therefore, **diminishing returns** were inevitable.

In this input-driven model, growth was pushed by commands from above and not pulled by market demands from below. There was a high priority to invest in

Table 1.1 Percentage growth rates in Soviet inputs, productivity, outputs and outputs per head (CIA estimates in parentheses). Note the steady decline in the productivity of inputs from 1950/60 on.

	1928/40	*1940/50*	*1950/60*	*1960/70*	*1970/5*	*1975/80*	*1980/5*
Gross National Product	5.8	2.2	5.7	5.2	3.7	2.6	2.0
GNP per capita	3.6	2.9	3.9	3.9	2.7	1.8	1.1
Combined factor inputs	4.0	0.6	4.0	3.7	3.7	3.0	2.5
Total factor productivity	1.7	1.6	1.6 (1.4)	1.5 (0.9)	0.0 (1.5)	−0.4 (−0.8)	−0.5 (−1.2)

Source: G. Ofer, 'Soviet economic growth', *Journal of Economic Literature*, December 1987.

capital equipment and military hardware, with a correspondingly lower priority for the production of consumer goods, and an ideological insistence on remaining independent and separate from western market economies. Such a political/ economic structure could not allow for failure to meet production targets in high priority sectors. That is, certain state-owned and -run production units operated with what was known as **soft budget constraints** – the Soviet authorities bailed them out if they squandered any inputs.

It should be apparent that there is no incentive for an economy so organised to strive to be efficient. The best materials and the best brains would be commandeered for the sending of highly advanced military hardware into space, but there would be little resource left, and strictly enforced censorship on ideas to serve the lengthening queues of consumers wanting more than the bare essentials. And who places orders for consumer goods? Production was according to planned targets handed down by bureaucrats and was not responsive to customer demand. This is a recipe for abysmal service. In the end the Soviet Union broke up not because of any external influence or the arms race but – note the falling growth rate on GNP per capita in Table 1.1 – simply because it could not produce a standard of living that was satisfactory for the ordinary citizen.

Since the fall of the Berlin Wall in 1989 the old Soviet Union has been dismantled; East and West Germany have been united, and other East European nations formerly held within the Russian iron embrace have attained independence and have turned to utilise market systems of economic organisation.

The future progress of these transition economies depends crucially on the strength of the foundations on which they have based their market systems. These criteria were identified earlier. How secure are private property rights? Are enterprise, labour and capital free to move between alternative investments, and across frontiers? Is industry characterised by competition or dominated by monopoly? Is there freedom of information and expression to challenge the status quo? The economic record has been most successful for those nations further to the west which retain a memory of market organisation prior to Soviet domination (see Figure 1.4). For Russia and its immediate neighbours, still rich in resources, they may enjoy growth so long as they can extract and export oil and other minerals and prices remain high. But for the longer term, if old and entrenched command traditions of controlling ideas and trampling on dissent are not reformed, then free markets cannot flourish, technological development will be constrained and diminishing returns will reappear again to inhibit growth.

China's road to the market

In the 1970s, China was a poor, centrally planned, autarkic country, hostile to outsiders and opposed to radical reform. Its population was three times greater than that of the old Soviet Union and Eastern Europe combined, but it was crammed into half the land area. After the self-inflicted economic disasters of the (misnamed) 'Great Leap Forward' (1958–60) and the 'Cultural Revolution'

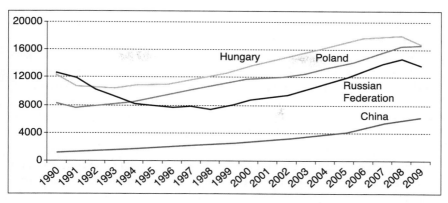

Figure 1.4 GDP per capita (constant 2005 US$, PPP) 1990–2009. Note the contrasting fortunes for East European states and Russia, consequent upon the break-up of the old command system run by the Soviet Union. Generally speaking, those countries closer to Western Europe had a less traumatic transition to market than Soviet states further east. China is included for comparison – a nation of much lower income per head but witnessing a steady and increasing growth.

Source: World Bank Development Indicators.

(1966–76), China's economy was only half the size of Russia's, its per capita income only 15 per cent and its future looked bleak.

Since then, China has transformed itself from a poor, sluggish, highly inefficient command economy into a dynamic emerging market society with one of the highest growth rates in the world. By 2010 its **Gross National Product** was the planet's second highest, it has become a major trading power with its growth in exports dwarfing all others (>500 per cent in a decade) and its income per head reaching almost 50 per cent of that in Russia. How did it do it?

The answer is by being alert to the adoption of new ideas, taking one step at a time, and learning from the process. Characteristic of the Chinese way has been the introduction of market incentives first of all in a pilot or experimental fashion, and then, depending on results, broadening the scope of reforms across the country. Secondly, China has not confused ends with means. Best practice institutions – such as complete private ownership and perfect competition in industry, fully flexible market prices, free movement of capital, labour and enterprise, all in a stable economic environment – represent goals to be achieved in the long term and not to be gained straight away. Efforts were thus devoted to employ transitional institutions that would lead to this end eventually. Thirdly, the development of the economy took place alongside political evolution, not revolution, so the overall reform programme has been consistently managed, uni-directional and not subject to sudden reversals.

It started in agriculture with the introduction of **dual track pricing** and the **household responsibility system**. Official planned targets were still maintained where outputs were purchased by the state at administered (low) prices, but individual households were allowed to sell any surplus above these quotas at local market prices.

Chinese agriculture had earlier, after the communist revolution of 1949, been collectivised in massive communes which proved to be massively inefficient. Since individual effort was not rewarded, there was the perverse incentive to do little and instead benefit from the hard work done by others – the **free rider** problem. Challenging official practice and re-allocating collective land to individual households was originally a subversive idea pioneered by a group of peasants in Anhwei province in 1978 – but the effect it had on farm outputs brought official sanction instead of punishment. By 1980, 14 per cent of all collective farm production teams had changed over to the household responsibility system, rising to 80 per cent by 1982 and 99 per cent by 1984.

Annual growth of farm outputs from 1957 to 1978 increased by 2.3 per cent, but from 1978 to 1987 this had increased to 5.8 per cent per annum. Even more revealing was the rate of growth of farm labour productivity: *minus* 0.19 per cent per year from 1957 to 1978 but plus 5 per cent from 1978 to 1987 (A. Maddison, *Chinese Economic Performance in the Long Run*, OECD, 1998.) With household property rights now state-sanctioned and more efficiently allocated, and with price incentives, labour was working much more efficiently.

Agricultural revolution releases resources that can be redeployed elsewhere. The institutional form this next step led to was small-scale town and village enterprises (TVEs) which were market driven and originally local authority owned. In the absence of full privatisation, this novel arrangement served to increase the incentives for profit-seeking entrepreneurs and it bought the support of local government officials who could use these TVEs as revenue-raising devices. Once started, the idea grew and soon privately owned TVEs overtook publicly owned ones. Collectively owned TVEs peaked at 1.73 million entities in 1986, but between 1985 and 2002 private enterprises soared to more than 20 million in number (Y. Huang, 'Private ownership: the real source of China's economic miracle', *The McKinsey Quarterly*, 2009).

Opening the country to the stimulus of world trade was similarly begun in an experimental fashion: four coastal special enterprise zones (SEZs) or free trade areas were set up in 1980 where imports and exports were duty free, where wages were low by world standards and where new enterprises enjoyed substantial tax holidays. International trade boomed, along with economic activity and internal migration to the region, resulting in another SEZ being created in 1988. Since then Chinese trade has continued to expand, its exports providing relatively low-cost merchandise for Europe and North America, at the same time as sucking in imports from primary producing countries like Australia (see Figure 1.5).

Western market liberalisation

A significant shift towards increasing market liberalisation and reducing the role of government direction took place from 1979 onwards in western economies

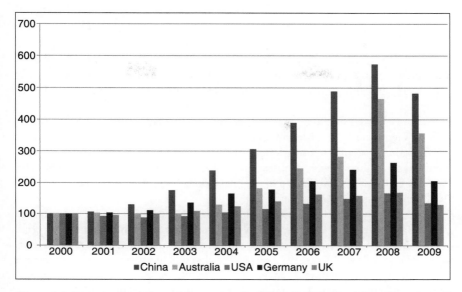

Figure 1.5 Export value index, various countries, 2000–9. Calculated from base year of
2000 = 100, this illustrates the percentage increase in each country's exports to
2008 (and the subsequent decrease, 2008–9).

Source: World Bank Development Indicators.

also, especially under the administrations of UK Prime Minister Margaret Thatcher
and US President Ronald Reagan. This major change in policy direction was a
response to a revolution in economic thinking in an era of oil price shocks and
what was believed to be the inflexible, sclerotic response of over-regulated
economies (see also Chapters 3 and 9).

A fateful consequence of this policy shift was the liberalisation of financial
markets, in particular. Making money is the business of banking (see Chapter 7)
and, following the philosophy that private markets know best, the creation of
credit and its allocation between competing uses was thought safest and most
economically productive if the misguided (and typically self-serving) influence of
politicians and bureaucrats was minimised.

The two decades of the 1980s and 1990s therefore saw a progressive deregulation
in the rules of banking and finance that had been in place ever since the Great
Depression. Originally designed to prevent ordinary customers' bank deposits from
funding speculative capital market activity, regulations ensured that retail or high
street banks were kept separate from building societies and different from investment
or merchant banks, from hedge funds, insurance companies and stock markets, etc.

Of course, profit-seeking financial enterprises always have a natural incentive
to try and evade regulatory constraints, but now after 1979 they had the support of
economic theory and free market politicians to loosen the reins that restricted their
operations.

The efficient market hypothesis (see Chapter 9) argues that unregulated, undistorted capital markets will always price securities efficiently. Any enterprise that wishes to raise a loan will issue a security that will be priced according to the risk it offers to the prospective buyer. All available information is taken into account by market traders, such that the riskier the asset, the lower the price it will carry, and the higher the rate of return it will have to promise, to attract a buyer.

Not only was government regulation in such market calculations likely to distort this efficient pricing of risk and lead to a misallocation of investible funds but, furthermore, by removing restrictions and allowing financial institutions to grow in size and in their range of operation, so they would likely become safer. The bigger and more diversified the bank, the easier it would withstand any crisis of confidence in any one asset class.

Politicians averse to socialism, mindful of the increasing success of market policies in East Asia, and wishing to rejuvenate the spirit of private enterprise within their own nations, were entirely supportive of such theorising. A succession of measures followed from 1979 to 1999 to deregulate financial markets, free up the internal and international movement of capital, and promote competition and movement between retail and wholesale banks, insurance markets and others.

The result was an explosion of finance. Since the Second World War, global financial assets (the total of bank deposits, private and public sector debt, and equity capital) had grown more or less at the same pace as world outputs or GDP. The more sophisticated financial markets with deeper asset bases, like the USA and the UK, had a value of total financial assets of around 200 per cent of their respective national products, but that ratio had been stable for decades. From 1980 onwards, however, global financial assets soared from an amount approximately equal to the total value of world goods and services to *more than four times* the value of global real output by 2007. The structure of those assets changed also: by far the greatest growth of paper was in the form of private sector securities of a baffling variety of loans. See Figure 1.6 for the changes in the world's largest single financial market place – the USA.

By allowing private financiers to arrange their own affairs with only light touch regulation, western governments were declaring their faith in free markets to secure optimal outcomes – that is, sustained economic growth, free from the boom and bust cycles that had occurred in the past.

Through the 1990s, people generally thought that had happened. This was the era of 'the Great Moderation' when, throughout the developed world, inflation and unemployment rates both came down to low levels, interest rates were falling, economic volatility was reduced and it was the most benign financial environment seen for decades. True, house prices were rising rapidly in a number of cases, but this was seen as perfectly normal in markets where supplies took time to respond to rising demand. Housing was another 'efficient market', not a speculative bubble, it was alleged.

Confidence was high, incomes were growing. There were, of course, occasional blips and distractions in world economic progress (the Mexican 'tequila' crisis of

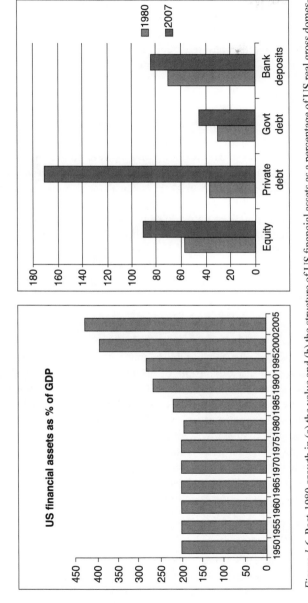

Figure 1.6 Post-1980 growth in (a) the value and (b) the structure of US financial assets as a percentage of US real gross domestic product.

Source: Roxburgh C., Lund S. *et al*, 'Global Capital Markets: Entering a new era', McKinsey Global Institute, September 2009.

1994, the East Asian financial crisis of 1997, the Russian rouble collapse of 1998, the 'dot-com' bubble and bust of 2000, the Argentine crisis of 2001, etc.), but these could be brushed aside as typical of immature sectors or markets and nothing to worry the great centres of global growth . . .

Pride comes before a fall. What was happening on a fundamental level within the world economy, but on so large and dispersed a scale that no one could fit all the pieces of the puzzle together and see it coming, was the conjunction of a set of circumstances that were profoundly destabilising.

Quasi-religious faith

The first guilty party was the semi-religious belief in the self-correcting tendency of free market systems. After years of allegedly misguided government interference, this return to classical economic theory, as explained earlier, argues that markets best secure optimal outcomes when left alone by government. It was a belief that had ensnared policy-makers – that is, governments and central bankers – and as Sir Howard Davies (the first chairman of the UK Financial Services Authority, 1997–2003) explains: 'a heavy burden of proof was placed on regulators who wished to question the rationality of market transactions and market prices'. He adds: 'On every occasion that I appeared in Parliament as Chairman of the FSA I was attacked for over-intrusive regulation' (comments at the Bank for International Settlements conference on financial regulation, June 2010). The paradigm of *laissez-faire* or 'leave alone' ruled.

Soporific environment

Secondly, the Great Moderation meant that the macroeconomic environment was relaxed. Independent central banks in the developed countries were following a successful strategy of 'inflation targeting' – that is, they were predominantly charged with keeping price levels low and stable. This was not difficult since China and other emerging markets were exporting volumes of cheap textiles and manufactured goods, which meant western prices remained low and the 'feelgood factor' was high. The effect on policy-makers was soporific: the longer such a benign environment lasted, the longer people expected it to last. 'Tail risks' or 'black swan events' (i.e. very infrequent but major shocks that by their nature are extremely difficult to predict) appeared remote.

Global trade imbalances

Meanwhile, through the 1990s and into the new millennium, the growth in importance of emerging market economies was having an impact on global trade that was quite unique. We have already seen (Figure 1.5) that Chinese export revenues were booming. This was also mirrored in the rising trade surpluses of India, Brazil and others, particularly oil and primary producing economies. What were they doing with this money? Contrary to economic theory which predicts that funds should flow from capital rich (developed) nations to capital scarce (less developed) nations, much of these trade surpluses were not being invested at home by the exporting nations, but instead were being deposited in banks, finance houses and treasuries in the West – principally in the US and UK financial markets. Why was this? To some degree it was because the accumulation of trade surpluses was so rapid that it could not be spent fast enough and thus savings were inevitable. It was also because the Asian and other financial 'blips' referred to above prompted emerging economies to bank large precautionary reserves of dollars, just in case their domestic currencies came under speculative attack again. Lastly, by saving their export revenues in dollars rather than converting them into domestic currency, countries like China could hold their exchange rates down and thus maintain an export advantage.

Official encouragement + financial innovation

With western financial markets flush with incoming funds, a seemingly low risk environment and a correspondingly low rate of return on traditional bonds and bills, and political support and encouragement to widen the base of home ownership, this was the perfect scenario for banks to invent high yielding paper assets. Brokers issued mortgages, then sold on these loans to investment bankers who would package them up in highly complex securities. In bundling up hundreds of loans (many very risky or 'sub-prime') into these **mortgage-backed securities**, some very fancy mathematical calculation was necessary to assess their specific risk/ price. However, rating agencies were paid to approve them, other traders would sell **credit default swaps** to guarantee them, and **special investment vehicles** (SIVs) were created to buy and sell these now highly profitable top-rated AAA fabrications.

Overconfidence + greed

But these fancy-named financial innovations were *underpricing risk*. Indeed, they were too complex for most traders to fully understand – financiers were buying them on trust and using them as assets to support the creation of further loans. Selling on loans was a way to make big profits – using these off-balance-sheet SIVs (which were not subject to central authority regulation), instead of going through normal banks, allowed traders to create more loans without having to raise more capital: a process known as **leverage**. Like an inverted pyramid, more and more credit was being extended on a smaller and smaller capital base.

Booming prices and incomes

Inevitably, circulation of all this paper money drove real asset prices higher. From the 1990s up to 2006, house prices boomed in the most inflated financial markets. (See Figure 1.7.)

Housing markets were not the only ones to which all this excess credit was directed. The world price of other commodities also rose – oil, gold, cereal crops – but, more importantly for those directly involved, the earnings of financiers boomed. Professor Robert Wade of the London School of Economics commented

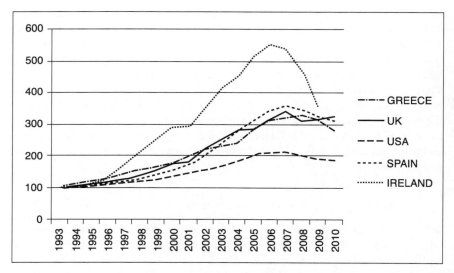

Figure 1.7 Index of house prices, selected countries, 1993–2010. These are crude annual
average prices of average properties (much greater price volatility can be
expected for select properties in certain densely populated areas). For example,
the average price trend for the USA, an immense housing market compared
with relatively tiny Ireland, is thus flatter but shows the same overall shape.

Source: Bank for International Settlement.

(LSE website blog, 8 January 2010) that in the USA, during the last four years of
the boom under President Bush, *the richest top 1 per cent of households captured
73 per cent of the gains from the country's economic growth.* Comparing the
average of all incomes, in 1980, the top 1 per cent of US households were earning
9 per cent of national disposable income; by 2007 this 1 per cent were now
creaming off 23 per cent. Meanwhile the average real incomes of the bottom 90
per cent of the US population actually *fell* between 1973 and 2006. Wade asserts
that the reason that this slow-growing and regressive redistribution of incomes did
not awaken political protest at the time was because the financial sector was
simultaneously stimulating a huge increase in debt (see *Private debt* in Figure
1.6). Banks, money makers and speculators had engineered a cultural shift: people
thought it was absolutely OK to live on borrowed funds – commonly at multiples
many times more than their annual incomes and frequently not backed by sufficient
collateral.

The situation could not last. Inevitably, some could not keep up the payments
on their mortgages. It started with the most heavily indebted selling property to try
and regain the capital to pay off their creditors. Property prices thus plateaued –
then slumped as others joined in the rush. The urge was to sell now while prices
were high rather than wait, but of course if everyone thinks the same, then prices
collapse, as panic sets in. The bubble burst in 2007/8 (see Figure 1.7).

But why should a housing bust in the US sub-prime mortgage market spark a worldwide financial crisis? This is where economics is learning from medical science and the spread of viruses: firstly, with regard to the virus and its ability to rapidly metamorphose, and secondly, in identifying the importance of 'superspreaders' – infected parties that have connections everywhere.

As the defaults on sub-prime mortgages gathered pace during 2007, there came the horrifying realisation that the mortgage-backed securities (MBSs) involved were far more infectious and difficult to pin down than originally believed. Instead of portraying a forecastable risk and thus a predictable loss, these MBSs had been bought, sold, reproduced, insured, moved off balance sheets (i.e. hidden) and generally morphed into a class of **collateralised debt obligations** that nobody really could properly evaluate and understand. And they were underpinning financial institutions everywhere.

This toxic virus changed characteristics according to the institution which carried it . . . and some of these institutions were very big indeed and interacting with others all over the world.

In theory, the function of banks (more properly, **financial intermediaries**) is to pool savings from vast numbers of ordinary people and recycle these funds to productive investments in industry – backing winners and avoiding losers in the process. (See Chapter 7.) The profit-seeking intermediary will only back a risky investment if, firstly, it has investigated the venture and, secondly, it has calculated that the projected returns more than compensate for the perceived risk. There is no need for excessive government intervention: the efficient market hypothesis asserts that financial markets are close to perfect with fast-moving information and intense competition.

The reality, as we have all seen to our cost, is very different. Banks loan massive amounts of funds *to each other*; they invent new forms of debt, sell this on to others, hold securities that have emanated from somewhere else, and in many cases do not have the time or inclination to fully assess the risks involved, especially if they can quickly pass commitments on to others. This merry-go-round can continue spinning so long as confidence holds and prices and incomes are rising. But if there are any doubts about the solvency of any one particular bank, what this means is that you need to examine, not only your own exposure to that specific financial institution, but also your exposure to all other banks to which that party is indebted. If Bank A is in trouble and cannot pay you back as promised, and neither can it pay banks B, C, D, etc., what about your exposure to these other institutions? Will they all collapse? If so, if the plague spreads, you are in real trouble, and so is everyone else who has been in contact.

Fears of this sort were developing throughout 2007 and 2008, until the crunch came on 15 September 2008 when the US administration refused to bail out Lehman Brothers. This investment bank (the fourth largest in the USA) was thought to be too big and too internationally connected to fail. Not so. As a result, there was a rush to sell off a whole range of asset-backed securities, supposedly guaranteed by big-name banks all over the world – but now no one trusted anyone.

The problem this created was that intermediaries could now no longer perform

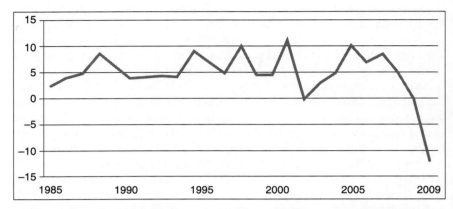

Figure 1.8 Annual percentage change in world merchandise exports, 1985–2009. Over this period when the free market paradigm ruled, world export growth varied around a mean of 5.6 per cent . . . until 2008–9.

Source: WTO.

their proper role of investing in productive enterprise. In what was called the *credit crunch*, everyone, everywhere, wanted their money back. Smaller, vulnerable banks and businessess had to close down. Mortgages could not be raised, houses could not be built. Half-finished properties stayed that way as construction companies could not be paid. Finance for any and all consumer goods became expensive or unavailable. Cars went unsold, production lines slowed down, shipping stayed in port, employment and incomes fell – particularly amongst those businesses most interconnected in North America and Europe.

Globalisation is fine when growth in some parts of the world economy stimulates growth everywhere else. Unfortunately the converse is also true – a slump in markets unites consumers and producers in a progressive and collective gloom worldwide (see Figure 1.8). Note that the crash in world export volume illustrated here (*minus 12 per cent* in 2008–9) was actually steeper and deeper than that which occurred between 1929 and 1931 which heralded the onset of the Great Depression.

Conclusion

The world economy is undergoing momentous changes. The major market economies have had to bail out their banks – for without trustworthy finance there can be no trade and no growth, and the contraction of incomes would be savage and prolonged. But this has meant that richer country governments have had to penalise taxpayers to pay off bankers' debts: the financial crisis thus converts into a national or **sovereign debt crisis** (see Chapter 9).

Richer countries are not so rich as they thought, therefore, and nor can they be quite so confident and domineering in world economic relations as they used to be. The fact is that the less wealthy countries of Latin America, Africa and Asia were not responsible for, nor have they suffered so much from, the implosion of world finance. Indeed for those important primary producers amongst them, their economic fortunes have improved relative to Europe and the USA as commodity prices have recently increased (see Chapter 5).

In the realm of economics, the biggest casualty has been the free market paradigm. There is no doubt that for those hamstrung by central controls, the process of confirming property rights, liberalising individual enterprise, fomenting competition and freeing the exchange of information may together release powerful forces conducive to economic growth. But, like all forms of immense power, economic power can just as easily be abused. Apart from certain fanatics

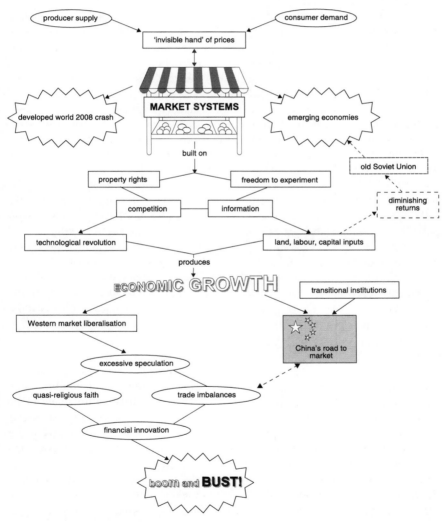

Figure 1.9 The themes of Chapter 1.

who hold on to their idealistic models with religious certainty, it is now generally recognised that market traders will rarely secure efficient outcomes without being policed. Government oversight and regulation, for better or worse, must be an essential, irreplaceable and continually revisited component of the modern economy. We go on to examine the further theoretical implications of this statement in the next chapters.

Key words

Collateralised debt obligations or CDOs are created by banks and finance houses to pool a large number of unrelated debts of varying risk, which are then sold off in tranches or slices to others. They offer a rate of return which is supposedly finely calculated on the risks of the underlying debts, bonds, mortgages or whatever they are based upon. Both buyers and sellers, of course, greatly overestimated the true value of these CDOs and underpriced the risks involved in the build-up to the 2008 crash. Because they stayed on the balance sheets of many interlocking financial institutions, the risks that were supposed to be diversified were in fact sitting like time-bombs in many banks thought too big and important to fail. CDOs were not publicly traded in stock markets, but passed over the counter in many private deals, and so the total indebtedness that was created is difficult to measure. One source (*New York Times*) put it at US$534.2 billion in 2006.

Command economies are those that employ central planning, rather than the price mechanism, to allocate society's resources; they typically employ a well-publicised mission statement or manifesto to promote their official ethic, and in the case of the communist command economies of the late twentieth century, they organised production into huge, state-owned, monopolistic enterprises.

Consumer sovereignty This is the principle that, in a market economy, the consumer is 'king'. By the pattern of the public's purchases the consumer determines which products will be successful, and thus which producers will make most profits and which will fail. Consumer sovereignty is only half the story, however, in that innovative businesses can create new products, employ sophisticated marketing techniques, engender demand and create a market for new gismos that consumers were previously unaware of.

Credit default swaps (CDSs) These offer a form of insurance against loss to someone who buys a CDO. If you think that a third party to whom you have just extended credit may default – that is, fail to pay up – you can sell off or swap that debt with another. The provider of a credit default swap will charge a price for this service which supposedly reflects the markets' valuation of the risk of default. However, in any *real* insurance contract the insurer will interview the debtor in great detail to evaluate the risk and keep the contract on their books, whereas CDSs are priced in simple and quick calculations that allow the paper to be bought and sold rapidly between traders who may not hold them for long and simply wish to make a speculative gain.

Diminishing returns One of the oldest and most reliable laws in economics. Employing more and more of one factor with a fixed amount of other resources (e.g. more and more workers in a given enterprise or farm) will secure an increase in outputs, but in steadily diminishing amounts. Eventually total output may fail to rise at all.

Dual track pricing A transitional innovation in China where target farm outputs were originally planned and priced, but any surplus over target was allowed to be sold off at whatever price the farmer could get. Since official prices were much lower than could be obtained locally and informally, peasant farmers strained to produce surpluses and local customers came to prize this unplanned, private bounty. Dual track pricing rapidly led to the emergence of flourishing local markets where before the state had commandeered everything.

Financial intermediaries is the generic term to describe all banks and other financial enterprises that intermediate or recycle funds from those that have surplus to those who have insufficient. They make a profit on the difference between the rate of interest they offer on deposits and the rate of return they charge on loans.

Free rider problem Originally coined to describe those who cheat the public tranport authorities by taking a ride without paying. Now used to label any party that benefits from consuming a good or service that all others have paid the sacrifice for.

Gross National Product An estimate of the value of everything a nation produces in a given year. It is notionally the same as all the income a nation earns and all the expenditure a nation makes in a year, since what one produces and sells, another must buy. Calculation is complex to take account of losses on imports, gains on exports and measuring the output of public goods and services – many of which are not marketed.

Household responsibility system Chinese agricultural communes, created after the 1949 revolution, relied upon the individual working for the benefit of others. But indoctrination alone was not an enormously successful incentive. The leasing of collective land, machinery and other assets to individual households began as a private initiative in Anhwei province in 1978 but, in harnessing individual incentives, it proved to be remarkably productive. The Chinese state accepted the result. Communal ownership and organisation was thereafter doomed.

Laissez-faire Roughly translates as 'leave alone'. Otherwise interpreted as 'business knows best', or let the market decide.

Leverage A very popular, overused and abused term. It refers to the way in which any agent may use an asset they possess to lever an advantage, or gain an opening. Typically used to describe how a financial enterprise may pledge its equity capital to raise a hefty loan. As debts increasingly accumulate on top of a slender capital foundation, the firm is described as 'highly leveraged'.

Mortgage-backed securities The infamous and specific debt instrument or CDO that represented hundreds of different mortgages – loans to house-buyers – bundled up together in one complex document. Thus the value of one piece of paper or security might be backed by countless loans to others – the value and riskiness of these loans being impossibly difficult to calculate quickly. But that doesn't matter if you buy it and sell it on to others at a profit . . . and then they do the same . . . and round and round the money goes, bidding up higher and higher prices until some day, some time, somebody blows the whistle, and whoever ends up holding this paper loses out, since at that point no one, anywhere, wants to buy it.

Soft budget constraints A term made famous by the Hungarian economist Janos Kornai to describe any enterprise (typically state owned) that is politically difficult to close down and is thus forgiven for running over budget, being awarded more funds to deliver on its promises. Such enterprises may thus come to expect to be bailed out and to never have to face the constraint of a tight budget.

Sovereign debt crisis This occurs when a sovereign state runs up immense debts so that financial markets eventually come to doubt that 'there is a lot of ruin in a nation' (Adam Smith). See Chapter 9.

Special investment vehicles SIVs were designed to take financial dealings off the balance sheets of commercial banks and thus away from the eyes of the central authorities. They therefore formed a sort of shadow banking system and were highly profitable up until the great 2008 crash, since SIVs could issue huge volumes of loans above and beyond what regulators would insist was prudent for the formal banking sector. They earned great profits – so long as prices were rising and no one defaulted.

Questions

1   What are the causes of technological revolutions? Why, despite possessing technologically advanced military hardware, did the old Soviet Union experience 'diminishing returns'?
2   Why did Chinese economic performance lag behind that of the West for so many years and what have been the causes of its radical transformation?
3   Is an agricultural revolution necessary before a country experiences an industrial revolution?
4   What are the criteria for an efficient market?
5   Of the combination of factors that caused the 2008 crash and subsequent Great Recession, which in your view was the most important?

Further reading

Cleaver, T. 'A world in upheaval', Chapter 1 in *Economics: The Basics*, London: Routledge, 2011.

Maddison, A. *Explaining the Economic Performance of Nations*, Cheltenham: Edward Elgar, 1995.

Qian, Y. 'How reform worked in China', Chapter 11 in D. Rodrik (ed.), *In Search of Prosperity: Analytical Narratives on Economic Growth*, Princeton University Press, 2003.

2 Market failure and the great debate

Eugene Fama, the father of the efficient-market hypothesis, declared that: 'the word bubble drives me nuts,' and went on to explain why we can trust the housing market: 'Housing markets are less liquid, but people are very careful when they buy houses. It's typically the biggest investment they're going to make, so they look around very carefully and they compare prices. The bidding process is very detailed.'

Quoted by Paul Krugman, 'How did economists get it so wrong', *New York Times*, 2 September 2009

Introduction

An understanding of prices is absolutely essential to an understanding of market societies. As was emphasised in Chapter 1, the price mechanism is the key organising agency of the modern market economy – the invisible hand that directs the pattern of all consumption, production and distribution. It determines what is produced, which industries and economic practices will succeed or fail, and which resources will, or will not, be employed.

How well, or efficiently, each and every price signals what people want and what society is able to produce is absolutely critical to the workings of the market economy. High prices should indicate a shortage in supply, for example, providing the profit incentive for suppliers to invest in mobilising resources to increase production. But if entrepreneurs subsequently find that the price signal is false, this will have brought about massive wastage – scarce land, precious labour skills and vast amounts of capital may have been redeployed at great cost only to find they are not now needed. Unemployment is not just uneconomic; it is socially and politically harmful.

Alternatively, erroneously underpriced goods and services lead to an equally dangerous extreme. Such items will be eagerly snapped up by consumers, and if price signals do not change, this will leave society with seriously diminishing resources that perhaps will be discovered, belatedly, to be highly valued and now at risk of loss or extinction.

Therefore how prices are determined is at the heart of economics. This has been the case since the beginnings of the subject in the eighteenth century, and chapters on **microeconomics** and the theory of price still appear at the start of textbooks on the subject today.

The theory of price

Classical economics, as it has evolved from the earliest economists like Adam Smith and others, was and is concerned with the workings of individual markets – that is, how to make the most efficient, economic use of given resources. This is microeconomics: the study of consumer and producer behaviour in the trade for specific goods or services.

Where demand, supply and the price of any product are all freely variable, we can see how their interaction secures economically efficient outcomes. There are many factors that influence consumer and producer decisions. Take the example of a local newspaper, on sale every day in a particular city. On the occasion of a major news story – perhaps the success of the local football team – there might be a rush in demand and the newspaper sells out, leaving many dissatisfied customers. How is the market likely to respond to this *disequilibrium* situation where demand exceeds supply at the ruling market price? In this example we can predict that on the following day, assuming continuing interest in the story, local shops and stallholders will order more newspapers to meet anticipated demand, and the printers will run off more copies. It is also possible that, to avoid disappointment, some consumers will leave the market – perhaps following the story on local TV and radio – rather than risk unfulfilled demand a second time.

In these circumstances, if suppliers have guessed correctly, the quantity of newspapers will adjust to secure the necessary equilibrium between demand and supply. Sales increase; all consumers are satisfied; the newspaper price remains unchanged.

A different scenario may operate in the market for housing. Suppose a big new business opens up in a small town and very quickly there is a great supply of jobs on offer. Further consider that, in response to this, there may be many people who now wish to move to this town and so start looking to buy, or rent, somewhere to live. If the consumers concerned are anxious to find somewhere quickly, then they have to accept that the available supply of property is fixed. If the supply of housing cannot increase, therefore, the most anxious consumers will have to pay inflated prices in order to secure a roof over their heads. In this scenario the shortfall between supply and demand is closed by a movement in prices, while the quantity stays the same. Existing house owners will find their properties are scarce, relative to demand, and thus those wishing to sell up or rent will be able to hold out for the highest prices.

For most goods and services, a combination of both these scenarios will ensure demand equals supply: there will be some adjustment in prices and some change in quantities traded to bring about market equilibrium.

The key point to emphasise here is that there are a number of different influences affecting demand and supply. Consumers' incomes change, their tastes and preferences vary, credit may or may not be available – all these factors, as well as a change in prices, may influence demand for one product rather than another. In production, costs will alter, technological possibilities differ, random shocks (from earthquakes to exchange rates) have their effect. These issues, as well as the prospective price the entrepreneur is seeking, will influence the quantity of the product eventually supplied. (See Box 2.1.)

Box 2.1   Demand, supply and price determination

The quantity that consumers will demand of any one product tends to fall as its price rises, *given all other factors influencing their decision remain unchanged*. This is illustrated by DD in Figure 2.1. Suppose, however, that some factor other than price now changes – perhaps people are assured that they can double their spending this month thanks to banks extending cheap credit. Whatever the price of the product on offer, twice as much will now be demanded. The **demand curve** shifts to D1D1.

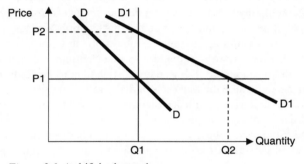

Figure 2.1 A shift in demand.

If the supply of the product in question can be rapidly increased to meet the demand (as in the case of newspapers), the quantity Q1 moves to Q2, tracing out a **supply curve** that is horizontal, and the price remains unchanged at P1. If, however, the product is fixed in supply (extra housing cannot be rolled out as easily as running a printing press), then as demand booms, price surges to P2. The short-term supply curve in this case is vertical at Q1.

A high price for housing will inevitably tempt construction firms to build more. These will take time to come to market, and costs of available land may mean that the supply cannot expand sufficiently to bring house prices down to their original level. Thus the longer-term supply curve may evolve to a shape SS – see Figure 2.2 – with an eventual market-clearing price of P3 where demand now equals supply at quantity Q3. Clearly some consumers (Q3–Q2) who cannot afford this eventual price will have to leave the market; by the same token, construction firms will be unwilling to increase the supply of housing beyond Q3 since this price P3 is insufficient to tempt them to produce more.

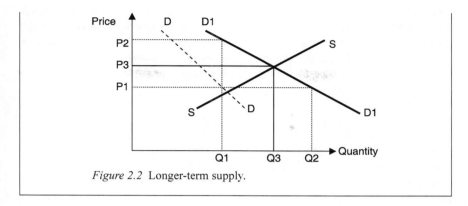

Figure 2.2 Longer-term supply.

Some of these factors are more variable than others, and the 'art' in the science of economics is to identify – in the case being studied – which is the key variable, and which factors in comparison are relatively unchanging. A theory of demand, supply and price can thus be constructed and, given factor x changes and y remains constant, we can thus predict the market outcome.

Whether, of course, economists' predictions are fulfilled depends on whether or not they guessed right on the variables that changed. If x was constant and y changed – or, worse, x and y stayed the same and unexpected z varied – then their theories need revising. Here you can begin to see the source of controversy in the subject.

The examples above raise an important point. In the case of newspapers, the rapid responsiveness of supply to changes in consumer demand means that the sale price need not alter. Where this responsiveness (or **price elasticity of supply**) is much reduced – in the case of housing where no short-term increase in quantity is possible – then price changes may be very large.

This poses the key question, when price changes are significant, of whether this reflects the functioning of an efficient market – signalling an essential movement of resources required to resolve a disequilibrium situation – or does it instead reflect a speculative bubble or some other artificial interference in the market place?

The housing market in the USA showed great volatility up until the 2007/8 price crash referred to in Chapter 1. With the benefit of hindsight we can now see that this was a speculative bubble that burst – as was the collapse of the immense bubble in finance that went along with it. But what makes the difference between a bubble and an efficient market?

Paul Krugman, a Nobel Prize-winning US economist, began the opening quote of this chapter with the comment that there was a general belief amongst mainstream commentators that bubbles just did not happen, that the prices of housing and all classes of financial assets simply reflect the underlying economic fundamentals – that is, the 'real' forces of demand and supply.

Eugene Fama certainly believed in what I have referred to as this quasi-religious faith of classical microeconomics and also in its modern expression – the pricing models employed by financial analysts. The price of any one specific asset is determined, according to formula, by its expected return *vis-á-vis* its risk, compared with all other asset prices in the market. All available information is taken into account; prices are very carefully calculated. There can be no mistakes.

If prices are correct and market equilibrium is always secured, then there is no need for any oversight or heavy-handed government intervention. If, however, demand or supply is somehow inflated (or, conversely, restricted) so that it does not really reflect what people are willing and able to pay for, then there is the danger that a sudden, significant readjustment may be necessary. Speculative bubbles build up until they burst.

It is short-sighted to focus only on the microeconomics of individual markets. You cannot spot a bubble in a market by looking at all the other traders alongside you – all are caught up in the same myopic frenzy. The price of one asset is bound to reflect the price of similar, substitutable assets. A wider view of the world is needed to compare the trend of price movements in one market place with all other (some very different) markets. Clearly, the price of a house in one region may well be precisely related to the price of alternative properties in another region, but if average house prices are increasing many times faster than average *incomes*, something must be wrong. What is driving the increase in prices if not a commensurate increase in incomes? (See Figure 2.3.)

Financial intermediaries have a real economic function to fund productive investment, but they can also act as gambling houses. The products they develop and the prices that they carry then reflect short-term speculative desire. I have explained in Chapter 1 that greed, innovation and faith in the free market was responsible for the explosion of finance created on the slimmest of foundations. The price of housing prior to 2007 was booming because financiers were creating increasing amounts of credit and suckering people in to take it. It was like feeding gamblers in a casino to put more and more money on the table – reassuring them that they could not fail. What happens when the winning streak ends and creditors want their money back?

Whose fault?

I should emphasise here that some critics after the crash have insisted that the excessive creation of credit was all the fault of central authorities intervening in the private market place: encouraging financiers to support poorer families in buying their own homes; holding down the central bank rate of interest for too long; implicitly promising the biggest banks and mortgage providers that they would not be allowed to go bust.

The Great Recession has, yet again, opened up the Great Debate amongst economists: are the swings in economic fortunes that bedevil us the result of intrinsically unstable markets, or the effect of destabilising government interventions? Should the 'invisible hand' be left alone or not? Believers assert that flexible markets, free from any interference from central authorities, will always secure equilibrium outcomes where demand automatically equates with supply. Resources will transfer

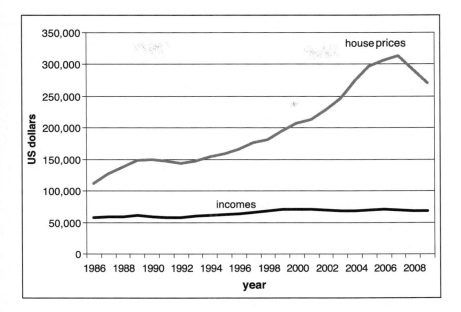

Figure 2.3 Average household incomes compared with the average purchase price on new homes in the USA, 1987–2009. How can house prices rise so spectacularly fast if incomes are not keeping pace? There must be an increase in borrowing that is filling the gap – an increase that must be paid for some day!

Source: US census bureau.

their employments according to efficient price signalling – and it is only governments intervening with prices that distort market outcomes. The glaring mismatch illustrated in Figure 2.3 is a case in point, they allege.

There is undoubtedly some truth in this – and it is not just US governments that promote home ownership for poorer people and also tend to guarantee banks. The first is a desirable social aim for many countries and, with regard to banks, no self-respecting government can allow the store-houses of people's savings to be sacked if private financiers get their sums wrong.

Before the credit crunch, no one saw what was coming. Not believers in efficient markets, not government officials, nor even central bankers who are supposed to police financial services.[1]

The tremendous financial bubble that was inflating larger and larger was thought to reflect real values such as the price of insurance, the low rate of risk, the real demand for property. Fancy innovations like collateralised debt obligations were thought to be of genuine service to the financial community, and central authorities trusted private markets to know best.

The notion of free markets has a particularly strong hold on classical economics. Price flexibility and the evolution of an equilibrium price that 'clears the market' is a theoretical process that has a powerful influence on the mindset of microeconomics. The economics profession, and particularly Keynesian economists who distrust classical theory, should have known better and spoken out earlier (very few did). Whether you blame private sector innovation and a desire to circumvent controls, or public sector laxity in policing the banking industry, something went badly wrong. Ballooning credit creation and asset prices were symptoms of massive (worldwide) market failure, not the efficient operation of sound finance.

But we shall return to consider the world of banking and finance in more detail in Chapters 7 and 9. Let us now turn to a further investigation of microeconomics, its theoretical underpinnings and other sources of market failure.

Positive and normative economics

There are two fundamental sorts of criticism of any economic system. One is that it does not work efficiently (**positive criticism**) and the other is that the system works, but produces outcomes of questionable value (a normative criticism).

There are some commodities which individual consumers may demand – such as sophisticated weapons or hard drugs or offensively racist or sexist publications – but which society may prefer to outlaw. Millions of dollars are spent each year on these commodities and there are undoubtedly enormous profits involved in their international trade. In a market economy, the more money that is forthcoming for these goods, the more of the world's resources will be devoted to producing them. But can this really go unchallenged? The fact that governments seek (not always successfully) to control these trades is an indication of the unacceptability of free markets for such products. This is a **normative criticism** (see also Box 2.2).

Box 2.2   Consumer sovereignty and widening inequalities

Consumer sovereignty means that the buying public dictates what should be produced in a market system according to the pattern of their purchases. This has been described as 'dollar democracy': consumers cast dollar votes in favour of those products they want. Businesses thus clamour to allocate resources and increase outputs for whichever product gains the most dollar votes.

The problem is that some people have far more 'votes' than others. Market systems only cater for those with the most purchasing power and ignore those with little or none. For example, there is an almost obscene variety of junk foods on offer for those who are wealthy, yet at the same time – and sometimes on the same streets – there are those who cannot buy a decent meal and are struggling with malnourishment or actual starvation.

Rich-world health services devote billions to cope with the ailments of excess, obesity, diabetes, heart disease, etc., yet nowhere near similar levels of funds are devoted to the treatment and research of poor-world afflictions such as infectious diseases. (According to the World Health Organization, infectious diseases are now the world's biggest killer of children and young adults. They account for more than 13 million deaths a year – one in two deaths in developing countries. The top child killers are, in order of importance: pneumonia and flu, diarrhoeal diseases, measles, malaria and TB. All are related to poverty, could easily be cured with more cash, and have been more or less eliminated in the rich world.)

It is not just that we start together in the world economy with a wide spectrum of inequality; many critics point out that liberalising markets actually leads to a worsening, a widening, of these differences. We saw in Chapter 1 how the financial boom in the last four years of the Bush administration in the USA had exacerbated inequalities. In both the developed and developing worlds alike, freeing up markets tends to reward the rich more than the poor. (See Figure 2.4.)

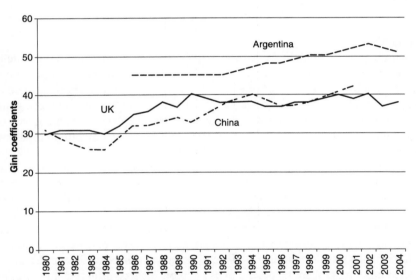

Figure 2.4 Liberalising markets and increasing inequalities: Argentina, the UK and China, 1980–2004. A rising trend illustrates increasing inequality; a flat line means no change. Check when these three nations introduced supply-side reforms to free up their internal markets: China from 1978 onwards; in the UK, the Thatcher decade of the 1980s; and in Argentina the Menem reforms of the 1990s. In all cases, inequality (as measured by **gini coefficients**) increases.

Sources: World Bank, UK Office of National Statistics.

Why is this? Free markets require **occupational and geographical mobility**. Those resources quickest to move in response to changing demands will earn the highest rewards; meanwhile land, labour and capital tied to traditional employments will be condemned to declining incomes. For those people who cannot pay for decent education or health services, they will never get far up the ladder of economic opportunity without a helping hand from the state. Market systems will only provide such merit goods to the wealthy few, which only reinforces their economic advantage. Similarly, small informal businesses that survive on very little capital will not have the collateral to borrow more, invest and grow in size to compete on the same terms as large, formal sector corporations that can access cheap capital from a variety of national and international sources. It is always easiest for those who already have money to make money.

This is a major normative criticism: free markets may work efficiently, but produce social outcomes that have attracted criticism (if not actual revolution) over generations. We will return to consider this issue later. The analysis of economic growth and development is further investigated in Chapter 10.

With regard to communal interests, markets fail to provide essential **public** or **merit goods** like decent roads, defence and police forces, sufficient health and educational services. A mind-boggling variety of cars, guns, cigarettes, breakfast cereals and glossy magazines can be attractively promoted and sold across the counter to the willing customer, but the market has no means of reaching out and demanding payment from everyone who benefits from street lighting or national security, for example. There is an in-built bias to produce anything (no matter how trivial or harmful) for which demand can be stimulated and access restricted to individual fee-payers. Other goods and services which bring immense benefits to all the public, and for which demand cannot necessarily be restricted only to those who pay for them, will find few producers. This is a positive criticism.

Further positive critiques emphasise that efficient markets require perfect information and perfect competition, and yet there are plenty of instances when one or the other of these conditions is missing. Situations can exist where one party to a deal knows more than the other and can exploit such **asymmetric information** to their own advantage. For example, unscrupulous traders have been selling snake oil, or its modern equivalent, to gullible bystanders for centuries. Where active competition between suppliers takes place, concerned consumers can always take their custom someplace else, but what if competition over time eliminates many and leaves the market place to a single dominant producer? In such cases prices may be pushed up and not signal scarcity at all – but only **monopoly** power.

Not only might market prices reflect some things they should not (like excessive corporate power; see above), but they also leave out important elements that ought to be included.

For example, in a market system the low price of travelling by car compared with rail transport into a city should be a reflection of the relative efficiency of the two services: if the cost to the private consumer of taking the car eventually increases (say, due to rising fuel consumption, or time lost in traffic jams), then there will come a point when rail transport is preferred instead. But such calculation of **private costs and benefits** – which is at the heart of the free market society – takes no account of the costs imposed on society. Cars kill and maim. They pour out pollution. They impose major transformations on urban landscapes. Lifestyles and social interaction are subtly but importantly affected.

The most efficient way to transport thousands of individuals from rural and suburban areas into city centres daily is not in separately cocooned and powered metal death-traps along massive land-gobbling superhighways. That is how consumers will choose to travel, however, so long as the price of car travel does not include the **social costs** of funeral and hospital bills, land purchase orders and environmental blight that such private decisions impose on others.

The price mechanism is thus not an automatic, objective, value-free device to organise an economy since the free market inevitably brings into the price calculus all sorts of hidden prejudices. The implications here are massively important. Not only will each and every price signal fail to some extent to reflect all the costs and benefits involved in its market determination, but by extension the sum total of these distorted market interactions will bring about an economy-wide outcome that must be far from optimum.

One result worth emphasising is the impoverishment of the environment. Priceless (literally!) natural assets such as clean air and seas are plundered without limit in unregulated markets and the long-term consequences for the planet are extremely worrying. Of course, command economies run by governments that care little about the environment can cause the same, if not worse, problems. The point is, however, that free markets embody no mechanism that is responsive to all the needs of the planet. Informed regulation is therefore essential to ensure sustainable development. (See Chapter 12.)

Another far-reaching implication is that market systems are chronically unstable. Of the numerous positive criticisms of market theory, the fundamental one here relates to the **fallacy of composition** – that is, the assumption that what works for the community in an individual market place will work for all market places throughout an economy added together.

Specifically, all the millions of independent decisions by consumers in markets up and down the country may add up to a general level of national demand for resources that is insufficient (or alternatively, too great) for the economy as a whole to sustain. Insufficient aggregate demand will mean unemployment and recession; too much demand means price rises and **inflation**.

The logic of microeconomic theory dictates that, if there are excess supplies of any good or service, then prices should fall to clear the market. Unsold fruit and vegetables, or magazines, or cars? Cut prices until they are all gone. Unemployment? People are asking for too much and not enough employers want to take them on. Classical economists have never argued that people have a right to work: the unpleasant truth is that labour is just another factor of production and businesses will only employ workers if they are worth their pay. If people ask for too high wages in any one category of work, there will be an excess of labour relative to employer demand. The remedy for unemployment, in this scenario, is to cut wages.

The problem is that cutting wages, in the hope of pricing people back into work, may work for individual occupations – say, if there are more unemployed car mechanics than are currently in demand from local employers. Being willing to work for less may get you a job in this case. But what works for one occupation at one time/place cannot work for all jobs in an economy added together. If this wage-cutting policy is implemented on a large scale, it must only serve to drive down the general level of incomes and consumption, thereby reducing employment prospects still further. Which businesses will take on more workers and produce more goods and services in a great depression if incomes and spending throughout an entire economy are falling? This argues for a wider approach to economic analysis. Aggregate demand in the 1930s was insufficient to keep the bulk of the labour force in employment, and John Maynard Keynes developed a new theory of **macroeconomics**, emphasising expansionary government policies (the very opposite of wage cuts) in order to remedy that situation. Many Keynesian economists all round the world argue precisely the same today.

Macroeconomic theory

Let us look at Keynesian macroeconomics in more detail. If we ignore the influence of governments for the time being, we can divide an economy into two sectors: producers and consumers. For the sake of simplicity we can say that all production is located in business firms and all consumption occurs in households (see Figure 2.5). There is thus a circular flow of money and incomes between households and firms within the economy. Incomes are earned at work and spent at home on those consumer goods and services produced by business.

All income in a market economy is derived from the production process. It may be earned in the form of wages or salaries for direct work, or it can be earnings from the ownership of capital or land. Either way, these resources of labour, enterprise, capital and land can only generate earnings if they are employed in production. And eventually all these incomes, from whichever source, will find

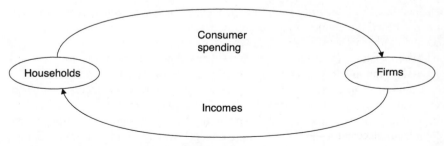

Figure 2.5 Circulation of money: incomes and spending.

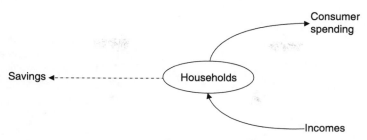

Figure 2.6 Savings are a leakage of incomes from the circular flow.

their way into someone's household where they will be spent or not as the case may be.

Looking at the household sector for the moment, we can say that any income received that is not directly spent on consumer goods and services is 'saved', that is, it is not passed on through the market place to producers. It therefore leaks out of the circular flow (see Figure 2.6).

If we consider now all expenditure in the economy, we find that it is made up of spending on consumer goods, plus some fraction spent by firms on business investment – that is, building capital goods to provide for future production. Either way, all spending goes through firms and contributes to the income they generate (see Figure 2.7).

We should add the qualification at this stage that households buy many imported goods and services. Thus some consumer spending will always leak out of the circular flow in one country and enter that of another. By the same argument, every trading country will receive some foreign spending on those exports it sells abroad.

Putting all these elements together, we can thus see the full picture for the whole economy (see Figure 2.8). According to this circular flow model, the economy is in equilibrium if net additions to money circulation equal net leakages and thus aggregate income equals aggregate expenditure. So long as the injections of export revenues and investment equal the outflows of import spending and savings then the amount of money flowing round the system must remain constant. What happens if this equilibrium is disturbed? If, for some reason, there is a general reduction in wages, then clearly incomes would fall, households would be able to

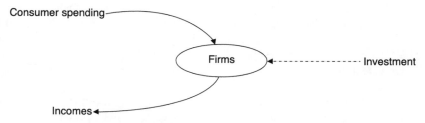

Figure 2.7 Firms' investment is an injection to the circular flow.

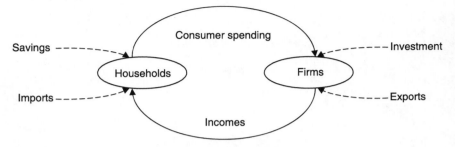

Figure 2.8 The circular flow of incomes and expenditure.

spend less and there would be a fall in the circular flow of incomes, consumption and therefore employment.

Key variables here are the propensities of households to save, spend, and spend on imports. The greater the fraction of households' income that is spent on domestic goods and services, the greater the impact any change of income will have on firms' revenues and production plans. An economy-wide wage cut will thus be rapidly transmitted through to increased unemployment. Conversely, any increase in incomes will quickly generate increased production and the creation of new jobs.

Because there is a circular flow involved here, any small change to the system has a cumulative, **multiplier** effect. Suppose, for example, wages are cut first in the construction industry. Falling incomes will not only impact on those families directly involved, but because their spending represents someone else's income then the recessionary impact spreads further. Local shops, transport firms and other related services will lose custom, and they in turn will pass on less spending and hence revenues to businesses dealing with them. Incomes and, therefore, expenditure fall throughout the economy. As the recessionary outlook begins to take hold, the spiral of decline gathers pace. Is there no bottom to the depression?

This was the fear expressed in the recent credit crunch and Great Recession when there was a real danger of returning to the situation seen in the 1930s. During that inter-war period, owing to the fact that one country's imports represent another country's export earnings, falling incomes and spending that occurred most markedly in the USA rapidly impacted on all other trading nations. The 1930s Great Depression was thus transmitted worldwide. To avoid just such a recurrence of this economic calamity and its world-changing aftermath, in 2008 leaders of all the major powers, and of international institutions such as the International Monetary Fund, the World Bank and the World Trade Organization, were united in agreement that the Great Recession should not lead to countries implementing protectionist, anti-trade policies.

As can be seen in the macroeconomic model above, incomes and spending will fall and keep on falling so long as leakages from the circular flow exceed injections. Stability is only attained when outflows equal inflows, and Keynes' great insight was that there was no inherent necessity for such an equilibrium to exist at full employment within an economy; it could just as easily obtain at lower levels of economic activity – an unemployment equilibrium (though see Box 7.1 in Chapter 7).

So countries could get stuck with a quarter of their workforce unemployed, and no private businesses still operating would see any reason to expand. If the private sector sees no future in investment, if no consumers at home or abroad have money to increase their spending, how is the gloom to end?

The answer, according to Keynes, was that governments could bring about an autonomous increase in injections. The multiplier process outlined above could thus be made to work in a positive fashion: if governments place orders, say, for building more roads and houses (and, in the 1930s, military spending), then 'first round' employment and incomes will rise. Subject to some fraction not being spent, the rest of consumers' incomes will be passed on as 'second round' expenditure, incomes and employment, which in turn stoke up a 'third round' and further recovery.

The economy will grow and grow until the cumulative total of leakages just rises to equal the size of the government-induced injections, and thus the circular flow rebalances itself – at a higher, aggregate total of national income.

As noted before, it should be seen that the speed and extent of the expansion (or contraction) of the economy depends on people's propensity to spend any slight increase in their incomes. That is, the greater their **marginal propensity to consume**, the greater will be the multiplier effect.

In 2008, the pressing economic problem was to recapitalise the banks and get them lending again; to try and get households and firms to spend rather than save; for governments to increase demand if the private sector would not. For example, as custom fell away and long lines of unsold, new cars were building up, subsidies such as 'cash for clunkers' were introduced to try and start people buying again. The last thing policy-makers wanted was for 'beggar my neighbour' attitudes to reappear – the notion that 'I want to sell as much as I can, make as much money as I can, but to spend little myself.' This is a clear fallacy of composition – a microeconomic, little world view that *cannot* succeed if everyone follows suit. No one would spend; all trade would cease.

Note that Keynesian macroeconomics is concerned solely with the general levels of income, output and employment of an economy. Governments must pump up their own spending to maintain aggregate demand if the private sector does not. The result means **budget deficits** must rise in the short term, but this is worth financing if economic growth is restored and thus private incomes and consumption grow in future. Tax takes will then rise and the government's budget will eventually return to balance. Note that microeconomic discussion about *where* to inject government spending, whether or not labour should be deployed here or there, released from industry A in order to transfer to industry B, is not the issue of first importance. Keynesians argue that such debate is irrelevant when aggregate demand is slumping, millions lose their jobs and all industry is below capacity.

Criticisms

There is no persuading some people, however. US President Ronald Reagan famously said: 'The nine most terrifying words in the English language are: *I'm from the government and I'm here to help.*' Adherents of this view insist that big government is bad; that the deficit is a symptom of all that is wrong with the country and it leads down the slippery slope to socialism. Without going to quite such ridiculous extremes, it is nonetheless worth examining the criticisms of the Keynesian policy recommendation to increase deficit spending in recessions.

Those who argue that governments should not increase spending to prevent a fall in aggregate demand must demonstrate that a free market economy will somehow rebound by itself, without help, and/or that increasing public expenditure will make matters worse.

The private sector will only increase investment to facilitate future production if business expectations of sales and profits are optimistic. This was hardly the case in 2008/9 as evidenced in Figure 1.8, when world trade slumped by minus 12 per cent – more steeply than in 1929. Indeed what subsequently caused the slump to bottom out and prevented a continuing 1930s-style decline was precisely the fact that the major powers had learned the lesson of the past and quickly resorted to massive government injections along Keynesian lines. The USA announced a $800 billion fiscal stimulus for 2010; the Chinese had earlier begun a massive public infrastructure spend (planned to exceed US$500 billion) on railway, road, irrigation and airport construction. The only two members of the **G20 nations** not following this example were the UK (which was already running a sizeable budget deficit) and Germany, which took the route of exporting its way to growth (that is, relying on other countries to increase spending on their products!).

How is an increase in public expenditure to be financed? One of the arguments against increasing budget deficits is that the shortfall between government spending and tax revenues must be met by borrowing. If governments borrow more from a given national pot of money, it means the private sector must make do with less. This is the 'crowding out' argument. If one party demands more and more money, it forces up the rate of interest on scarce funds and the other party is thus dissuaded from borrowing. This argument only holds, however, if the private sector *wants* to borrow and invest; a relevant point in normal times, but hardly applicable in a slump when business expectations are pessimistic. There is no crowding out if the government is filling up an empty vessel.

The criticism that public sector borrowing forces up interest rates is not so easily disposed of, however. Although interest rates are unlikely to rise in a financial market awash with excess funds, there nonetheless may come a point where the build up of government borrowing over time leads to a **national** or **international debt** that becomes excessive. Financial markets may then become doubtful whether the government will ever be able to repay all that it owes on time. If holders of public debt (**bonds**) judge that the government is becoming a credit risk, they will thus demand a premium on any loans. This makes a bad situation worse: the government is faced with the need to make ever greater interest payments on its borrowing, and if the economy is sluggish or sinking, then tax revenues will never rise to meet future demands on the public purse. This is the route to a sovereign debt crisis (see Chapter 9).

Governments will always find excuses to increase public spending, this argument runs, and they are not to be trusted. Instead the market economy must be freed and then left alone to rebound by itself, as it surely must.

Such faith in the unaided, recuperative powers of market systems, it must be said, is not shared by everyone. True, markets seem to go through cyclical stages of pessimism and then optimism, but it may take a very long time indeed for sentiments to revive and the economy to recover if employment must wait for business expectations to turn around – and unemployed people tend to vote for a change of government rather than just wait. 'It's the economy, stupid' was the slogan accompanying the successful challenge of Bill Clinton in 1992 to the incumbent US President George Bush Sr who, despite a successful foreign policy, was vulnerable to the charge of doing too little in a recession. The faith of free marketeers in a faltering economy rebounding by itself tends not to be shared by vote-conscious politicians – a point we will return to later.

The criticism that counter-cyclical government spending might make a bad situation worse has another side to it, however. A preoccupation with stimulating the level of aggregate demand, such that the circular flow of spending rises sufficiently to generate full employment in the economy, does not take account of what sort of employment, and what sort of industry, is being supported. The dominant criticism of Keynesian economics in the past has been that government spending is wasted on keeping alive industrial dinosaurs, or zombie companies, that should have been left to die long ago. The health of any economy rests on pushy, enterprising, growthful businesses, not on traditional sectors that may carry a great deal of political clout in establishment circles but whose innovative streak has run out, whose time is past.

New Classical, 'supply-side' economists were the dominant policy-advisers of the 1980s Thatcher/Reagan era (see next chapter) and they argued that recessions can be a good clearing-out time for an economy. Where too many resources in Europe and North America were tied up in inefficient, declining industries, unemployment *ought* to rise, freeing up workers to move to newer, growth areas. Unemployment thus becomes a measure that is necessary to reallocate resources within an economy. Wage rates should fall in 'sunset' industries that have failed to win market success, and this will tempt workers to leave these uncompetitive industries and move into 'sunrise', market-winning sectors. The key to long-term, sustainable growth, therefore, is the classic, microeconomic one of **allocative efficiency**. Any government policy focused only on stimulating aggregate demand fatally ignores this necessary redeployment of resources within the economy. If governments distort or prevent prices and wages from signalling where the market is heading, then the economy concerned will be condemned to decline. In a globalised world, other nations will be only too pleased to out-compete you.

Conclusion

The ongoing debate between supporters of active government intervention in the economy and those more in favour of *laissez-faire* is moving modern theoretical work forward. Both micro- and macroeconomic issues need to be addressed: the essential price-signalling mechanism in a market economy may fail to deliver efficient outcomes if markets are left unregulated *and* if government intervention is too heavy-handed.

There is an essential role for government in providing public and merit goods and services that would otherwise be missing in society; the abuse of corporate economic power needs to be policed, and financiers need to be supervised to safeguard their use of other people's money.

Central authorities need to intervene to smooth out the most severe swings in an unregulated market economy – but should not blindly inject money into the circular flow and prop up enterprises that have no future. Governments should help lead resources towards market opportunities, not to unconditional hand-outs.

As was indicated in Chapter 1, the opening up of trade and the extension of competitive markets worldwide has generated exponential growth in living standards for billions of people since the eighteenth century and, despite the recent crisis that engulfed the more developed nations, unshackling market incentives has lifted countless numbers out of poverty in much of the developing world. The free market is an impressively liberating and empowering engine for change. But it is an economic powerhouse that needs careful piloting if it is not to wreak havoc.

Key words

Allocative efficiency A given resource – say, a doctor – may be highly efficient and successful in his work of treating cases of sports injury on university campuses. However, if the country is suffering a major build-up of serious trauma cases in road accidents, then this doctor's services may be more economically efficient if allocated to this latter employment. Allocative efficiency is obtained when there can be no further net gains available to society by reallocating resources from one use to another.

Asymmetric information If one party to a deal has access to relevant information that the other does not, then the agreed bargain will be one-sided, or asymmetric. The price determined in such a deal will not reflect the true costs and benefits involved; the outcome of all such practices will be far from the social optimum. In fact, markets characterised by asymmetric information will eventually fail since dealers will not trust them.

Bonds Old English for promise. A bond is a written promise, a legal contract – usually a promise to pay a fixed rate of interest on a given loan. For example, you pay me $1 million and I will promise to pay you 5 per cent per year for as long as you have my 'bond'. My bond may be returned to me and cashed in at an agreed

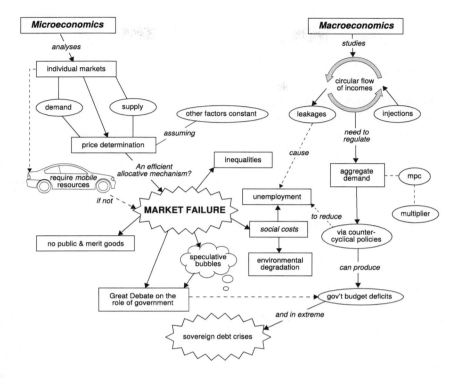

Figure 2.9 The themes of Chapter 2.

date, or you may decide to sell it to someone else (at whatever price you can get) in a *secondary market* (see Chapter 7).

Budget deficit This is where spending exceeds income over a fixed period. A government's budget contrasts its spending on all sorts of public goods and services against the income it receives from its (mainly tax) revenues.

Demand curve An illustration of how the demand for a given product varies with its price, all other variables being held constant. For normal goods, this is a curve sloping down from left to right.

Fallacy of composition The belief that what is a valid and successful course of action for one agent acting alone is equally valid and successful for all agents acting together. If I leave work early to go home and beat the traffic, that works for me, but it is a fallacy to assume that such an action would work if everyone tried to do it.

G20 nations A talking shop of the top twenty leading nations, supposedly to provide global leadership and governance. Heads of state, finance ministers and foreign ministers have all met and made their deliberations on a rotating basis since 2008. Inevitably more representative than the G8 nations that preceded it, the meetings of the G20 attract a great deal of publicity, but with such diverse interests involved, it is easier to make grand statements than to follow through on common action.

Gini coefficient A measurement of inequality – usually income inequality – from zero to 100 per cent, or from zero to 1, where zero means all national income is distributed equally between all households and 100 per cent or 1 means all income is concentrated in one household only.

Inflation The rate of change of an average of retail prices over the period of a year.

Macroeconomics The study of the economy as a whole, of all markets taken together, and thus it involves the movement of aggregate demand and aggregate supply.

Marginal propensity to consume (MPC) The fraction an individual, or a nation, will consume of an increase of income.

Merit goods These are excludable goods or services that can be restricted in supply and would be provided to those few who can afford them in a pure market economy, but whose benefits are deemed to be worth providing to all. Education is a merit good.

Microeconomics The economics of individual households, goods, services and markets which is typically calculated assuming all other things remain constant.

Monopoly One dominant supplier in a market, powerful enough to determine the price consumers must pay.

Multiplier The ratio by how much an increase (or decrease) in injections into an economy will generate an increase (or decrease) in incomes.

National debt How much a country's public authorities owe to the nation's public from whom it has borrowed; as distinct from **international debt** where government borrows from other nations.

Normative criticism A critique based on a difference of values: where one asserts what another should or should not do.

Occupational and geographical mobility The ease with which a resource (such as land, labour or capital) can move between occupations, or between different places of employment. Land in city centres can be highly occupationally mobile, but geographically fixed. Contrast this with an oil tanker . . .

Positive criticism A critique based on what will or will not work. This is not a matter of opinion; it is a testable proposition.

Price elasticity of supply A measurement of how rapidly an increase in the price of a commodity will induce an increase in its supply. For example, a 10 per cent rise in the market price of a product will increase the incentive for producers to supply more, although this may not be possible immediately (price elasticity of supply will be low). However, if prices and profits stay high, then production may increase by more than 10 per cent later on (price elasticity increases over time).

Private costs and benefits Those costs and benefits taken into account by the individuals who buy and sell the product or service involved. This does not include others who may be affected but are not party to the deal concerned.

Public goods These are non-excludable goods and services which cannot be provided by a private market since the producer cannot restrict the supply only to paying customers – who would thereby pay for the investment. For example, street lighting is a public good which does not discriminate between those who do, or do not, benefit from its provision.

Social costs These are costs imposed on society by the production and/or consumption decisions of private individuals. Sometimes referred to as 'negative externalities'.

Supply curve The illustration of the relationship between the price and the supply of a given good or service, assuming all other factors are unchanged. For normal goods, as the price of the product increases, so the supply curve slopes up.

Questions

1   There has been a recent sustained increase in world demand for various rare earth minerals used in electronics, lasers, mobile phones, etc. What are the implications if either (a) prices, or (b) resources, in this market place are insufficiently flexible?

2   How would you know if a rapid rise in the price of a given product was the result of a speculative bubble or due to real changes in economic fundamentals?

3   'The price mechanism is thus not an automatic, objective, value-free device to organise an economy since the free market inevitably brings into the price calculus all sorts of hidden prejudices.' Explain and discuss.

4   Central authorities inject $100 billion into the economy in an attempt to stimulate depressed aggregate demand. One-quarter of this amount is withdrawn from the economy in savings, imports and other leakages. By how much will the national economy grow as a result of the government stimulus until total leakages rise to equal the original injection and the circular flow of income is in equilibrium?

5   Should governments always aim to balance their budgets or, if they are allowed to run substantial deficits, how might this be financed over the long term?

Further reading

Any introductory text on economics will expand on the theories of price determination and on the macroeconomics of aggregate demand and aggregate supply. See:

Cleaver, T. *Economics: The Basics*, London: Routledge, 2011, especially Chapters 3, 4 and 5.

3 Unemployment and inflation

By far the most important thing the federal government can do to build confidence is to agree on a ten-year plan to deal with the budget deficit. Any such plan will require higher taxes and cuts in spending.

Martin Neil Baily

The single most effective thing that could be done to create jobs would be for the Fed to return total spending in the economy to its pre-recession trend level.

Ryan Avent

Two economists quoted on how to deal with unemployment; in *What Matters*, by McKinsey & Co., 18 July 2011

Introduction

Unemployment is not a natural phenomenon. No creatures in the wild are unemployed – you do not see any birds or animals lying idle. Nor are people in tribal or agricultural societies ever unemployed. In the Middle Ages mass unemployment was unheard of. There was simply too much to do: crops to be harvested; cloth to be woven; stone to be quarried, shaped and placed in construction. Today, in poorer parts of the world, in those remote corners untouched by so-called modern civilisation, you will not find anyone unemployed either. No. Unemployment is solely the creation of modern, industrial society. It is not natural. It is not even man-made. Unemployment is rich-man-made.

Since the industrial revolution, world economic growth and the accompanying sophistication and integration of international trade have brought with them increased specialisation, interdependency and thereby fragility. We call this process today **globalisation**.

The very success of trade means individuals specialise in those employments that can earn them most money. Sophisticated products such as a modern motor car are the outcome of millions of specialised tasks and production decisions spread across many different factories, regions, even countries. Every person's job is dependent on someone else's, and all are dependent on the final consumer demanding the finished product.

Creative destruction

What happens when new products and processes appear in the market place; or when consumer tastes change?

Austrian economist Joseph Schumpeter described modern economic and social evolution as a process of creative destruction – new products and processes are created at the expense of old ones. New jobs destroy traditional employment. There is no future in resisting this creative destruction, in demanding (long-term) government support or in protesting against the employment of modern technologies. Stagecoach drivers lose out to train drivers who will eventually lose out to automatic pilots.

A dynamic economy will always exhibit some industries that are on the way up, and others in decline. This must imply that every such economy will suffer some (hopefully) short-term **structural unemployment** where there is a mismatch between existing skills and changing job opportunities. Remedying this requires education and retraining of the workforce, not stopping the advance of innovative technology. So far as the economics profession is concerned, there is no real disagreement over the causes and remedies of unemployment here.

Academics are, however, seriously divided over whether there is, or is not, a problem with the overall pathway of aggregate demand. According to Keynesian economists, recent experience shows that even with modern, appropriate skills, there may be occasions when there are simply not enough jobs to go round to employ everyone. This is **demand-deficient** (or 'cyclical') **unemployment** which requires an injection of increased spending to prevent its continuation. The notion of cyclical unemployment takes as given the fact that a modern market economy is unstable – liable to booms and slumps. The responsibility thus falls upon the central authorities to manage the level of aggregate demand so that it does not fall too low – creating unemployment – or rise too high, where it may cause inflation.

As we have seen, others disagree. Check the first quote that opens this chapter. New Classical economists (see later) have argued that fluctuations in economic activity are perfectly normal in dynamic, market economies. Highly complex economic systems are simply engaged in a random walk in the process of coping with the real shocks, stresses and strains imposed on them by occasional resource restrictions or technological breakthroughs. Counter-cyclical government policies can do little to improve the innate flexibility and creativity of market systems and may do a great deal of damage instead. Governments should keep out of demand management and concentrate on balancing their budgets just like everyone else.

The great debate continued

As mentioned in the Introduction, what you see happening in the world around you to a large degree depends on the mental mindset you carry with you – and this is never so true as in the great debate over macroeconomic theory. What one economist sees as a recession caused by markets malfunctioning, others interpret as the result of government failure. These two viewpoints are referred to in the opening quotes above. We need to investigate this debate further – and to do that means tracking back to see the different experiences and philosophical starting points that inform this exchange.

The two intellectual adversaries at the bottom of this debate both lived through the First World War, the subsequent rise of socialism and fascism, the Great Depression years of the 1930s and the onset of the Second World War. Although living through the same events, however, this did not mean they drew the same conclusions. Their standpoints were perhaps influenced by their different experiences of British as opposed to Austrian economic governance.

The economic theory of John Maynard Keynes (1883–1946) can first be seen in his scathing attack on the Versailles Peace Treaty in 1919 where he argued, as a UK government adviser, that the reparations demands placed upon Germany would so seriously detract from that nation's circular flow of income that it would prevent its economic growth and condemn the nation to poverty. The full development of his new macroeconomics had to wait until *The General Theory of Employment, Interest and Money*, published in 1936, where he made the case for government contra-cyclical intervention (see Box 3.1) that many have argued saved capitalism in an era when socialism was rampant.

Box 3.1   The Keynesian cross

Keynes' *General Theory* stimulated enormous interest and debate from the moment it first appeared. His ideas were famously encapsulated and popularised after his death by US economist Paul Samuelson in what has been called the Keynesian cross diagram (equal vertical and horizontal scales, crossed by a 45 degree line).

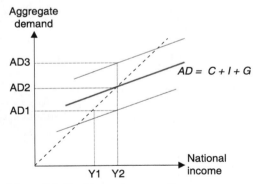

Figure 3.1 The Keynesian cross diagram.

Aggregate demand *AD* in an economy is made up of all consumer spending *C*, plus investment spending *I* and all government spending *G*. (Assume for simplicity that there is no international trade, no loss of spending overseas, or gains from foreign inputs.)

Consumer spending C is by far and away the biggest component of aggregate demand and its level *tends to rise slowly as national income rises.* (People's spending is determined primarily by the size of their incomes, but their marginal propensity to consume is normally less than 100 per cent. Think about it: if your income doubled, your spending would undoubtedly increase but most likely by a bit less than 100 per cent.)

The main determinants of investment I and government spending G are business expectations and political pressures, respectively. In the short term, they are not so closely related to national income Y. In sum, we can say that AD slopes as shown – increasing by less than 45 degrees as Y increases.

Assume that the economy is in *full employment equilibrium at a level of national income Y2, equal to a level of aggregate demand AD2.*

Consumer habits change only slowly. Changes in government spending also take time to be implemented. Business confidence and investment, however, tend to be volatile. Any shock in trade (positive or negative) will impact on investment first of all, only later on consumer and public sector spending.

At any given level of national income, aggregate demand may shift up or down as investment increases or decreases: moving to *AD3* or *AD1*.

What happens if there is booming business confidence and investment such that demand increases to *AD3*? With full employment at level $Y2$, it should be seen that there is no potential in the short term to increase production to meet the quantity of spending illustrated at *AD3*. Excess aggregate demand will cause inflation – unless the government acts to raise taxes and/or cut back spending by the amount *AD3–AD2*.

Conversely, should pessimistic expectations cause a collapse in investment, *AD* falls to *AD1*. There is insufficient spending in the economy to generate full employment. Indeed, aggregate demand now equals aggregate incomes only at level *Y1* – an unemployment equilibrium equivalent to a severe depression. The economy will not recover if the government does not close the gap in aggregate demand by cutting taxes, increasing its own spending, or maybe increasing the money supply to encourage others' spending by an amount *AD1–AD2*.

Conclusions: (1) inflation and unemployment are opposite evils caused by too much or too little aggregate demand, and (2) the government can avoid either extreme by implementing *counter-cyclical* **fiscal** or **monetary policies**.

The Austrian (later British) philosopher and social theorist Friedrich Hayek (1899–1992) witnessed the folly of Austrian and German governments in fomenting hyperinflation in 1923/4 and the excesses of centralised power in the regimes of Stalin and Hitler. As a consequence he became convinced of the virtues of classical liberalism and the perils of central planning, first emphasised in his text *The Road to Serfdom* in 1944. Hayek moved to Chicago in 1950 where his idea of a role of government limited only to controlling the money supply reached fertile ground. Freedoms were guaranteed by allowing countless consumers and producers to interact in the market place, with the central authorities placed under orders not to debase the value of the currency. They were not to be trusted with any other role.

The Keynesian revolution

Keynesian theory completely revolutionised previous classical thought. Unemployment in the 1920s and 1930s had been addressed in those days by wage cuts – economists then being persuaded that excess supplies meant the price of labour was too high. Keynes now showed that this was an entirely inappropriate response in a situation of nationwide, or international, depression.

Such theorising dominated policy-making in the world after 1945. Nations demobilising after the Second World War were fearful of returning to the unemployment levels of the Great Depression era and so embraced demand management policies with gusto, seemingly successfully (see Figure 3.2).

In contrast to the economic instability of the inter-war period when governments were generally non-interventionist, active post-war demand management policies coincided with steady growth and full employment in the western world. When A. W. Phillips published his famous findings on unemployment and inflation in

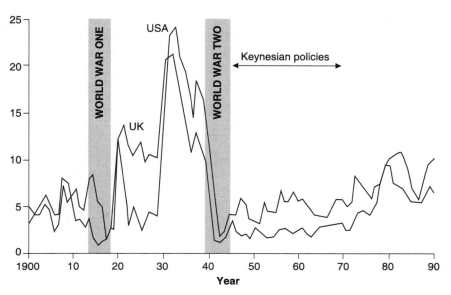

Figure 3.2 Percentage unemployed in the UK and USA, 1900–90. Note the great instability of the 1920s and 1930s compared with the post-1945 era when Keynesian policies were being implemented.

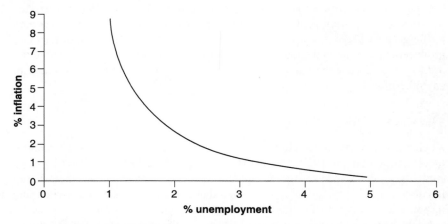

Figure 3.3 The UK Phillips curve, 1862–1958. Phillips' data supported the hypothesis that unemployment and inflation are inversely related: as unemployment falls, inflation rises and vice versa. It was this so-called trade-off that led governments to think they could opt for a little less of one in place of a little more of the other.

1958, the victory of Keynesian theory over classical views on unemployment was complete.

Professor Phillips was concerned about the link between the rate of change in money wages and unemployment. Working at the London School of Economics, he correlated UK inflation and unemployment performance for almost a hundred years from 1862 to 1958 and found that the relationship between the two was remarkably stable. The Phillips curve (see Figure 3.3) shows a clear **trade-off** between unemployment and inflation, with the unavoidable policy implication that, in the short run, if a country opts to reduce one it must exacerbate the other – exactly in accordance with Keynesian predictions.

The Keynesian 'revolution' of the 1930s had thus become the mainstream orthodoxy of the 1950s and 1960s. As always in economics, there was a continuing academic debate between adherents and critics of these views (Chicago holding out against Keynesianism), but this had little impact on the practical policy-makers. Keynesian demand management was predominant in western governments.

The classical revival

Ironically, although Hayek was in Chicago, his was not the key influence on the economist who first challenged the Keynesian revolution in policy-making. Milton Friedman (1912–2006) undertook exhaustive research which he published in *A Monetary History of the United States* (1963) and which led him to conclude that the Great Depression was nothing to do with insufficient aggregate demand, but was rather due to variations in the US domestic money supply – caused by bank collapses unsupported by the **Federal Reserve**.

Friedman's view was that central authorities should set the growth of money supplies to equal the long-run trend growth of the economy – and do no more. Any other intervention is essentially misguided and destabilising. (Note the clear parallel with Hayek's ideas.)

In the 1950s and early 1960s no policy-makers were listening to Friedman's views, although that situation was soon to change. Friedman was highly critical of government attempts to try and manipulate aggregate demand, opting for a little less unemployment (a vote-winner) in place of a little more inflation (less noticeable). In 1967, in a famous address given to the American Economics Association, Friedman opened an attack upon the theoretical basis of the Phillips curve. For a hundred years of non-interventionism, the periods when prices were rising roughly equalled those times when prices were falling. Inflationary expectations would thus be zero. From the early 1960s, however, with governments openly stimulating demand, this was no longer a reasonable assumption. Slowly creeping inflation had taken hold and, he reasoned, this must in time affect expectations and therefore wage bargaining.

If workers and their union representatives expected that prices would rise in the future, then they would build in this factor to their wage demands: asking for higher pay to protect their real incomes. If employers then granted such wage increases, they would thereafter try to pass on these extra costs by pushing up prices even higher. Inflation would begin to accelerate. Workers find prices are higher than expected and thus put in for even greater wage increases next time. The end result must be an inflationary wage–price spiral.

Milton Friedman of the University of Chicago published simultaneously with Edmund Phelps of the University of Pennsylvania and both independently argued that the stable function between the two alleged opposites of inflation and unemployment that had lasted for almost a century could not continue. So long as governments keep stimulating spending in the attempt to reduce the level of unemployment below the economy's natural level, excess demand will outrun the economy's capacity to produce and prices will keep rising. The original Phillips curve must transform into a vertical line (Figure 3.4). *Any* rate of inflation was

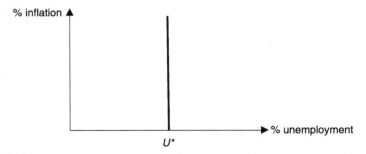

Figure 3.4 Friedman's 'expectations-augmented' Phillips curve. There is no trade-off between inflation and unemployment in this conjecture. Unemployment is stable at some natural level U^* determined by labour markets, and prices will rise to any level consistent with whatever amount of money is circulating in the economy.

Box 3.2   The natural rate of unemployment

The 'natural' rate of unemployment is a controversial notion and one first mooted by Friedman in his 1967 address. It is that level which obtains when all labour markets in an economy are in microeconomic equilibrium and thus the only unemployed are those unwilling or unable to offer their labour at the going wage rate in their line of work, i.e. they are *voluntarily* unemployed.

Note that workers will always be taken on in a market economy up to the point where what they produce and earn for their employers just compensates for their wage costs. Wages are determined in each respective labour market and governments cannot force businesses to take on more labour beyond the point where they are loss-making. But governments *can* inject more spending into the economy, thus increasing short-run revenues and fooling businesses to take on more of a diminishing pool of labour. In this case, prices will only rise faster than outputs and workers will come to realise their **real wages** are now less than they thought and thus will demand more. This extra will be given by employers providing these extra wage costs can be passed on to consumers in the form of higher prices – cranking up a wage–price spiral of inflation that will continue for as long as the government attempts to overstimulate the economy, trying to reduce unemployment below its 'natural' level.

(The corollary of this argument is that the unemployment rate will never rise *above* U^* in Figure 3.4 since it is postulated that labour will produce revenues in excess of their costs up to this point – and no profit-seeking business will pass up this chance of taking on such productive labour.)

---

consistent with the 'natural level of unemployment' (see Box 3.2) depending on how much money the authorities were pumping into the economy.

Friedman's argument of a vertical, expectations-augmented Phillips curve was a neat theoretical argument at the time that excited much academic discussion, but it wasn't until a decade later that his views suddenly became world-famous. What suddenly changed the picture were the 1973 and 1979 oil price shocks (see Chapter 5) and the associated recession that followed them. Rates of inflation *did* take off in the USA, Europe and indeed all round the world, as governments tried to spend their way out of trouble (see Figures 3.5). The previously stable Phillips curve relationship broke down just as Friedman had predicted and so too did the Keynesian paradigm that had dominated post-war policy-making. 'Stagflation' – stagnation *plus* inflation – seemed to dog the late 1970s and early 1980s, and the old Keynesian remedy of stimulating aggregate demand no longer seemed to work (with a world dependent on severely restricted oil supplies, more spending could not induce more production, only more inflation). Inflation and unemployment were not opposites now, but complements. Keynesianism was dead; a new and revived classical theory was triumphant.

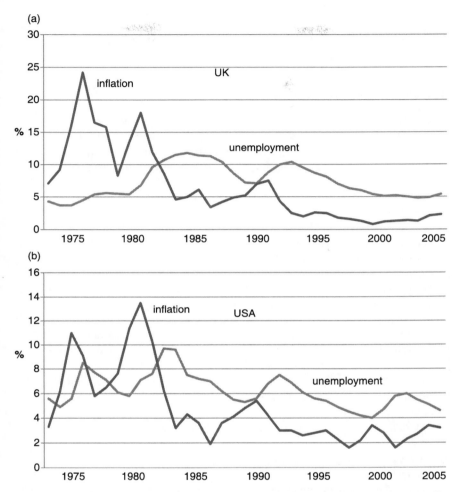

Figures 3.5 (a) UK and (b) US percentage rates of inflation and unemployment, 1972–
2006. Note how inflation and unemployment both trend upwards in the 1970s
until 1982, whereupon – in both countries – they cross over on their trend path
down. (Although the vertical scales are different these are very similar pic-
tures, and are similarly reflected in other trading nations over the same period.
They demonstrate just how interlinked our fortunes are in this globalised
world.)

Sources: Eurostat, rate.inflation.com.

What governments had ignored was that, in focusing on stabilising aggregate
demand (and in the US case, extending immense military and space commitments),
the steady advance of public sector spending and employment in the post-war
years had increasingly impaired the essential allocative functioning of (especially
labour) markets, frustrated economic growth, led to deficits getting out of control

and fomented creeping, and then galloping, inflation. The 1970s oil price shocks were just a wake-up call, simply the last alarm bell, to remind nations that long-term sustained growth requires the supply side, and not only the demand side, of an economy to be nurtured and kept healthy.

The expectations revolution

The expectations revolution, codified in a **New Classical economics**, was driven forward by a new generation of economists from the Chicago school, and it became the dominant paradigm of the post oil-crisis years, taking hold of economics departments everywhere and relegating Keynesian theory to the sidelines. It emphasised sweeping reforms to limit the role of government and liberate markets along Hayekian lines. In its extreme form, new classical theory asserted that government economic intervention was ineffective because, with **rational expectations**, liberalised private markets would always second-guess what policies would be introduced.

For example, if the central authorities announced a credible policy to cut back inflation, this would immediately affect expectations and private markets would quickly bring wage demands and prices under control even before the government acted. If implemented, of course, then cutting back money supplies and government spending might cause unemployment to rise, but this would only be a short-term phenomenon in circumstances where the economy was inflexible and expectations took time to adjust. Theoretically speaking, it should be possible to go straight down the vertical line in Figure 3.4, just as quickly as inflation went straight up. Solution: liberate the supply side of the economy. Restore the essential dynamism and flexibility to the market economy and there is no need to worry about any macroeconomic imbalance. The free market will right itself. Long-term unemployment cannot happen so long as prices and resources are mobile.

Key policy components of the new classicism were:

- remove all price ceilings and wage floors and permit all prices and resources to move freely;
- deregulate industry and commerce and promote competition;
- privatise any and all state-owned industry;
- cut taxes, reduce government expenditure and shrink the size of the public sector; fiscal policies should be confined to balancing the budget;
- monetary policy is critical: make the central bank independent and keep politicians' hands off the money supply.

Through the 1980s and beyond, the supply-side reforms listed above informed government policy-making circles in countries as distant and diverse as Chile and China, New Zealand and Norway, Eastern Europe and South-East Asia – as well as in the UK and USA where they were famously associated with Margaret Thatcher and Ronald Reagan.

Supply-side policies have had an immense impact on the world economy, liberating growth and lifting people out of poverty as mentioned earlier – but then so had Keynesian policies in the immediate post-war era before this, though the generation of Thatcher's and Reagan's children had forgotten or ignored that fact.

The introduction of expectations into theoretical models of how an economy works is clearly important, but the prediction of the new classical paradigm that flexible markets will always secure equilibrium without unemployment, providing governments do not interfere, flies in the face of experience.

New Classical economics has no satisfactory explanation for why aggregate demand can collapse and stay depressed. What caused the Great Depression of the 1930s? What caused the 'lost decade' of Japan in the 1990s? (See Box 3.3.) And what has caused the Great Recession of current times? It is a little too easy to blame it all on governments distorting the workings of private markets and to assert that all unemployment is voluntary.

Box 3.3   Japan, the lost decade and the liquidity trap

One nation that bucked the trend of the (particularly East Asian) booming 1990s was Japan. In contrast, it suffered what has been called a 'lost decade' (actually longer) of deflation and depression, and many pessimistic American commentators have argued that what happened there, then, foretells what will happen to the USA in the current era.

The similarities of Japan's experience with what was subsequently to follow for other nations is certainly striking, and it should have rung alarm bells around the world well before the sub-prime mortgage crisis.

More than a generation of tigerish growth, particularly in manufacturing exports that were pouring into Europe and the USA, had filled Japan's household and business coffers, pumped up the value of the yen and, after numerous overseas investments and takeovers that worried western business and political leaders alike, the Japanese were running out of places to put their cash. In the late 1980s, a combination of booming domestic property values and very low interest rates led to easily available credit, fuelling a massive speculative bubble.

In 1989 in central Tokyo, prime office space was going for US$139,000 a square foot and some were estimating that the value of the land covered by the Imperial Palace alone was worth more than the entire state of California! On 29 December of that year, the Nikkei 225 Index (a market measure of the value of Japanese industrial capital) reached its highest value of 38,957.44. These were insane heights that eventually prompted the Finance Ministry to prick the bubble by sharply raising interest rates.

The stock market then crashed. In less than a year, by September 1990, the Nikkei fell by almost 50 per cent, and it continued bumping along down until, by October 2008, the Japanese index had slumped to 6,994 – a decline of 82 per cent over nineteen years. By early 2004, houses were selling at 10 per cent of their peak price, and commercial real estate was selling for less than one-hundredth of its peak-market value. What all this meant was that people's savings in property were disappearing into thin air: wealth was being vaporised.

This was no recessionary blip, but a full-blooded depression along 1930s' lines. Economic growth for much of the 1990s was stagnant; unemployment was rising and inflation was negative, that is, prices were actually falling over time. This was dangerous. Domestic consumption, already hit by declining wealth, had no incentive to increase – people will withhold spending today if they think prices will be lower tomorrow. But, of course, if everyone stops spending, the circular flow just gets smaller and smaller. Japan had fallen foul of a Keynesian fallacy of composition called **the paradox of thrift**.

Domestic investment was not going to get them out of this – despite interest rates being close to zero, expectations were extremely pessimistic. (US Economist Paul Krugman commented in 1998 that the ten-year bond rate was less than 0.7 per cent; that is, financial markets were then betting that the depression would last for at least another ten years.)

The required remedy was to stimulate aggregate demand by fiscal and monetary policy. With regard to fiscal policy, the size of the demand deficiency was so great that such a large increase in budget deficits for so long (ten years?) would be simply politically impossible to achieve, given the highly conservative nature of Japan's ruling elite. As for monetary policy, Japan was stuck in what Keynes had described as a **liquidity trap**. (Keynes had originally dreamed up this concept as a theoretical possibility only – fifty years after his death, Japan was faced with its reality!)

According to standard microeconomics, an excess supply of funds – where an economy's aggregate savings exceed investors' demand for loans – should mean that rates of interest (the price of loanable funds) will fall until eventually supply equals demand. But what if interest rates are already close to zero? Do they become negative? That is, must banks offer to pay businesses to borrow money? Somewhat unlikely. (Actually, in 2009 in the USA, just as in Japan during part of the 1990s, domestic inflation rates were higher than nominal interest rates. That is, the *real* interest rate was negative. Anyone borrowing money at those times could pay it back later at less real value! Yet still there were too few takers . . .)

Insofar as Keynesian macroeconomics is concerned, if governments wish to stimulate private sector investment in order to initiate a multiplied increase in the circular flow of incomes, then an expansionary monetary policy in these circumstances will be ineffective. Zero interest rates mean a country already has more than enough liquidity, and increasing supplies of money will not be taken up by businesses which are not interested in investment.

So what could Japan do with both fiscal and monetary policies unworkable? Krugman claimed that reforming the banks and financial practices would not work either since too many bad loans meant they would be cleaning up their balance sheets and contracting trade for years to come. (Does all this sound familiar?)

If deflating prices was holding back consumption, then the only hope to persuade the Japanese to bring their spending forward, he suggested, was for the Japanese central bank to make a credible promise to *increase* inflation. A novel recommendation! (The Japanese have traditionally had a high savings ratio, compared with the West, which in booming times was a great asset since it could fund higher investment and growth. However, such a virtue in the good times when supply is constrained converts into a major obstacle in bad times when aggregate demand has slumped.)

At the time of writing, Japan has still not completely worked its way out of depression and returned to its 'miracle' growth trend of the 1980s. This experience and the lessons for academic economics are lost, of course, on those who will not see.

Former US Treasury Secretary Lawrence Summers argued (in the *Financial Times*, 13 January 2011) that a sick economy works differently from a normal one:

> After bubbles burst there is no pent-up desire to invest. Instead there is a glut of capital caused by over-investment during the period of confidence – vacant houses, malls without tenants and factories without customers. At the same time consumers discover they have less wealth than they expected, less collateral to borrow against and are under more pressure than they expected from their creditors.

This is a textbook illustration of a lack of aggregate demand; it perfectly sums up what happened in the 1930s, in late twentieth-century Japan and in the early twenty-first-century developed world. Freeing up the supply side of an economy and assuming that this is all that is necessary and sufficient; insisting on governments' reducing deficits in order to 'build confidence' when trade has collapsed – this is simply quasi-religious, dogmatic claptrap. Businesses need orders before they can become confident in the future.

A Keynesian restatement

In the longer term, economies must invest in labour and capital in order to secure growth. Technological innovation that increases the productivity of a nation's natural endowments is essential. Efficiently allocating resources among growth-promoting employments, and present and future needs, requires a flexible market system (see Chapter 10 on growth theory). But to get to the long term you first have to solve the short-term problems that are paralysing you, and this is not achieved by simply waiting for recessions to cure themselves. The 'invisible hand' is simply too invisible in such times.

With regard to New Classical economics, supply-side reforms are appropriate *when* the supply side is constrained. Over the longer term, inflation and unemployment might well go up and down together as this theory predicts.

But take another look at Figure 3.5. What do you see happening from 1980 to 2006? To be sure, both inflation and unemployment *did* fall more or less over this period – now referred to as the Great Moderation – but was the Keynesian notion of a short-term trade-off between these two variables entirely discredited? I think not. The two lines do seem to swing up and down in opposition to each other remarkably consistently, albeit over a declining trend.

The precise relationship between inflation and unemployment has been through a number of changes since Phillips' day, but nonetheless these two economic objectives do appear to be short-run alternatives – at least in the evidence featured here.

US economist Alan Blinder uses a very helpful analogy to illustrate how managing a national economy in the stable world environment of the 1950s and 1960s compares with the crisis-ridden 1970s. It is like driving a car – there is always a short-term trade-off between speed and safety. The faster you go, the more dangerous it is: speed and safety are alternatives. Now consider what it is like driving in clear weather on a good road, compared with driving in blizzard conditions in unknown country. The same trade-off still exists, but now the relationship shifts to a completely different level. Hazardous external conditions have transformed the way these two alternatives operate on your driving.

The Phillips curve thus shifted to a different level in the mid-1970s compared with the previous situation – and in so doing it discredited Keynesian economics. The Great Moderation through the 1990s saw changing conditions (a 'good road') which seemingly supported new classical theory, but I would suggest this was simply a shift back towards the original Phillips curve. Certainly what has happened since 2008 undermines all notions of the impossibility of long-run unemployment if markets are flexible. The supply-side reforms – which were undoubtedly effective – have not prevented the current Great Recession from widening the gap again between inflation and unemployment (see Figure 3.6). And so, with a return to a more hazardous world economy, it is now Keynesian economics that has come back to the fore.

Rewriting economics

Global economic and financial crises lead to a rewrite of economic theories. The Great Depression led to the Keynesian revolution; the stagflating 1970s led to the expectations revolution; the theoretical and policy implications of the Great Recession are still being argued over but here are some early conclusions.

Microeconomic issues are very important. Labour with the wrong skills, financiers who fund speculation and not investment, self-seeking businessmen and public officials who favour hand-outs rather than enterprise – they all inhibit growth in real outputs and condemn an economy to stagnation, if not boom and bust. Perfect markets with efficient price signalling are essential – but cannot be assumed. They must be policed. Liberalising prices and deregulating trade and commerce can lead to market failure just as surely as excessive government intervention can hamstring the private sector and deaden entrepreneurial dynamism.

Macroeconomic demand management is still necessary. Deficit spending in a major slump cannot be avoided since market systems are unstable and not self-

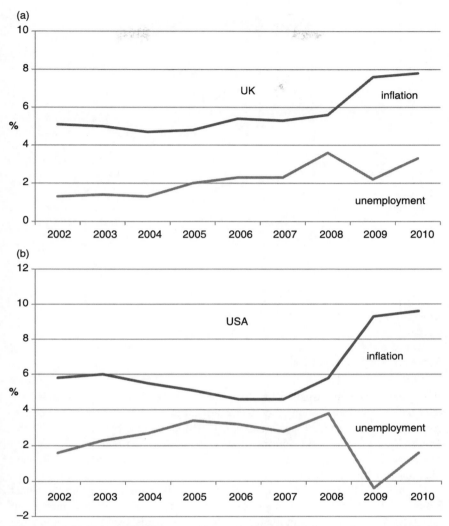

Figures 3.6 (a) UK and (b) US percentage rates of inflation and unemployment, 2002–10. The return of the Phillipsian trade-off.

Sources: As Figure 3.5.

equilibrating at a level consistent with full employment and no inflation. The clear message here, therefore, is 'fix the roof when the sun shines'. That is, governments should aim for budget surpluses when times are good because we have learnt that they do not last.[1] Inflation and unemployment remain opposite evils and require *both* demand-side *and* supply-side, macro- and microeconomic medicine to keep them in check.

To stabilise the aggregate supply of money, government monetary policy cannot be confined just to making central banks independent, limiting the amount of

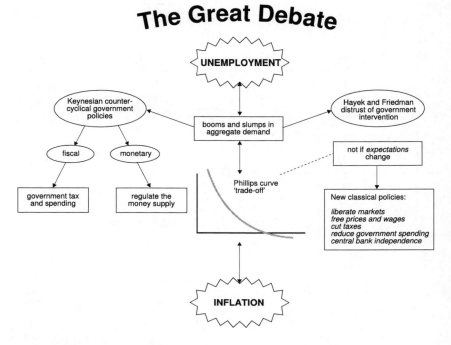

Figure 3.7 The themes of Chapter 3.

credit they create, and trusting financial markets to balance their books and look after their own affairs. Such markets are subject to extremes of over- and under-confidence, extraordinary delusions and herd-like animal behaviour: quite the opposite of rational expectations. National and international regulation and supervision of banking and finance therefore needs to be tightened; supply-side liberalisation needs to be reversed (see Chapter 9).

The one area barely touched upon so far is international trade. From the outset I have claimed that increasing trade accompanies and facilitates increasing incomes. The theory and evidence for this now needs examining, as do the implications for specific policies. You should not be surprised by now to learn that there is a wide variety of trade-oriented policies that can be employed by any country towards its neighbours, partners and rivals in the world, and there are just as many differences of opinion as to which policies and strategies should be employed by any one nation, and to what consequence. Much of the rest of this text is devoted to these questions.

Key words

Demand-deficient or 'cyclical' unemployment Market economies tend to experience booms and slumps over time as aggregate demand either outpaces, or falls behind, the rate at which aggregate supply grows. At the phase of this cycle where aggregate demand is less than aggregate supply, then general unemployment will rise.

Federal Reserve The central bank of the USA. Its prime responsibility is to conduct the nation's monetary policy, and in this regard, though notionally independent of the government and political interference, its actions have an inevitable political impact and it is thus subject to conflicting pressures. The Fed's chequered history includes periods when it was alleged to be too slow in dealing with the country's economic problems (in the 1930s) or misguided (in allowing the speculative bubble leading up to the 2008 crash).

Fiscal policies Government policies on what, and how much, to tax and spend. Such policies impact on the level and direction of private consumption and production in the economy.

Globalisation   A much used and imprecise term to describe the international impact of economic affairs. It refers to the wider and wider reach of markets – bringing together buyers and sellers around the globe – and this in turn relates to the 'four freedoms': the ease of movement of goods, services, labour and capital about the world.

Liquidity trap A situation where the supply of loanable funds has increased to exceed its demand and thus the rate of interest has fallen to zero. A possibility thought to exist in a severe recession where, if the central bank engineers a further increase in supply, it is unlikely to induce entrepreneurs to borrow and invest and thus generate an increase in economic activity.

Monetary policies Central bank policies aimed to determine either the rate of interest or the quantity of money operating in the economy. Central banks have been charged to use such policies to control the rate of inflation in the country, or to affect the rate of economic growth, or to contain unemployment. With conflicting targets, with the explosion of private financial intermediation, and the many different forms of money they create, central banks have an increasingly difficult time in making their monetary policies impact in the ways they wish.

New Classical economics A school of thought which emphasises the primacy of private markets. Economic agents are alleged to be rational, quick to learn and to move faster than politicians such that government economic policies may be ineffective. New classical recommendations are to privatise and liberalise markets and 'get government off people's backs'.

The paradox of thrift The fallacy of composition emphasised by Keynes that if one person saves, he or she may be better off in future – but if everyone saves it implies aggregate spending must fall and so everyone must earn less.

Rational expectations The notion that economic agents will base their future production and consumption decisions on all information available to them, such that if prices are forecast to rise next year they will base their current behaviour (e.g. investment decisions or wage demands) on such an expectation. Expectations have always been important in economic theorising, but the New Classical School employs not only feedback from past experience, but also complex formulas and rules for predicting the future in its characterisation of 'rational' expectations.

Real wages The value of wages, not in terms of money, but in the amount of real goods and services they will buy.

Structural unemployment That which results when the structure of an economy changes so that traditional industries fail, new industries emerge, and people laid off from the former may not be employed in the latter.

Trade-off A key concept in economics: to gain one thing you want may mean you have to sacrifice another.

Questions

1   If wages are fully flexible, can there be such a thing as long-term unemployment? Why or why not?
2   If Friedman is correct that the Great Depression was caused by a contraction of the US money supply unrelieved by the Federal Reserve, is there any role for Keynesian counter-cyclical fiscal policies to alleviate unemployment?
3   'Governments should not attempt to counter recessions – they are both inevitable and necessary to clear out the dead wood in industry.' Discuss.
4   In what ways is the modern Great Recession similar to the 1930s' Great Depression, and in what ways is it different?
5   What are the strengths and the limitations of implementing New Classical or supply-side economic policies in times of global recession?

Further reading

It is difficult to be totally objective and also difficult to simplify the academic controversies that have opened up in the various analyses of unemployment and inflation, but see Nobel Prize-winning economist and regular *New York Times* columnist Paul Krugman in his excellent portrayal of what I refer to as the Great Debate in: *How Did Economists Get It So Wrong?*, www.nytimes.com/2009/09/06/magazine/06Economic-t.html. See also his blog: http://krugman.blogs.nytimes.com.

The best in-depth study of the main macroeconomic schools of thought can be found in Brian Snowdon and Howard Vane, *Modern Macroeconomics, its Origins, Development and Current State*, Cheltenham: Edward Elgar, 2005.

4   Free trade, regional agreements and job losses

Piece by piece, job by job, factory by factory, [American industry] is being carted off to foreign soil.

Pat Buchanan (one-time US presidential hopeful)

Most economic fallacies derive from the tendency to assume that there is a fixed pie; that one party can gain only at the expense of another.

Milton Friedman

Introduction

Free trade in world markets randomly visits misery on groups of workers and business people whose products seem suddenly to go out of favour. Most countries can find examples of established industries that – thanks to changing technology and the costs of production, or some fickleness in consumer demand – have lost their markets to new competitors.

- In the early 1980s, Hong Kong, South Korea and Taiwan together accounted for nearly a third of the world's clothing exports. That has now fallen to less than 8 per cent as world demand snaps up cheaper produce from China.
- In the late 1980s and early 1990s, as communications and transport costs fell, US carmakers transferred assembly plants to Mexico; Volkswagen invested in the Czech Republic; Philips consumer electronics went further afield to China.
- The outsourcing of jobs offshore, which used to occur in pursuit of cheap manufacturing labour, is increasingly undertaken in the search for high-end service skills. Legal process outsourcing is now a US$61 million business for India. When large US multinationals fight a case at home, the corporations need only one lawyer in court now since they are backed by entire legal departments on the Indian subcontinent.

The process of creative destruction that causes distress to some brings opportunity to others, of course, but the differential impact on costs and benefits means that the misery can be painfully concentrated in certain regions and countries at certain times. The benefits may seem too often to be more accessible to other people, other places. During periods of instability and wrenching change, the political impetus for protectionist policies – to cushion certain communities and industrial sectors from the harsh realities of international competition – may thus prove unstoppable. It often plays on the short-sighted sentiment that a country's wealth and welfare is best ensured by denying foreign advantage.

Trade protection

Mercantilism has a long and sorry history. It advocates securing trade gains at the expense of other countries, erecting barriers against imports whilst aggressively promoting exports. At the extreme, it drove eighteenth- and nineteenth-century European empire-building and colonialism – the rush to carve up resource-rich and militarily less-powerful American, African and Asian lands before rivals could do likewise. In the 1930s, mercantilist 'beggar-my-neighbour' policies were pursued in the attempt to escape the Great Depression – only to make matters worse. The same protectionist, nationalist sentiments emerged across the world during the stagnating 1970s and have reappeared again during the current Great Recession.

In the new millennium, myopic attitudes to trade have taken a novel twist. Laudable, but fundamentally uninformed concern for the welfare of poorer nations has fuelled protests against the international gatherings of trade ministers and government leaders. Diverse meetings in Seattle, Prague, Washington and Davos have witnessed angry demonstrations against the supposed representatives of 'global capitalism' which allegedly set the rules of world trade against the poor. The irony is that if there is to be any general rule to lift incomes for the whole world – poor as well as rich – then it must be to free up trade for all and not to resort to blinkered protectionism. Both reason and empirical evidence reveal that international trade benefits those that support it – it is not a zero-sum game where if one gains another must lose – and so the best solution is to extend the opportunity to trade to all. (However, note concerns about distribution; see Box 4.1.)

Protectionist thinking never goes away. As implied above, it is simply more apparent at some times and places than at others. When the world economy is booming it becomes less relevant since all are becoming richer; when world economic growth slows, becomes stagnant or shrinks, however, then the protectionist barriers go up and one country's economic fortune can be at the expense of another's.

At such times it requires considerable diplomatic effort to prevent trade restrictions from spreading. A general collapse in world trade, everyone agrees, is bad for all, but what does it matter if my country alone subsidises its exports and protects its vital industries? Such is the argument of the free-rider – who benefits most if everyone else agrees to the rules. But protectionist policies are dangerously infectious. Once one party breaks ranks and erects a trade barrier, then other countries will retaliate and, without any international forum to consider the global implications, within a very short time frame trade and incomes slump for all.

The General Agreement on Tariffs and Trade (GATT) was set up in 1948 precisely to prevent such narrow protectionism from occurring. It formed an

---

Box 4.1   Trade, growth and income distribution

Trade between rich and poor nations may benefit both parties, but this says nothing about the *distribution* of the gains between and within participating countries.

For example, Country A with national income equal to 100 and Country B with income of 40 may both double their incomes in a decade of increased trade between them – but this would then result in A reaching an income level of 200 and B only reaching 80. The income gap between them has widened.

Alternatively, now consider that, due to trade, the poor country grows on average *faster* than the rich country (China, for example, has grown more rapidly than the UK since 1978). The principle above still holds for the distribution of gains *within* each country. As national incomes have doubled overall in the poorer country, and increased by only 10 per cent in the richer country, the richer fraction of the population in both may have widened the gap between them and the poorer fraction of the same nation (see the indices of inequality in China and the UK in Figure 2.4).

Conclusion: freer trade, in general, will benefit *all* parties involved – certainly it is better than autarky (where a nation tries to cut itself off from all international commerce and thereby condemns itself to no, or very slow, growth). But the distribution of the gains from trade needs monitoring since *those with skills in demand will inevitably gain more*, and thus active government policies are essential to ensure that some people are not left out from playing their part in the market place than would otherwise be the case.

Issues of growth and inequality will be analysed in more detail in Chapter 10.

---

important part of the attempt to rebuild a positive world order after the disasters of two world wars and an intervening depression. Despite all the difficulties, it has been outstandingly successful and in 1995 it graduated to become the World Trade Organization (WTO). Originally, 23 countries participated in the first GATT round of discussions in Geneva. At the last count in 2008, the WTO claimed 153 members. In the meantime, the average tariff on world trade has come down from around 40 per cent to less than 4 per cent; the global economy grew six-fold up to the new millennium and international trade shot up almost off the graph (see Figure 4.1).

Trade clearly correlates with economic growth. Economic historians have identified three great phases of globalisation when trade restrictions have been reduced, when costs of world finance and transport have been falling, and when major exogenous shocks have been absent:

1.   between 1870 and 1913, with the opening up of rich resources in the New World;

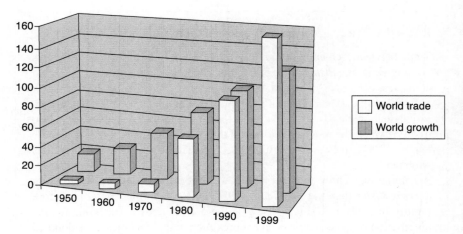

Figure 4.1 Index of world trade and growth, 1950–99 (1990 = 100).
Source: WTO.

2.   from 1945 to 1973, with recovery and dynamic growth after the Second
     World War; and
3.   from 1980 to 2008, after oil price shocks and the deregulation of world finance.

Negotiating worldwide reductions in trade barriers, although worthwhile, is
extremely slow going. The binding principle that drives the WTO is the commitment
to end discrimination in trade and to generalise 'most favoured nation' status to all.
Thus any advantage granted to one trading partner must be extended to every
signatory. This is time-consuming to arrange. The issue that inevitably slows
progress the most is the *distribution* of gains involved in any new round of cuts (as
mentioned in Box 4.1). Why should one nation agree to reduce **tariffs** and **quotas**
if these seem to give greater competitive advantage to another? Poorer countries
dependent on the export of a precious few products are wary of the exploitative
power of rich nations with highly developed industrial bases; old rivalries amongst
mature economies are easily awoken; there is also much disagreement between
poor nations themselves. The most recent round of talks launched in Doha, in the
Gulf state of Qatar, in 2001 was designed to embrace a wide range of issues – trade
in manufactures, agriculture, services, intellectual property rights, environmental
protection – but has been struggling on and off ever since without much progress
owing to widespread distrust. After the latest breakdown, WTO Director General
Pascal Lamy reported (July 2011): 'The differences are . . . profoundly political,
rendering compromise impossible without a shift in position.' Each nation claims
legitimate concerns and all this requires much time and diplomacy to address.

   Despite such disappointments, the WTO remains important, and perhaps its
greatest success recently was its ability to insist that member countries keep to a
rules-based multinational trading system, to prevent a return to beggar-my-
neighbour policies in the aftermath of the 2008 global financial crisis.

Along with the slow progress of multilateral trade negotiations, two other, relatively recent developments in international trade are of increasing concern: firstly, the rapid increase in regional and bilateral trade agreements, and, secondly, the growth in outsourcing/offshoring deals.

Regional deals

The fewer the parties involved in any negotiations, and the more they have in common, the easier it is to secure agreement. It is for this reason that regional trade agreements (RTAs) have grown rapidly, against the background of a WTO-inspired, general expansion of international trade. So long as the regional deals involved do not lead to a raising of barriers to outsiders, then, somewhat pragmatically, WTO rules do not prohibit such arrangements. Realistically, the post-war movement towards the construction of the European Union (EU) in particular – although highly discriminatory with respect to farm trade – has been unstoppable. The very success of the EU has been an added reason for the growth of other regional associations, both in the desire to emulate its success and in the fear of losing out in a world increasingly subdivided into power blocs.

Of the 484 RTAs notified to the WTO as of 31 December 2010, 293 were active; all WTO members except Mongolia are members of one deal or another (some belonging to as many as 20!), and the overall result has been what Indian-American economist Jagdish Bhagwati has called a tangled spaghetti bowl of overlapping trade regulations – making life very difficult for trade officials, not to mention those actually wanting to do business.

It would be helpful at this stage to define the different types of trading agreements between nations before going on to discuss in further detail some of the issues involved. There are various levels of relationship possible – from negotiating a limited reciprocal reduction of tariffs on certain goods only, all the way through to the full integration of entire economies. The spectrum of choices involved appears below in order of increasing complexity:

1. *Independence.* A country may opt not to join any regional trade grouping and choose instead to arrange its own policies on a bilateral, country-by-country basis. This way it is not constrained by any rules set up by prior agreement with others. Minimum levels of commitment, sovereignty loss and gains from trade are involved.
2. *A free trade area.* Here a number of countries may agree to reduce tariffs and quotas on designated items between themselves, but leave each individual country to pursue independent policies with respect to the rest of the world. Intra-area trade may thus be completely free of all restrictions on goods and services, or (more realistically) tariffs may be reduced but not entirely removed on some, not all, items.
3. *A customs union.* In addition to free trade between member countries, a common external tariff may be erected against all outside trade. This barrier will be of different heights for different goods, and erected against some

countries and not others, but what makes a customs union different from a free trade area is that it has a common trade policy for all member countries with respect to all external parties.

4. *A common market.* This involves free trade not only in goods and services between member countries, but also in the unrestricted movement and employment of labour and capital. Additionally, a common market usually implies an increasing number of common policies (e.g. in Europe, the Common Agricultural Policy) and – with regard to trade – a progressive reduction in non-tariff barriers also. This implies that all the rules and regulations, different specifications and standards embodied in member countries' goods and services become 'harmonised', or that mutual recognition is accepted.

5. *Economic union.* Many common policies are pursued at this stage, in particular a common currency and monetary policy. This would therefore necessitate a common central bank and other economic institutions, coordinated fiscal policies, convergent financial performance, an industrial and competition policy, and almost certainly a 'structural fund' or regional policy to address the possible problem of differential growth rates between regions/countries.

6. *One nation.* With an increasingly integrated union economy, political sovereignty will inevitably be pooled between member countries. Central political institutions tend therefore to parallel the growth of common economic structures. A common parliament and legislature grows up at this stage and, with them, well-defined political and economic relationships are established between member states and the centre. Common fiscal, social and regional policies will evolve from economic union; a common foreign and defence policy will similarly evolve from a common external trade policy.

(Note that these stages have been delineated as primarily an economic process; the sixth above, however, could be characterised instead as the ultimate stage of a separate political process which examines the degree of integration of political institutions and constitutions.)

It should be emphasised that once started on this process, there is no inevitability in progressing through this sequence of increasing economic integration, nor do these stages themselves represent discrete and well-marked steps along the way. As will be seen, a free trade area may still be rather slow in reducing internal trade barriers yet achieve breakthroughs in other common policies, such as with the mobility of capital, or in exchange rate agreements.

The European Union provides the best example of a regional association of nations that has both deepened and widened its trading relationships through the various stages outlined above. This supra-national development, which began with the Treaty of Rome in 1957, has provoked different reactions from other countries around the world – from applications to join from near neighbours, to negotiations for concessions from distant partners fearful of being shut out, to the establishment of other regional groupings of countries seeking to rival the EU's growing economic influence.

The most notable example of another regional association is the North American Free Trade Agreement (NAFTA), signed between the USA, Mexico and Canada in December 1992. Unlike the EU, there is no political momentum in this agreement to progress from freer trade to economic union. We will return to examine some of the issues involved in these two regional trade associations a little later.

Moving jobs overseas

Since 1980, in the third wave of globalisation referred to above, the fastest growing dimension of world trade has been the rise of developing country manufacturing exports. Traditionally the suppliers of raw materials to rich western nations, now a growing group of former primary producing countries have broken into world markets for manufactures and, even more recently, services. In 1980 only 25 per cent of the exports of developing countries were manufactures, but by 1998 this had increased to 80 per cent. In the early 1980s, commercial services made up only 9 per cent of the exports of developing countries, but by 1998 this had risen to 17 per cent. These are truly momentous changes that have impacted on the incomes and consumption of all parties.

Driving these developments have been a number of factors. We have already mentioned the post-1980s phase of liberalisation and reduction of tariff restrictions. Greater inflows of capital – foreign direct investment – have also been important. Multinational corporations have increasingly taken the opportunity to invest in developing countries both as a low-cost base from which to export to western markets and also to take advantage of the booming domestic scene. Thirdly, the costs of transport and especially communications have tumbled such that geographical distance between supplier and customer, or particularly between different participants in the supply chain, need no longer be the barrier it used to be.

Especially noteworthy of course has been, skill for skill, the cheaper source of labour available to western businesses in developing countries. This involves both hiving off some of the work that multinationals previously performed in-house ('outsourcing') and giving the contract to overseas businesses or, alternatively, setting up an offshore affiliate of the parent country in a lower-cost location. With the explosion of developments in digital technology, businesses can be increasingly footloose and not necessarily committed to locating next door to either raw material supplies or consumer markets. (See Box 4.2.)

As a result, low-income countries and companies can now compete on more level terms with richer-world businesses and take this competition into high skill services, rather than stay with the original low-tech manufacturing sector. According to a report to the US Congress in 2004, a total of 3.4 million American service sector jobs might be 'lost' abroad by 2015 (Linda Levine, Congressional Research Service report, 18 June 2004).

Such developments always trouble those with a vested interest in keeping the status quo, especially rich-world politicians and business folk who want to retain their supremacy over upstart emerging nations. But firstly, they are fighting a

Box 4.2   Outsourcing offshore: the Indian connection

Outsourcing or subcontracting business to foreign or offshore locations can take many forms. The principal firm may place an order with another company for the manufacture of parts (car manufacturers buying in components such as seat belts, for example). Commercial subcontracting may involve the principal company – a predominantly marketing enterprise – distributing, say, sportswear that has been manufactured in foreign workshops. Business process outsourcing (BPO) involves front office staff subcontracting IT, administrative and service functions to large teams of back office staff offshore.

Why? What is driving the increasing trend to outsource business offshore?

1.   As markets expand for final products, upstream specialist firms can grow and serve a number of different customers in different countries. Small start-ups find this a route to grow to **optimum size**.
2.   Transactions costs have fallen in the digital age: search costs of finding quality products, writing and enforcing contracts, monitoring processes, safeguarding finance – all become cheaper and the attractions to principal firms of disintegrating the supply chain across borders has thus increased.
3.   Uncertainties of market demand have made it more strategic for principal firms to employ a small staff of full-time, guaranteed workers and subcontract out much work to an unprotected sector that can more easily be made redundant if and when sales fall.
4.   Domestic outsourcing in India has always been practised, given its long history of segmented, formal and informal labour markets. The former are well paid, (over)regulated, and governed by union-negotiated contracts. With little wriggle-room for local entrepreneurs and many poor people hungry and enterprising, the tradition for formal sector business has thus been to establish a trading company of very few, formal staff and to subcontract manufacturing and other processes to the informal sector. With the major deregulation reforms of the Indian economy since the 1980s and the simultaneous blossoming of international trade, this Indian business model has since spread overseas.

India is the world's leading country for offshore outsourcing. The industry started in the late 1980s and the IT and BPO export sector grew to US$47 billion in 2011, capturing more than half the world's offshore trade (The Stony Hill Group and *Sourcingline.com*). The Americas and Europe are the largest customers and account for 60 per cent and 31 per cent respectively of India's IT and BPO exports. The dominant sectors are financial services (41 per cent), telecoms (20 per cent), manufacturing (17 per cent) and retail (8 per cent). In 2009, the Indian IT and BPO export sector employed about 2.2 million people.

The large, English-speaking, low-cost workforce has always been the main attraction. The industry grew rapidly through the 1990s aided by rapid US technological development – the 'dotcom' boom and continuous IT upgrades (e.g. to prepare for the potential millennium bug – remember that?). Outsourcing to India provides western businesses with significant direct cost savings. Wages, the largest component of costs, are much lower than in the USA or Europe. For example, software/web designers with one to four years' experience are paid about 11 per cent of those in the USA. Senior, more experienced staff comprise about 30 per cent of comparable resources in the USA. More savings are possible in tax bills, office rents and other overheads but these vary according to location. A major qualification to set against these savings is the problem of infrastructure in a developing country (roads and electricity supply can be variable; regulations and ease of doing business can be frustrating), but outsourcing has been a welcome resort for multinational enterprise in a recession-hit, uncertain world and it has certainly brought benefits to India as well as to other developing nations. It is just one aspect of how international trade is changing and evolving.

losing battle against the tide of economic advance, and secondly – for those willing to commit themselves fully to the opportunities offered in liberalisation – the growing volume and dispersal of world trade makes for a win-win situation for all participants. There need be *no* long-term loss of jobs for those countries that engage in offshoring work to lower cost climes.

The theory of comparative advantage

What is the justification for such a claim? It is time now to examine in more depth the economic argument for free trade that underlies all the developments outlined above. What precisely is the argument that reducing trade barriers should lead to increasing wealth and welfare for the countries concerned? The economic theory of international trade and comparative advantage is at the heart of this debate and we need to understand this analysis more fully if we are to understand the drive behind the WTO, bilateral and multilateral regional trade associations like the EU and NAFTA, and the increasing trend to offshoring.

Consider the theoretical case of a number of trading countries, each with its own unique endowment of natural resources. It should be seen that instead of each one trying to provide for its domestic needs independently, all countries benefit by specialising in what they are best at and then trading with others in order to purchase, at less cost, what others produce. Free trade thereby enables specialisation, increased production and thus higher standards of living for all participants.

The same principle acts for any individual student: on leaving college, a large market society enables the graduate to specialise in his or her chosen employment, selling skills for an income that allows him/her to purchase a far wider range of goods and services than could ever be provided by the student in isolation.

Although particularly relevant to European nations of similar size and development, it should be emphasised that the theory of free trade as just outlined is also relevant to a relatively small, less-developed country doing business with a larger, wealthier neighbour – say, Mexico with the USA.

It might be asked, what has a rich country got to gain in trade with a poorer neighbour when it can produce everything more efficiently itself? Or, conversely, might not a smaller country suffer exploitation from its larger trade partner?

Clearly these arguments are incompatible. They cannot both be true.

The same can be said for the following pair of arguments: producers in high wage countries can often be heard claiming that they can never hope to compete with cheap labour industries in the developing world and so some government support is thus argued as essential. Equally, in poor countries other critics can be heard demanding exactly the same sort of assistance because they cannot compete with western high technology, i.e. cheap capital.

All these arguments are false. Even where trading partners are completely mismatched, economics can demonstrate that both parties may benefit from free trade. This principle was first established in 1817 by economist David Ricardo: the principle of comparative advantage.

Consider again the case of individuals. Why should a doctor, for example, employ a secretary to type letters which she could do more quickly herself? This is exactly the same question as: why should the USA buy manufactured goods, clothing and foodstuffs from Mexico that it could just as easily produce itself?

I hope you can see the answer. It is a better, more cost-effective use of resources for the doctor to devote her time to medicine than to devote twenty minutes or so typing a letter. Her less-competent secretary may spend half an hour on the same task, but her time is less costly and the doctor can meanwhile get on with some more productive employment. Similarly, US resources could be devoted to self-sufficiency in clothing, but it is more efficient to import much of this and concentrate on higher-tech products. For their part, the (currently) less-efficient Mexican producers can find a market for their produce, will gain better incomes than if they were confined to domestic sales alone and may start the process of improving their skills and development prospects.

In economics, we say the doctor possesses absolute advantages in both medicine and typing, but a comparative advantage in only one: the former. The secretary has absolute disadvantage in both practices, but a comparative advantage in typing. Similarly, in trade with the USA, Mexico has a comparative advantage in lower-tech, labour-intensive industries like manufacturing assembly and clothing.

It is this important principle of comparative advantage which determines the direction of trade. Once this is understood, a country is well on its way to concentrating its resources, establishing trade and increasing economic growth.

This point is sufficiently important to warrant further explanation. Consider the case of Japan. There are those who once considered that this country was a Far Eastern power-house that could outcompete European and American business in all sorts of world markets. From the analysis just presented you should be able to see that it was impossible for Japan to possess a comparative advantage in all its industries. In practice, the growth of Korean, Taiwanese, Hong Kong, Singaporean, Malaysian, Thai and (particularly) Chinese manufacturing industries – Asian dragons that have awoken in Japan's own backyard – prove the point. This leads to an important finding: comparative advantage is a dynamic, not a static, concept. In 1950 Japan had no advantage in producing cars and motorcycles. Nor in 1960 did Mexico possess any advantage in producing consumer durables like cars, computers and other electronic products; nor even in producing sizeable quantities of oil and gas. But in a free market society where (1) prices are flexible, (2) consumers exercise choice and (3) resources are free to move their employment, then industries will grow and decline. Comparative advantage will keep changing.

A secretary may not want to be a secretary for ever – he may want to train to be a doctor. Mexico may not want to specialise in cheap-labour industries for ever; it may want to secure economic growth and, in time, produce sophisticated high-quality goods and services. Free trade offers a pathway to progress. Countries have to start somewhere. Unless Mexico (with all other countries) can sell its produce in unrestricted markets, it cannot begin to reap the benefits of specialisation, trade and growth.

Where does this leave the developed nations of the world, those that have 'lost' jobs to fast-developing nations? They should specialise in those higher-value-added activities in which they enjoy their comparative advantage and which support higher wages and salaries. Experience suggests that most of the expansion into higher-value-added employments comes not from a revolutionary shift into entirely new industries, such as high tech, biotech or nanotech businesses (important though these cutting-edge areas are), but from the natural evolution of companies within existing industries.

In Italy's textile industry, for example, most clothing manufacture has now moved offshore to lower-cost locations, but domestic employment remains stable because companies have put more resources into tasks such as designing clothes and coordinating global production networks. UK engineering and construction firms increasingly work overseas, such as on large contracts in the Gulf states (e.g. the famous seven-star hotel Burj al Arab, Dubai), and so employ relatively few building site workers at home, but have grown instead to running large domestic offices of design teams and support staff.

Jobs change over time as technology and the market place change. Wells Fargo does not employ stagecoach drivers anymore. The top ten jobs in demand in the USA in 2010 *did not exist* in 2004. With globalisation, the world moves ever faster and faster and we have to move with it or be left behind. In the long term, however, countries should not shrink back from increasing trade in fear of being robbed of employment. It is the collapse of trade has that consequence.

Long-term benefits

According to theory, as large and small trading partners reduce barriers, separate markets increasingly become one. There can only be one price for each good or service traded in a single market and inevitably the dominant influence on prices will come from the larger, richer economy. For example, within NAFTA Mexican exports – and Mexican labour services – will thus increasingly sell for higher, US/ Canadian prices. The distribution of gains from free trade is thus predicted to be greater for the smaller economy. This is known as 'the importance of being unimportant'.

The macroeconomic impact of increasing export earnings will be magnified thanks to the **foreign trade multiplier** – injections to the domestic economy stimulate a rise in national income commensurate with the marginal propensity to consume (refer back to Chapter 3). This may at first be regionally focused where export industries are located in certain development zones (e.g. in the Mexican case, in border towns such as Ciudad Juarez, Tijuana and Nogales), but eventually the beneficial effects must ripple through the entire economy as second- and third-round incomes rise.

The most important gains from trade, however, come from the long-term impact of increasing international competition for local industry. Providing the immediate trauma of adjusting to change is phased in carefully, local businesses learn to adapt to international prices, quality standards and the demands of consumers. Efficiency gains are high. National resources move to employments that are internationally competitive. **Economies of scale** can be enjoyed in selling to far larger markets than are available within the domestic economy alone. Even where such free market changes are not phased in but impact with a big bang, the evidence from such countries as far apart as the People's Republic of China, Poland and Chile is that short-term costs are eventually outweighed by long-term recovery.

Short-term costs

This analysis of free trade does not deny, however, that there *are* very real costs involved. This chapter started with the assertion that the dynamics of creative destruction impose misery on selected communities in all trading countries. It is for this reason that free trade agreements are usually phased into operation over a number of years. Additionally, public authorities and vested interests in the negotiation process have an important responsibility to monitor the distribution of costs and benefits involved amongst the people affected.

The experience of Mexico certainly confirms the prediction that there will be winners and losers from trade. The impact of NAFTA in its first decade (as recorded in *The Employment Consequences of NAFTA*, by Sandra Polaski; testimony submitted to the Senate Subcommittee on International Trade, 11 September 2006) is very instructive in this regard:

• Income inequality has been slowly rising in Mexico since NAFTA took effect, reversing a brief declining trend prior to the 'Tequila crisis' of 1994. Compared to the period before NAFTA, the top 10 per cent of households have gained their share of national income, while the other 90 per cent have lost out or seen no change. Regional inequality within Mexico has also increased, reversing a long-term trend toward convergence in regional incomes.

- NAFTA has produced a disappointingly small net gain in jobs in Mexico. Employment created in export manufacturing has barely kept pace with jobs lost in agriculture due to imports. There has also been a decline in domestic manufacturing employment as China has increasingly taken US market share, due to its lower-than-Mexican labour costs.
- Mexican agriculture has been a net loser in trade with the United States, and employment in the sector has declined sharply. US exports of subsidised crops such as corn have depressed agricultural prices in Mexico. The rural poor have borne the brunt of adjustment to NAFTA and have been forced to adapt without adequate government support. This is a serious indictment and argument against the supposed benefits of free trade.
- Productivity has increased in Mexico over the last decade. NAFTA likely played a significant role, because Mexico cut tariffs deeply and was exposed to greater competition. The rise in productivity has the short-term cost, however, of releasing labour since now fewer workers are needed to produce the same outputs as before.
- The net impact of NAFTA on overall employment in the United States has been small. A widening gap between the wages of skilled and unskilled workers is partly attributable to trade, and NAFTA probably accounts for a small portion of that.
- Increased trade and outsourcing of employment has led to a weakening of US workers' bargaining power and NAFTA is one factor, among many, causing that effect.

Note that in Canada, NAFTA's predecessor – the Canadian/US Free Trade Agreement – led first to a significant net decrease in jobs in traded sectors, followed by a slow recovery of employment to pre-CUFTA levels after ten years, then a modest continued increase in subsequent years. This history is a potential signal of how things may later develop for the three partners to NAFTA.

The challenge for developing countries

To seize the opportunities available from trade, and to reduce the costs involved, requires that trading nations are responsive to market incentives. If developing manufacturing industry is composed only of screwdriver plants where skills transmitted are few, if all inputs are imported and if there is little involvement of the local economy in producing components and providing services, then **dualism** results. (McKinsey & Co., global management consultants, calculated that in the first foreign-owned and Mexican joint ventures set up south of the US border, the locally produced intermediate inputs employed by these *maquiladoras* represented less than 2 per cent of the value of their outputs!) Thus a rich, westernised enclave co-exists with a poor hinterland, but none of the economic benefits from trade are transmitted across the barbed-wire fence which divides them. The gulf between the modern enclave and the surrounding community within a developing country can be culturally and economically as wide as the distance between North and South America.

'Underdeveloped' countries are defined as such in the western, economic sense. They may be highly developed with regard to their own cultural identity, which has evolved over centuries. They may, however, be relatively unresponsive to modern market signals. Development, therefore, means building bridges across the divide. Early foreign investments in offshore assembly plants were not motivated by this ideal, and most are still not. But enlightened self-interest on the part of business management and government officials, at local and national levels, can do much to dismantle barriers and to encourage positive economic interchange.

Many entrepreneurial talents lie dormant in poor communities, and the appropriate skills and opportunities to develop them require nurturing. Cultural differences, values, hierarchical and dependent social relationships that are embodied in traditional patterns of land ownership and the colonial inheritance cannot be simply wished away and rapidly assimilated into modern industrial structures.

NAFTA can bring, and is bringing, the benefits of free trade to Mexico, but the distribution of these benefits is inevitably uneven. It takes time and a determined sense of direction in government to build bridges to all sectors of the community. The fewer restrictions on social and economic mobility, the more the gains from trade will be widespread. Mexico, like many middle- and low-income countries, is, however, a profoundly unequal society where the income gap between rich and poor widened during the 1990s. Increasing free trade, liberalising markets, removing exchange controls and privatising state industries without doing more to reform law enforcement, ownership patterns, regressive tax systems and restricted entitlement to education and health programmes runs the risk of further concentrating wealth in a capitalist elite and alienating the rest. Just as NAFTA has been celebrated in affluent districts of the country, so drug-running criminal gangs in the north and Zapatista rebels in the southern states have forcibly reminded their country-folk that if the national economy lacks the flexible political, social and economic framework to engage all its people in the development process, then they will resort to more direct, more violent means to improve their share. Poor people are not disposed to starve quietly.

In purely economic terms, the arguments in favour of free trade are far greater than those against – any elementary textbook will emphasise this. But all the economic benefits which flow from the application of the principle of comparative advantage are based on the assumption that the countries involved possess the preconditions, the infrastructure, the social dynamism and cohesion to make the necessary changes and enjoy the rewards therefrom. Where the foundations for a flexible market are absent – for example, property rights are restricted to the few; law enforcement is inefficient or corrupt; there is geographical and occupational immobility of resources – then the gains from trade will bid up the wages and profits of those with scarce talents or political connections and will increase the sense of frustration and loss of those excluded from the wealth-creating process.

Applying the principle of comparative advantage needs careful management, therefore. This is usually recognised in theory in the case of **infant industries**: that is, granting a level of protection to fragile industrial start-ups that are not yet strong enough to withstand the gales of international competition. The protection is supposedly removed when the infant is strong enough to look after itself and thus free trade may return again to rule. In poorer countries where large fragments of the economy may be underdeveloped, the infant industry argument can be used to justify more widespread protection and intervention. If coordinated in a national, integrated manner, rather than in a piecemeal, business-by-business fashion prompted by powerful interest groups, then the overall result can be a *strategic trade policy*, as used with effect by Japan and certain newly industrialised countries such as South Korea, Taiwan or Singapore.

The flying geese paradigm

The paradigm of 'flying geese' has been used to describe how a number of East Asian nations have followed each other in achieving rapid economic growth thanks to their success in exploiting their dynamic comparative advantage. The catching-up process is said to move through a regional hierarchy consisting of, firstly, Japan; then the first-tier newly industrialising 'tiger' economies (NIEs) of South Korea, Taiwan, Singapore and Hong Kong; next the second-tier NIEs of Malaysia, Thailand and Indonesia; then China, Vietnam and perhaps other countries in the region.

This paradigm of a set of neighbouring countries that have followed one another in achieving take-off remains arguably the most widely held conceptual framework to understand the unprecedented economic record of the region.

The paradigm postulates that certain East Asian nations, by pursuing similar strategic trade and investment policies with regard to the developed world, have transformed low-income economies into middle- and then high-income economies in a remarkable catching-up process that refutes all those who argue that western hegemony can never be challenged.

A deeper version of this paradigm emphasises that there is a lead nation (Japan) that acts as a growth pole and exemplar which points the way to increasing regional interdependence, and that all nations following enjoy positive economic **externalities** that spread at first from the one centre and thence outward from other subsidiary poles as, one by one, each nation follows the leader.

The idea is neatly summarised in Figure 4.2. This illustrates how the process begins in each country, starting with relatively low-tech employments (say, textiles in Figure 4.2a), moving through higher and higher value-added industries, as the product in each industry goes through a life-cycle of increasing growth, then a slowdown, and eventual decline as the lead country then takes up a new industry and leaves the older one for countries that follow. Figure 4.2b shows the hierarchical pattern of take-off of one country after the other.

The development process starts with strategic **import substituting industriali-sation**: the government targets certain sectors for protection, and the chosen businesses, through a process of reverse engineering, have to replicate the technology and quality standards of imported products they wish to specialise in. Much experimentation, or trial and error, is involved here, but the emphasis is on

a. For each country
index of comparative
advantage

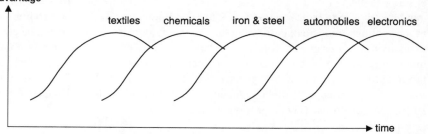

b. For each industry
index of comparative
advantage

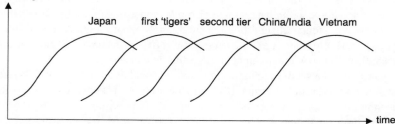

Figure 4.2 The flying geese paradigm. Industrial development moves through higher and higher value products (a), as do different countries (b), following one after the other.

Source: S. Kasahara, *The Flying Geese Paradigm: A Critical Study* , UNCTAD Discussion Paper 169, 2004.

producing goods that replace imports and go on to eventually succeed as exports. Protection is then phased out and the industry has to compete and win orders in the international market place.

Equally important, though less well known, is to facilitate *dis*investment in those industries selected to be run down. Businesses are encouraged over time to diversify into more profitable product lines, being given depreciation allowances to write off old capital, and subsidies for new plant and equipment. Similarly, both unions and employers are involved in the planning, retraining and redeployment of labour. The notion here is that, in time, goods originally chosen to be exports will eventually reach the end of their life-cycle and thus end up being imported from 'follower' countries, and resources within each country need to redeploy as costlessly as possible.

The paradigm is persuasive and the growth of the East Asian nations has been impressive . . . though the follow-my-leader theory has not been fully corroborated by reality.

Firstly, the character and economic performance of each economy in the region is not so similar that any one theory fits all. Hong Kong started its growth process with a textbook market economy where competition between rival enterprises was rife and barriers to international trade were minimal, as was the intervention of central authority. Korea, however, took off under a regime of authoritarian government (at first) and with a set of large, interlocking business conglomerates, or **chaebol**, that resorted to collaborative collusion more than competition. Singapore developed on the back of foreign direct investment, with a government that directed technological transfer, invested heavily in public infrastructure and leapfrogged the entire import substituting, protectionist stage and went straight for export promotion. China, an immense economy, followed its own independent trajectory to move from a centrally planned, command system to a market economy, implementing unique reforms (see Chapter 1), and so has not followed the example of any other nation.

Not all of the countries of the region progressed neatly through the sequence of low- to middle- to high-tech industries as illustrated in the paradigm, and most critical of all, these 'flying geese' countries did *not* develop through promoting interregional trade between themselves. All, in fact, have achieved economic growth by increasing and exploiting their dependence on North American and European markets.

The flying geese paradigm is thus an overly simplistic analysis to completely explain the recipe for successful economic growth and increasing trade in East Asia. It contains some important truths, but there is no one simple theory that fits all nations: each has found its own path to progress. (A deeper analysis of growth theories is undertaken in Chapter 10.)

Conclusion

The final conclusion offered here is that the principle of comparative advantage provides for substantial benefits in trade, but market economies must be flexible enough to respond to the changing dynamics of international commerce.

Comparative advantage used to be based on the differing factor endowments of countries – those rich in primary resources exchanging raw materials for manufactured products and services from the developed world. The great growth of world trade over our lifetimes – due to the rapid development of emerging markets from East Asia, through Eastern Europe to Latin America – has, however, transformed this simplistic picture. *Dynamic* comparative advantage comes from removing trade restrictions, exploiting international capital and skills, and building economies of scale in serving world markets from a domestic base.

In less developed countries in particular, where the geographical spread of the modern market sector may be limited and entrepreneurial resources may be scarce, governments need to work with business to design the appropriate policies in order to establish the institutions, the infrastructure and the preconditions necessary to secure economic development for all. Get the reforms right and manufacturing and service industries have shown some great successes in seizing the opportunity to serve world markets. Agriculture, in particular, stands to lose out with free trade if domestic, feudal patterns of land ownership and farming practices are suddenly subject to low-cost imports from rich-world agri-businesses. Farming sectors in many low-income countries around the world need protection and reform first before they can face international competition.

For the developed nations, the global economic order is changing rapidly and a loss of influence for the older, richer economies and their businesses is inevitable. So 'if you can't beat them, join them': outsourcing production to lower-cost offshore locations offers a way for US and European multinational corporations (MNCs) to keep up with the thrusting new MNCs domiciled in the emerging markets. Such developments offer a win-win situation: technology transfer improves skills, raises incomes and enriches markets for all. During the new wave of global integration since the 1980s, world trade has grown massively and markets for merchandise are now much more integrated than ever before. When the Great Recession eventually recedes, the pattern of global trade will have shifted; it will return to be bigger than before . . . and its centre will be further to the East.

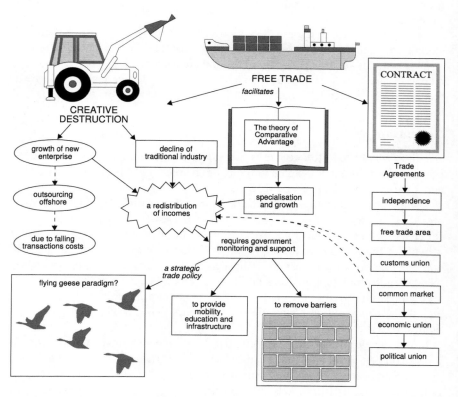

Figure 4.3 The themes of Chapter 4.

Key words

Chaebol Relatively few, large, conglomerate business associations of South Korea, with strong links to the government, which are active in construction, manufacturing and banking, and thus dominate their country's economy. They possess famous brand names, exported all over the world: Daewoo, Samsung, Hyundai, SsangYong, LG, etc.

Dualism The appearance of a modern, wealthy economic sector in an economy side by side with the traditional, poor and informal sector. At worst, the two are never integrated. People in the former will lock the doors of their cars, homes, factories and shopping malls against the latter so that incomes generated on one side of the divide will never percolate across to the other.

Economies of scale Where a business becomes more efficient and profitable as it grows in size. There are various technical reasons for this – for example, if you double the dimensions of a container its costs may increase by a factor of four but its volume increases eight-fold – relevant to all transport, storage and bulk processes. Big businesses can also afford to negotiate for lower cost credit, may buy up smaller competitors and secure trading advantages. (Note that bigger enterprises employing many more people may not always be easier to manage – leading to *diseconomies* of scale.)

Externalities These may be positive or negative. They refer to the impact of a given deal on others not directly involved. A government's decision to stop subsidising a coal mine may have a positive effect on the climate but a negative effect on local employment. Similarly, a decision to open a new fast food outlet may have a positive effect on local offices whose staff now have access to cheaper lunches – but there may be a negative impact of discarded food wrappers polluting the street.

Foreign trade multiplier The multiplied impact on a country's circular flow incomes caused by a change in its imports or exports.

Import substituting industrialisation Where a country starts to industrialise by first concentrating on producing at home those goods and services that it previously imported. This usually implies placing restrictions on foreign goods and services and thus protecting domestic industry from overseas competition.

Infant industries Businesses at an early stage of their development. Newly created enterprises tend to be smaller than their foreign competitors and many argue they need to be protected until they have grown big enough to survive on their own.

Mercantilism The nineteenth-century (and earlier) doctrine that asserts a nation must export more than it imports, build up its gold reserves and secure an advantage over all other rivals. It is a vision of the world as a dog-eat-dog, or zero-sum game where one economy must always strive to expand at the expense of another. Classical economists like Smith and Ricardo argued instead that the wealth of nations was best assured by specialisation and free trade.

Optimum size The best or most efficient size of firm that utilises its capital at the lowest attainable average cost of production. This obtains where the business expands to the point at which its economies of scale exceed the diseconomies of scale by the greatest margin.

Quotas A fixed limit to the volume of goods allowed.

Tariffs The rate of tax charged on imported goods.

Questions

1   Consider the costs and benefits involved in promoting freer international trade for a country of your choice.
2   Some governments have played a more active role, and have gained greater success, in guiding strategic trade policies than those of other nations. Why is this?
3   Assess the reasons for the increase in outsourcing business offshore and the costs and benefits involved. Are the poor and unskilled workers of developing countries being exploited by this trend?
4   How might Mexico improve the distribution of benefits to be gained from NAFTA? If it gains more in future, does this imply that Canada and the USA must gain less?
5   If the 'flying geese' syndrome is not sufficient to explain the success of many East Asian nations, what is?

Further reading

A comprehensive theoretical analysis is offered by P. Krugman and M. Obstfeld, *International Economics*, Pearson, 2009.

A fascinating contrast between East Asia and Latin America is offered in the following articles:

Kay, C. 'Why East Asia overtook Latin America: agrarian reform, industrialisation and development', *Third World Quarterly*, Vol. 23, No. 6, 2002.

Rodrik, D. 'Getting interventions right: how South Korea and Taiwan grew rich', *Economic Policy*, Vol. 20, April 1995.

Sokoloff, K. L. and Engerman, S. L. 'History lessons: institutions, factor endowments and paths of development in the New World', *Journal of Economic Perspectives*, Vol. 14, No. 3, Summer 2000.

5 The trade in primary resources – blessing or curse?

Twenty years ago, it took one ton of sisal for us to buy a tractor. Ten years ago, it took two tons. Today it takes three tons. And this is proof of a conspiracy by the developed world to keep Africans in poverty. We have to work three times as hard just to stay in the same place.

Attributed to Julius Nyerere, President of Tanzania, speaking in 1975.

Formula for success: rise early, work hard, strike oil.

J. Paul Getty

Introduction

Raul Prebisch and Hans Singer, two economists working independently after the Second World War, documented the thesis that the prices of primary produce compared with manufactures had a long-run tendency to decline. The evidence for this, and the implications for trade between developed and less developed nations, has stimulated much research, debate and controversy ever since.

According to the principle of comparative advantage, resource rich but technologically poor countries should specialise in exporting primary produce to the industrialised world, which should exchange them in turn for manufactured goods. The pattern of world trade in the nineteenth and early twentieth centuries could generally be seen to have followed this pattern, allegedly to the benefit of both parties. Certainly by 1914, countries like Canada (wheat), Argentina (beef) and Australia (wool) had grown as rich as some of the European markets they supplied. To this day, for many countries this pattern of world trade still exists – though a number of 'tiger' economies have grown to become wealthier by industrialising, diversifying and escaping from overreliance on primary resources.

Being reliant on the export earnings of primary produce is to have incomes dependent on the prices that these commodities fetch in international markets. That is fine when those prices are high, but not so good, maybe, if those prices are falling. Why is this? There are many issues here that need to be examined.

Firstly, consider that primary commodities like agricultural products, metals, fuels, etc., are dominant in the export portfolios of certain less developed countries, as evidenced in a selection of such nations listed in Table 5.1.

Table 5.1 Export concentration in selected countries, 2009.

Country	Dominant export	% share of this commodity in total export earnings
Iraq	Oil	99.8
Venezuela	Oil	94.1
Paraguay	Soybeans, animal feed	88.7
Malawi	Tobacco, tea, sugar	87.7
Nigeria	Oil	86
Ethiopia	Coffee	84.8
Nicaragua	Coffee, bananas, sugar	82.3
Sudan	Oil	74
Zambia	Copper/cobalt	64
Kenya	Tea, coffee, flowers	55.5
Côte d'Ivoire	Cocoa, coffee	52.8
Argentina	Soybeans, cereals, beef	50.6
Ecuador	Bananas, shrimps	39.7

Source: WTO.

The implication here is that with such export concentration, the earnings generated by the sale of these few commodities has a significant impact on the incomes of the countries concerned. Small wonder that in each nation listed here, the price of its principal export is closely followed and commented upon almost daily in the domestic media.

The nature of the market in which these commodity prices are determined is important. In nearly all cases, although the primary product in question may loom large in the exports and the economy of the individual nation, each producing country may have very little influence on the overall market supply, and thus price, of that product. Certain oil producers have tried to band together since the 1970s to form a **cartel** (OPEC, see later) in order to have a persuasive impact on the market concerned, but in fact the difficulty of securing a common policy for any substantial period of time has most often frustrated their designs. The result has been that the exporter of primary produce is generally dependent on the often unpredictable international forces of demand and supply in determining those prices that determine their main income streams. All sorts of exogenous shocks – natural disasters, political conflict, financial crises – can cause commodity prices to swing wildly from one extreme to another. Not only that, but a disaster that ruins the output and incomes of any one region – say, a coffee blight in Latin America – may cut back supplies and push up world prices that immediately benefit producers elsewhere – e.g. in Africa. Developing countries' interests are thus set against each other.

Price volatility

The market supply of a given commodity tends to be fairly inflexible in the short run. Supplies of minerals, energy and agricultural produce cannot be quickly increased even if the price incentive to do so is significant. It takes time to invest more capital, grow more crops, dig ever deeper. Supply is thus price-inelastic.

Since commodities are in demand as inputs for production by manufacturing industries, their consumption is closely related to the level of industrial economic activity in the developed world. This is fairly predictable in the short run: manufacturing industries require steel, rubber, copper, oil, etc. in well-known ratios; the demand for foodstuffs is perennial. Again, the demand for basic materials tends to be price-inelastic – such that even if the price of animal feed, petrol or coffee goes up, consumption will not drop drastically at first. (See Box 5.1.)

Box 5.1   Price inelasticity of demand and supply

We can illustrate the inflexibility, or inelasticity, of demand and supply of a chosen primary product with respect to its price in Figure 5.1. That is, demand and supply curves *DD* and *SS* are both relatively steep in relation to price. A relatively large change in price from *Ph* to *Pl* would only cause a small increase in quantity demanded from *q1* to *q2*. Similarly you can see that the same large fall in price causes a smaller fall in supply from *q2* to *q1*. The market equilibrium in this example will stabilise at price *P**, quantity *q**.

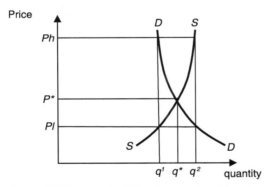

Figure 5.1 Price inelasticity of demand and supply.

The implication of a large price/quantity relationship as illustrated here becomes apparent if we now consider the impact of an exogenous shock imposed on the market on either side. It might be some natural disaster that wreaks havoc with supplies or alternatively it might be a financial crisis in the consumer countries that reduces spending and incomes. Take the first example – a random shock like a hurricane or, alternatively, a civil war that reduces supplies from a key producer region. See Figure 5.2. Whatever the price that prevailed in the market before, now there is less available: q* moves to q1. The supply curve *SS* shifts back to *SS1*. It might, in world terms, be a relatively small quantity change, but it causes a much larger price change: *P** to *Ph*.

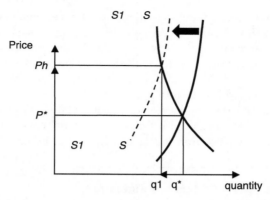

Figure 5.2 The price effect of a sudden cutback in supplies (q* to q1) of a primary product. Note that total spending on the product equals the price of each unit, times the quantity sold. In this case, the original total revenue earned (P*.q*) by producers is less than that revenue earned *after* the supply cutback (Ph.q1).

One important consequence of this scenario should be emphasised here: consider the area in the diagram bounded by the high price Ph and low quantity q1. This is far greater than the original price and quantity given by P*q*. That is, the total revenue earned by sales of this commodity post-shock is greater than that which obtained pre-shock. For those producers who are still able to bring supplies to market, they earn much more than before. Those that are wiped out by the disaster, of course, earn nothing, but their misfortune is more than compensated for by the riches earned by others still in the market. Consumers, meanwhile, have to pay much greater sums than before to make sure they obtain their supplies. This is one of the paradoxes of primary production: less produced earns more (which is why producer associations often try to artificially restrict supplies).

Given this example of shifting supplies, you should also be able to work out the effect of a sudden decrease in demand due to the Great Recession. In this case, it would be the demand curve for a given commodity that shifts back a little and this would therefore cause a large price fall: a large price fall that also means a large producer income fall.

The effect of short-run inflexibility is that, should some exogenous shock disturb either side of the market, the impact on the price of the commodity in question is both immediate and severe. Since neither demand nor supply can react quickly, most of the equilibrating movement required to balance trade must come via price changes.

Whatever the shock, the market is thus characterised by swings in prices that are more magnified than the changes in quantities that cause them. It is precisely this short-run price volatility that characterises commodity markets and thus

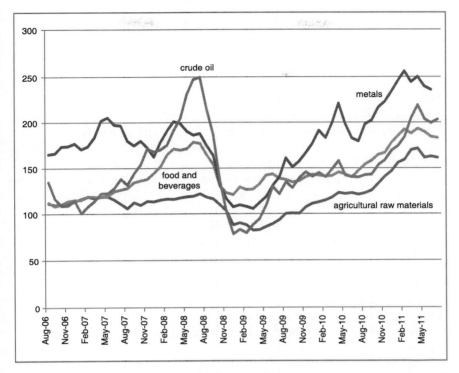

Figure 5.3 Monthly changes in the index of commodity prices, 2006–11 (2005 = 100). All
prices hit a low at the end of 2008 in the depths of the financial crisis. Since
then there has been a general recovery in demand – metals being affected particularly by strong growth in China, which is at a metals-intensive stage in its
economic development. Supply constraints have also had their effect: political
unrest in the Middle East and North Africa (the 'Arab Spring') has pushed up
crude oil prices; various droughts and floods have affected agricultural supplies. In addition, since these indices are all measured in US dollars, the gradual depreciation of the dollar against a broad group of other currencies since
2008 has inflated the rise in prices illustrated here.

Source: IndexMundi.

provides such a destabilising effect on all those whose livelihoods depend upon
them (see Figure 5.3).

Clearly, price volatility in important commodities is unwelcome. Neither
producer nor consumer countries would be content with frequent and unexpected
changes in fortunes, and in consequence market economies take steps where they
can to reduce such fluctuations. International stockpiles are thus maintained to
offset sudden exogenous shocks – and financial centres operate futures markets
and insurance services to mitigate the risks involved. Such interventions may not
always be able to smooth out exogenous shocks in their entirety (as can be seen in
Figure 5.3), but they may do much to moderate them nonetheless.

The success, where it is possible, in compensating for these short-run fluctuations in commodity markets, however, does not remove the problem of the *long-run* decline in the prices or **terms of trade** for commodity exports that is, it is alleged, a major barrier to the economic development of low-income countries.

The Prebisch–Singer hypothesis

Is it in the long-term interest of a country to specialise in the export of primary produce and thus remain dependent on the custom of richer countries? There are many who subscribe to **dependency theory** and argue that this economic relationship condemns low-income countries to a subservient role. It is alleged that the world economy is divided into 'core' and 'periphery' nations where the latter provide the former with unsophisticated, low-skill, raw material inputs that are priced in markets over which they have no influence. Richer, industrialised, 'core' nations, meanwhile, convert the commodities they have purchased from the periphery into high-technology products and manage to retain control of the much higher prices that these manufacturers now extort from their customers. Moreover, the wages paid to those who toil to supply basic raw materials are many times lower than those paid to the workers in manufacturing industry – who are most often more organised in trade unions and can thus benefit from collective bargaining with their rich-world employers.

In serving a processed product that is as relatively simple as a cup of coffee, for example, most of the value added to this product is retained in the consumer country. At the time of writing, the average daily wage earned by the workers on Ethiopian plantations, for example, is approximately £0.50, that is one-third of the price paid for a single cup of espresso in a UK coffee bar.

In addition to the lack of market power that producer countries are able to wield in determining their export prices, there are two other issues that affect world trading relations over time. Firstly, there is a tendency for the rich world to apply their technology to invent substitutes for raw materials – especially where there is the possibility of a restriction of supplies: artificial fibres therefore replace cotton; plastics are used instead of timber and metal; synthetic rubber for natural rubber; renewable energies for Arab oil and gas. As soon as poor countries begin to think they are gaining some price advantage over their richer customers, it is argued, so the demand goes elsewhere as alternative supplies are developed.

Secondly, and partly related to this first point, there is the well-observed tendency for those with rising incomes to spend a greater fraction of their earnings on high-tech products with a lower raw material content. Take two examples: poor people spend a high proportion of their incomes on basic foods; richer consumers will spend only a small fraction of their weekly budget on food, and that food will anyway be more processed/manufactured. Also, as incomes rise, nations' production, employment and consumption patterns naturally evolve away from agriculture, through industry and into services. As a result, the **income elasticity of demand** for primary produce is much lower than that for manufactured goods and services. Thus as world incomes rise, a rising proportion is spent on manufactures and services; a smaller and smaller portion flows in the direction of primary producers. A long-run diminution of aggregate demand for commodities thus produces a long-run tendency for falling prices, compared with all processed products.

How does the evidence for this hypothesis of Prebisch and Singer stand up? Numerous statistical surveys have been undertaken over the years and across a variety of commodities. Out of the mass of data studied, selecting the twelve most influential articles published on this matter – from the original argument in 1950 up to an IMF staff paper in 1994 – ten out of these twelve have corroborated the thesis. There are few hypotheses in economics that can claim such support. It is thus worth quoting from Singer's original:

> It is a matter of historical fact that ever since the [eighteen] seventies the trend of prices has been heavily against sellers of food and raw materials and in favour of the sellers of manufactured articles. The statistics are open to doubt and to objection in detail, but the general story which they tell is unmistakable.
>
> (Singer, *American Economic Review*, 1950)

The 1994 survey by Reinhart and Wickham (IMF Staff Paper No. 41) extended these findings to 1990 and, in consequence, made the recommendation that resource-rich developing countries should make efforts to stabilise price volatility by hedging strategies, stockpiling and – over the longer term – following a process of diversification into manufacturing and less material-intensive exports.

Ironically, at the time of this publication alleging sustained decline, the world was undergoing a period of increasing economic growth (the Great Moderation) shared by developed and emerging market economies alike, and the prices of all commodities were undergoing a sustained rise. See Figure 5.4 for the fifteen-year price trend.

To sum up: much evidence from the 1870s until 1990 seems to indicate a long-term falling terms of trade for primary produce and a lack of economic power among poorer countries to influence the prices on which their exports and incomes depend. The picture since 1990, however, reveals that although dependency on foreign market price determination remains, and despite short-run volatility, growth in world demand – particularly from China – has pushed up the prices of commodities and led to improving fortunes for many primary producers. Soybeans (Argentina, Paraguay), copper (Chile, Zambia), gold and iron ore (South Africa) have all brought increasing riches. Nowhere is that more evident than in the particular case of crude oil.

Oil

Crude oil is *the* world's most valuable internationally traded item. It is a vital source of energy, an irreplaceable transport fuel, and an essential raw material in many manufacturing processes.

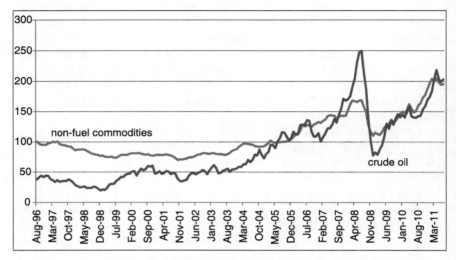

Figure 5.4 Price index of fuel and non-fuel commodities, 1996–2011 (2005 = 100). Despite
the major hiccup of 2007–8, the rising trend is clear. Note that non-fuel commodities as well as crude oil prices share similar profiles, the latter being the
more volatile.

Source: As Figure 5.3.

The countries that export and import oil are – for the most part – geographically,
economically and culturally separate. It is for this reason that oil – both in volume
and value terms – has become the world's most important marketed commodity,
and changes in this trade have had enormous financial, political and socio-cultural
repercussions for all parties involved. (Wars, revolutions and mass migrations are
only perhaps the most visible manifestation of these.)

Crude oil is a source of great economic power. Since its production cost in many
places is far below its selling price in world markets (see Table 5.2), the ownership
and control of oil reserves has been a means by which great wealth has been
earned and lost.

Because of its unique characteristics, the market price of oil behaves in a
way different from that of all other commodities. The oil market is dominated by
three interests – the consuming countries, the producer countries and the
international oil industry which mediates between them. This relationship was
described as a trilateral **oligopoly** (A. Roncaglia, *The International Oil Market*,
London: Macmillan, 1985), that is, each of the three parties referred to above is
dominated by a relatively small number: the wealthy industrialised countries
amongst the world's consumers, OPEC amongst the producer countries and the
major international oil companies in the industry. How the nature of relationships within and between each power group has changed leads to a greater
understanding of the determination of oil prices and the myriad other issues that
spill out from this.

Table 5.2 Oil extraction costs, various locations.

Oilfields/source	Estimated production costs per barrel (US$ 2008)
Saudi Arabia	4–6
Iraq	4–6+
United Arab Emirates	approx. 7
Algeria, Iran, Libya, Oman and Qatar	$10–15
Nigeria	15–30
Kazakhstan	10–18
Venezuela	20–30
North Sea	30–50
Middle East/North Africa oilfields	6–28
Other conventional oilfields	6–39
CO_2 enhanced oil recovery	30–80
Deep/ultra-deep-water oilfields	32–65
Enhanced oil recovery	32–82
Arctic oilfields	32–100
Heavy oil/bitumen	32–68
Oil shales	52–113
Gas to liquids	38–113
Coal to liquids	60–113

Source: Reuters, July 2009.
Note: Reuters, the international news agency, reports that oil companies are often reluctant to give precise cost information on their operations, but the country data in this table are collected from traders and industry analysts around the world. It also includes a more general assessment derived from the International Energy Agency. Note that these are well-head extraction costs and do not include the cost of transportation and delivery which are much greater for some inland sources at some distance from sea ports and/or markets (such as Kazakhstan).

A brief oil price history

In the first decades of the twentieth century, as the use of the motor car was growing and the world's navies were switching from coal to fuel oil propulsion, the Middle East was dependent on the international oil industry for the exploration, discovery and development of its oil resources. Only the major multinational oil corporations ('the majors') possessed the necessary capital and expertise to carry out this work. Additionally, the nature of the political relationship between the fledgling states of the Middle East and the Allied Powers was one still locked into colonial protectorates. Long-term concessions were thus granted by host governments to the majors to produce oil for a fixed royalty: the first big concession was made in 1901 by Iran to the Anglo Persian Oil Co. (later BP). Similarly, Iraq in 1925 awarded its oil rights to the Iraq Petroleum Company – a consortium of BP, Shell, Compagnie Française des Pétroles (later Total), Exxon and Mobil. In the 1930s the big Arabian Gulf fields were discovered and concessions were given to the Kuwait Oil Company (jointly owned by BP and Gulf) and in Saudi Arabia to Aramco (Exxon, Socal, Texaco and Mobil).

The world's oil supply was thus effectively controlled by the oligopolistic majors. Classic cut-throat competition between them ended in 1928 in a cartel

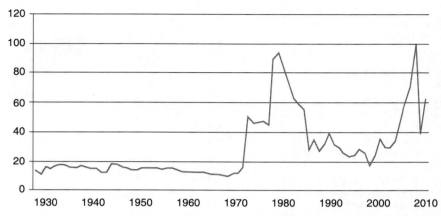

Figure 5.5 Crude oil prices, 1928–2009 (at constant 2009 US$). This profile reflects the changing influence of the three main price determinants: the multinationals' cartel from 1928 to 1973 (the flattish line, except for the increase due to the Second World War); the OPEC cartel from 1973 to 1985 (note in particular the price hikes of 1973 and 1979); and the recovery and growth in demand of the main consumer countries from 1985 until the 2007/8 crash.

Source: Forbes.com.

agreement to supervise joint production and to apportion downstream market shares. (Note that cartels work best where there are few parties involved, each one's actions are observable to all and penalties for cheating hurt. These three conditions were all met in the joint concessions on production: any one major trying to take more oil from a joint source could not hope to go undetected and unpunished by its partners.) Prices were stabilised by a unique agreement whereby oil sold anywhere in the world was priced equal to that of Gulf of Mexico oil plus transport costs – irrespective of whether it had come from the Middle East at half that figure. Such outrageous exploitation was amended slightly by 1945 at the insistence of UK and US navies, which were fuelling up in the Arab Gulf yet paying as though the oil had been shipped across the Atlantic!

The 1930s up to the 1960s, therefore, saw an unparalleled control of the world's oil market (see Figure 5.5) where prices, stability of flow, market shares and **joint profit maximisation** were all secured by the majors. With the main producer countries' sources of supply at their disposal, and with vertically integrated business empires stretching forward to every market place, there was, in effect, no free international trade in oil. Majors that were 'crude long', that is, with a supply of crude oil greater than their market outlets (such as BP), were tied in to 'crude short' companies (such as Shell) by long-term contracts, and so the scope for competition from any other suppliers was strictly limited.

Producer countries were increasingly unhappy with this arrangement. Western businesses were seen as being rich and powerful thanks to their exploitation of poor countries' oil. In 1951 Iran unilaterally nationalised its oilfields, but such was the power of the majors' cartel at this time that they could close down all Iranian production and compensate for this loss by producing more from other sources. Iran was thus forced into signing a humiliating, 25-year further concession in order to start up producing again.

Such a victory for the majors, however, proved to be their last. Iraq in 1961 similarly nationalised 99 per cent of foreign oil capital and subsequently became involved in a long drawn-out series of negotiations with the oil companies which were never concluded to the satisfaction of the latter. Meanwhile, Libya had shown the way by excluding all majors from tendering for concessions in its newly developed oilfields. In limiting the bidding only to the less-powerful independent oil companies, Libya had wrung from them a higher share of the profits and, simultaneously, had increased the downstream competition for the majors.

On 14 September 1960, the Organisation of Petroleum Exporting Countries (OPEC) was born. Iran, Iraq, Kuwait, Saudi Arabia and Venezuela were the pioneering members of this organisation which was formed in reaction to the oil majors deciding to reduce prices and with them producer countries' revenues. Although its initial impact was limited, OPEC became the forum through which producer countries could exercise increasing bargaining power, where follow-my-leader nationalisations could catch on, and where eventual control of oil supplies could be wrested from the grip of the majors and passed into the hands of host country governments.

As well as increasing success in gaining ownership and control of their own oil supplies and in weakening the competitive strength of the majors vis-à-vis the independents, two other events strengthened the producer countries' resolve to become more active players in the world oil market. The first was the floating of the dollar in 1971, which effectively devalued OPEC revenues since oil has always been denominated in dollars. The second highly significant development was the shift of the USA in 1972 from being a net oil exporter to a net importer. Low prices relative to other fuels had stimulated post-war western dependence on oil and now tight world demand coincided with OPEC being, at last, in control of its own supplies.

The political trigger was the 1973 October War between Israel and its Arab neighbours. OPEC shut off all oil supplies to the USA and the Netherlands (Rotterdam was Europe's major oil port) in retaliation for the West's alleged support of Israel. In three months the price of oil shot up 400 per cent and the shock waves reverberated around the world.

Western oil demand was price-inelastic – there were no short-run alternatives to buying OPEC oil if modern industry and trade were to continue functioning – and as a result the OPEC economies quickly accumulated enormous wealth at the expense of the **OECD** consumer countries.

In 1979, the Iranian Revolution, which deposed the (pro-western) Shah and ushered in the rule of fundamentalist ayatollahs, caused the second oil cutback and shock to oil prices. Again OPEC incomes leapt upwards, while the consumer countries were faced with stagflation – a slump in growth, large trade deficits and double-digit inflation.

This time OPEC was in danger of killing the OECD goose which was laying the golden eggs. Whereas the 1973 price shock did not choke off world demand, by

1979 its effect had brought onstream North Sea and Alaskan oilfields, and simultaneously stimulated western industry to invest in smaller cars and more fuel-efficient technology, plus research into alternative energy supplies. The 1979 shock provoked a further slide into world recession so that now, after decades of a relentless rise in oil consumption, western demand went into decline.

Oil prices fell in the 1980s. OPEC thus attempted to exercise the same control over supply as the majors' cartel had done before so successfully for all the time up to the 1970s. It failed. The three criteria for a successful cartel mentioned earlier did not apply: the producer countries were greater in number, had widely diverging interests and their actions were less open to observation and joint control than had been the case for the majors. The temptation to sell that extra barrel of oil at a price far above its production cost is irresistible if you can get away with it, and for those OPEC countries with pressing development needs and smaller reserves, there was always a strong case for trying to maximise revenues now, rather than later.

OPEC has therefore never succeeded for any length of time as a cartel. Quotas to restrict oil production have been set regularly for member countries and just as regularly broken. In the early 1980s, Saudi Arabia was willing to act as OPEC's controlling safety valve – always cutting back on its own output as others cheated on theirs – but in 1985 it refused to keep sacrificing its own income for others. It opened up production again and the world oil price collapsed.

Apart from a short price spike in 1990/1 due to the first Gulf War when Iraq invaded Kuwait, oil prices were now declining, reaching their lowest as a result of the Asian financial crisis in 1997/8. From then on the predominant influence was the strong growth in demand from the consumer countries. In the new millennium, Russia's desire to increase its oil revenues, consequent upon its troubled transition, resulted in that country becoming the most important non-OPEC source of oil, and this compensated for disruption in output from war-torn Iraq and industrial strikes in Venezuela. However, the dominant influence on oil prices was now booming world demand, and particularly the increasing appetite of China, despite the great crash in 2007/8.

Oil revenues

Crude oil is a basic raw material in the production of all sorts of petroleum products, petrochemicals, plastics, paints, and a countless array of manufactures. Owing to the transport, distribution and marketing costs involved, oil refineries, petrochemical industries and various processing plants are best located close to the final market places in the dominant consumer countries. As always, the value added by these downstream activities means much profit is captured by the consuming nations but, particularly for those oil producers where extraction costs are low, very large revenues can still be enjoyed by the exporters of crude.

The pattern of oil revenues earned by OPEC over the years since it rose in economic influence is shown in Figure 5.6. The similarity to the profile of oil prices illustrated since 1975 is clear to see. A snapshot of just one year's earnings on a per capita basis is illustrated in Figure 5.7. (Note this latter graph is only a

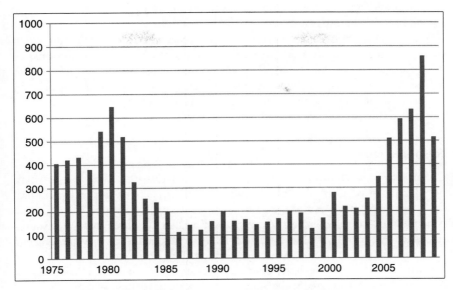

Figure 5.6 OPEC net oil export revenues, 1975–2009 (in US$ billions).

Source: US energy information administration.

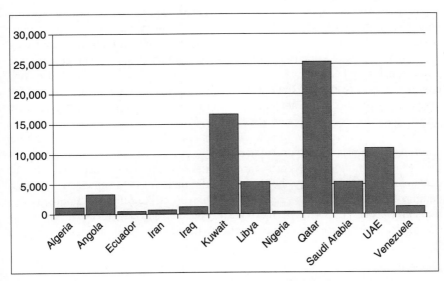

Figure 5.7 Estimated per capita oil revenues (in US$), selected countries, 2009. Although Saudi Arabia earns far and away the greatest revenues, Kuwait and tiny Qatar have smaller populations and so, on average, earn more per person.

Source: US energy information administration.

statistical average – it does not mean every person in those countries illustrated actually received these revenues.)

Saudi Arabia, OPEC's dominant producer, earned an estimated US$184 billion over the period January to November 2010, according to the US energy information administration (Qatar 'only' earned US$33 billion). These are significant revenues and make the Prebisch–Singer argument about the dangers of falling primary produce earnings seem a little redundant. They raise other issues, however, which are related to what has been called 'resource curse'.

Resource curse

Countries richly endowed with natural resources relative to the size of their populations – whether they be oil and mineral deposits or fertile agricultural lands – clearly have assets that are capable of generating high incomes and economic growth. Perversely, however, we find that countries that are resource rich, such as Nigeria, Zambia, Sierra Leone, Angola, Saudi Arabia, Venezuela and Argentina, amongst others, have demonstrated sluggish growth records over the past fifty years, whereas resource poor countries such as Japan and the Asian 'tigers' of Hong Kong, Singapore, South Korea and Taiwan, have all grown rapidly.

Such evidence has given rise to the notion of a 'resource curse': that somehow the possession of mineral and agricultural wealth condemns countries to a less than satisfactory economic performance.

There are, of course, exceptions. Botswana has been one of the fastest-growing countries in the world since 1965 and 40 per cent of its national income comes from diamonds. The USA began its growth trajectory in the nineteenth century by first extensively exploiting its natural resources. Nonetheless, on average, resource rich countries lag behind those that are resource poor. A recent survey of forty-two countries where resource exports represented more than 10 per cent of their GDP over the period 1965–90 found a significant negative relation between economic growth and resource abundance. (See Figure 5.8.)

Note that the correlation just described is *not* attributable to Prebisch–Singer overreliance on primary exports of declining prices and earnings – this is a concern that where commodity exports earn substantial revenues these are actually detrimental to growth. Why should a wealth of natural assets somehow impede a country's rate of economic progress? If countries strike oil or diamonds, is it a blessing or a curse? This has been extensively debated and a number of mechanisms by which rich resources can derail a nation's development can be identified.

Dutch disease

In the 1960s, large discoveries of natural gas in Dutch territorial waters of the North Sea attracted much international capital, increased the demand and thus the exchange rate of the guilder, and made it difficult for the Netherlands to export any non-gas-related products. The recession this then provoked in manufacturing industry was termed the 'Dutch disease', that is, a boom in the relatively narrow

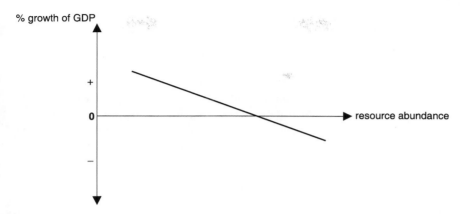

Figure 5.8 Resource abundance correlates with slow or negative growth. This relation is derived from a scatter plot of forty-two different countries where oil, precious metals, minerals and agricultural products feature strongly in their exports. Some nations, like Botswana, are placed way off this trend in the top right corner, but the average pattern overall is as shown.

Source: Derived from Mehlum *et al.*, 'Institutions and the resource curse', *The Economic Journal*, 2006.

natural resource sector provoked widespread decline in much other industry. This syndrome is relevant to any economy that earns sudden resource riches, typically from the oil sector, but it is also related to mineral extraction and even rapid, large-scale agricultural expansion.

The effect of a resource boom can firstly push up exchange rates and export prices – which might be fine for commodities with price-inelastic demand (see earlier), but is disastrous for manufactured exports that need to compete in very price sensitive international markets. Secondly, increasing resource earnings tends to lead to increased domestic spending (by governments if the resources are publicly owned or heavily taxed, or by the industry if privately owned); this may push up the prices of local goods and services, especially property, increasing the domestic cost of living. As a result, rather than buy domestically produced goods, people buy imports and so local manufacturing industry withers away. Thirdly, resource booms may create a reallocation of domestic capital and expertise to the export sector and away from alternative industry and commerce, and this may not be equally employment-, enterprise- and wealth-creating. Large-scale extractive industries may be very capital intensive, reliant on foreign inputs and provide high wages for an elite, but may generate relatively few growth-enhancing externalities. (This is particularly true if, typically, the resource is exploited using foreign technology and expertise and is exported unprocessed. The employment of and skills transmitted to local people may be very limited. In this case, the domestic development potential of such economic activity is little.) The ultimate expression of Dutch disease is indicated in places like Kuwait and Saudi Arabia – the creation of lopsided economies with little competitive industry outside the resource sector.

Rent seeking and corruption

A sadly well-observed result of accumulating sudden wealth when (particularly, but not always, less developed) countries strike it rich is that rapidly rising revenues are misspent, wasted or spirited away, rather than invested in productive enterprise. In some cases, fortunes are spent on spectacular but unproductive public works or monuments, allocated to idealistic but ill-thought-out development projects, or spent on hugely expensive military hardware. In other cases, billions may be diverted into the pockets of public officials, their relations, favoured friends and those whose political support needs to purchased (see Box 5.2). Even

---

Box 5.2   Corruption in Angola

Human Rights Watch is an international non-profit organisation dedicated to investigating and publicising human rights violations. Its 2004 and 2010 reports on Angola reveal massive misuse of oil revenues, corruption, distortion of government agencies and arms dealing.

For example, the 2004 publication states that the Angolan state oil company Sonangol was unable to account for how, between 1997 and 2002, oil revenues to the value of *US$4.2 billion* disappeared and bypassed delivery to the nation's central bank.

Not only could the state oil company not fully explain its actions but, the report adds:

> in recent years, as oil revenues surged, the Angolan government has refused to provide information about the use of public funds to its population, undermining their right to information. It has failed to establish hundreds of courts and allowed the judiciary to become dysfunctional, undermining Angolans' ability to hold government officials and others accountable. And it has not fully committed to free and fair elections, thus removing another avenue of accountability.

The 2010 report compounds the misery, raising questions about the source and use of funds of Angolan president Eduardo dos Santos' 'philanthropic foundation' FESA and its links to arms dealing. And as for the central bank, it emphasises the 'ultimately unsuccessful attempts by Dr Aguinaldo Jaime, formerly the central bank governor of Angola and later the country's deputy prime minister, to transfer US$50 million from Angolan central bank accounts to private accounts in the United States during June and August 2002 while he was the central bank governor.'

(Human Rights Watch Reports, *Some Transparency, No Accountability. The Use of Oil Revenue in Angola and Its Impact on Human Rights*, 12 January 2004, and *An Update*, 13 April 2010.)

if corruption is not excessive, local businessmen learn rapidly that the best way to get on is to find some way of accessing the incoming **resource rents** – via cosying up to influential officials, seeking exclusive contracts and lobbying for political influence – rather than engaging in the entrepreneurial risk-taking that is at the root of economic dynamism. The end result is that the economy begins to revolve around whomsoever controls the oil/natural resources tap – efforts are directed towards how to gain access to this, not how to compete, innovate and produce goods and services of real developmental potential.

Conflict

Natural resources can be geographically widespread, as in the case of fertile farmlands, or concentrated in specific locations, as in mineral wealth. The latter 'point resources' are more likely to provoke conflict as people squabble over access. If great riches are attributable to isolated mines or oil installations, then even if heavily guarded they may still be prizes that are simply too tempting to resist for people excluded from sharing the spoils. Fertile lands, on the other hand, have usually been widely settled for generations and, with the exception of clandestine production of illegal drugs in remote locations, are unlikely to cause disputes over unique ownership and control.

Paul Collier, perhaps the world's leading economic expert on conflict in Africa, has emphasised that the combination of low incomes, slow growth and dependence on natural resources substantially increases a country's susceptibility to civil war. When (especially) young men compare the benefits of a life struggling in poverty to the risk of death or injury in capturing access to oil, diamonds or drugs, many may calculate the risk is worth taking. The **opportunity cost** of joining a rebel army may be very low. (A similar, more detailed economic appraisal of terrorism is undertaken in Chapter 11.)

Examples of where resource wealth has been both an important cause of civil war and a source of finance for its continuation are the cases of Sierra Leone (diamonds), Nigeria (oil), the Democratic Republic of Congo, formerly Zaire (diamonds, cobalt and other precious minerals), and Angola (diamonds, oil). The human tragedies that have occurred in these and other war-torn countries are too vast to document here, and resource riches may be just one of the contributory factors involved, but suffice to say that fighting over the spoils of mineral wealth has put the course of economic development in these countries into reverse and condemned them to a continuation of poverty, disease and stagnation.

Some key statistics relating to the Democratic Republic of Congo (DRC) sum up the effect of devastating civil wars and serve as convincing evidence of the extremes of resource curse:

- *Population*: approximately 68 million (second largest in Africa, eleventh in the world).
- *Income per head*: approx. US$300 (PPP adjusted; ranked 223 out of 224 by the World Bank).

- *Human Development Index*: ranked 168 out of 169 by the United Nations Development Programme (declining by 0.4 per cent annually from 1980 to 2010).
- *Corruption Perception Index*: ranked 164 out of 178 by Transparency International.
- *Poverty headcount*: 71.3 per cent (World Bank).
- *Civil war*: on and off since independence in 1960. The BBC reports that, in the DRC between 1998 and 2003, 'millions died' in what it called 'Africa's world war . . . fuelled by the country's vast mineral wealth'.

Wikipedia sums up the country's situation thus:

> Although citizens of the DRC are among the poorest in the world, having the second lowest nominal GDP per capita, the Democratic Republic of Congo is widely considered to be the richest country in the world regarding natural resources; its untapped deposits of raw minerals are estimated to be worth in excess of US$24 trillion.

Conclusion

Specialisation in the export of natural resources carries risks. Sales revenues are certainly volatile and possibly destabilising in the short run; in the long run, earnings may be subject to decline for some but may promise rich rewards for others – no general rule can be derived with confidence.

Particularly in the case of poorer nations lacking the developed, transparent and accountable institutions that give a voice to all citizens and can expose and punish corruption, the concentration of resource wealth in the hands of a few may allow funds to be misspent and provoke conflict.

It is worth emphasising that export dependence on one or two products – be they primary resources or even industrial goods – is an unlikely development strategy. If successful it can lead to a lopsided economy and this cannot offer economic opportunity to all nor provide the longer-term security of a diversified export base. Note that this does not mean that all primary producing countries must inevitably aim to move resources into manufacturing or service industry. Diversification may be possible in primary produce. Growthful economies like Chile have developed vibrant agri-businesses that export fruit, vegetables, fish, forestry products and wines, and this Latin American exemplar has moved far from its traditional reliance on copper. Wealthy economies such as Australia have also grown rich by exporting a wide range of traditional and non-traditional primary produce such as wool, meat, wheat, coal, iron ore, gold and other minerals.

Referring back to Table 5.1 we can see that primary product specialisation does seem to be typical of less developed nations. This is inevitable – growth has to start somewhere and sophisticated skills and capital cannot be accumulated without first generating revenues and then investing them in productive assets. The fact

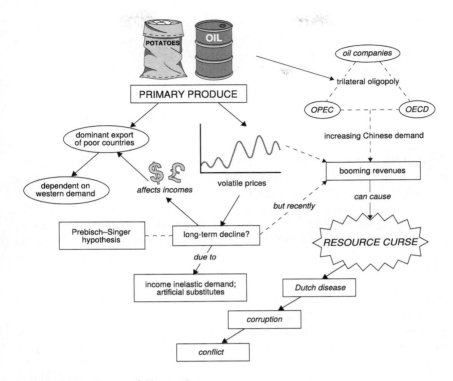

Figure 5.9 The themes of Chapter 5.

that some, indeed many, countries waste or misspend their resource rents does not mean this is an inevitable outcome, nor are they – even then – condemned to economic stagnation. Mistakes can be rectified. All developed nations have progressed (not always continuously) through stages of primary, then manufacturing, then service specialisation, and some, as referred to above, still retain a strong natural resource sector. Further analysis of the pathways to sustained economic growth and development are considered in Chapter 10.

Key words

Cartel A cartel is a small group of rival producers who decide to act together, formally or informally, legally or illegally, to jointly profit maximise (see below) as if they were a monopoly or single seller.

Dependency theory Not so much a theory, more an argument shared by many observers and political commentators that asserts that rich countries exploit poor ones and the latter are dependent on the former to sell their exports of primary resources. A number of influential Latin American economists allege there are various mechanisms by which dependent nations are locked into a pattern of international subservience, from unequal influence over prices to exploitative banking practices, but the implication that poorer nations are powerless to determine their economic destinies is questionable and dependency theorists' lack of agreement on viable policy recommendations is a major weakness.

Income elasticity of demand This measures how responsive is the demand for a given product to a change in the consumer's income. Luxury goods tend to have a higher income elasticity of demand than basic commodities.

Joint profit maximisation If oligopolists agree they can increase prices together, or at least refrain from price cutting, revenues and thus profits may be maximised for the group as a whole. (The temptation always exists, however, for one producer to break ranks, cut prices and win a larger market share at the expense of its rivals. Hence the typical oligopolistic outcome is long periods of price stability and joint profit maximisation where competition takes place in the realm of advertising and marketing, interspersed with shorter, violent price wars where the relative standing of the rivals is reassessed.)

OECD The Organisation of Economic Co-operation and Development. This was set up to promote economic growth and financial stability amongst countries of the developed world. Its members include Australia, Austria, Belgium, Canada, Denmark, Finland, France, Germany, Greece, Iceland, Ireland, Italy, Japan, Luxembourg, the Netherlands, New Zealand, Norway, Portugal, Spain, Sweden, Switzerland, Turkey, the UK and the USA. The OECD is therefore a club of rich countries.

Oligopoly A few, large rival producers in the same market, where the effects of one's actions, say to alter prices or advertising in order to increase sales, are immediately felt by the others. There is an inevitable incentive in oligopolies to try and strike an agreement between the parties involved and thus form a cartel (see above), but this is strictly illegal in most markets. In the case of oligopoly, price competition can be unpredictable, costly, even fatal to the interests of one or more of the rival producers. In such situations, non-price competition may be safer: rivalry in advertising, packaging, special gift promotions and other marketing gimmicks. Cutting prices to win sales can always be matched by a rival. A really clever advertising campaign and slogan, however, can be unanswerable in the short run.

Opportunity cost The most basic concept in economics. A choice has to be made whenever scarce resources are employed – the cost of opting for one course of action is losing the opportunity to follow another. (If there is no opportunity cost involved, then the resource in question is not scarce; there is no need to economise on its use.)

Resource rents This is technically defined as the surplus between production costs and the going price earned by a resource that has no alternative market. If I am sitting on a reserve of oil that costs little to extract beyond turning a tap, then almost all that I earn from its sale – whether it be at a high or low price – is in the form of economic rent.

Terms of trade The price at which an internationally traded item is determined.

Questions

1   Which countries are particularly dependent on the export of primary produce? What determines whether or not they should increase the production of alternative produce?
2   Is the Prebisch–Singer hypothesis now out of date and irrelevant?
3   What factors influence the demand for crude oil? How are these factors likely to change over the next decade?
4   What would be the consequences of a sustained and long-term rise in the price of oil (or any other primary product)?
5   What makes for a successful cartel? Contrast the fortunes of the oil majors' cartel and that of OPEC. Would a cartel be possible in the market for any other primary product?

Further reading

Adelman, M. A. 'The real oil problem', *Regulation*, 2004, www.cato.org/pubs/regulation/regv27n1/v27n1-1.pdf.

Frankel, J. A. 'The natural resource curse: a survey', *Working Paper 15836, National Bureau of Economic Research*, 2010, www.nber.org/papers/w15836.

World Trade Organization. *Trade in Natural Resources.* World Trade Report 2010.

6 Customs unions and common markets

> The Community shall have as its task, by establishing a common market and progressively approximating the economic policies of Member States, to promote throughout the Community a harmonious development of economic activities, a continuous and balanced expansion, an increase in stability, an accelerated raising of the standard of living and closer relations between the States belonging to it.
>
> Article 2 of the Treaty of Rome, 25 March 1957

> Capitalism is man exploiting man; communism is just the opposite.
>
> Eastern European proverb

Introduction

Freeing up trade between partner countries brings increasing economic benefits and such results may thus fuel arguments for even closer integration. In the case of the European Union, this drive for closer relations began on 1 January 1958 with the creation of a customs union between the original six founder members – Belgium, the Netherlands, Luxembourg, Italy, France and West Germany – with the objective of forming a common market with overtly political as well as economic aims. The Treaty of Rome, signed on 25 March 1957, committed the participants to the 'promotion of peace', 'increased prosperity' and 'ever closer union among the peoples of Europe'.

Other European countries were not ready at this time to commit themselves to such binding objectives, and so the United Kingdom, Norway, Sweden, Denmark, Austria, Portugal and Switzerland preferred instead to establish the European Free Trade Area (EFTA) in 1960. As it turned out, however, the greater economic success of the (then) European Economic Community (EEC) later drew in the UK, Ireland and Denmark in 1973; Greece became a full member in 1981, and Portugal and Spain joined in 1986. EFTA effectively dismantled itself, with Austria, Finland and Sweden in 1995 all becoming members of the now formally titled European Union (EU).

Over the period 1999–2002 convergence took place towards the adoption of a common currency, the *euro*, which was formally adopted by twelve nations in 2002. In May 2004 a historic eastward expansion of the EU took place to admit the most progressive of the transition economies that had formerly been under Soviet influence: Estonia, Latvia, Lithuania, Poland, the Czech Republic, Slovakia, Hungary, along with Slovenia, plus the two Mediterranean islands of Cyprus and Malta.

At the time of writing, after the accession of Romania and Bulgaria in 2007, the EU member countries number twenty-seven (for the euro, seventeen), but this very growth has given cause for much concern and prompted calls for reflection on where Europe is headed: should the kaleidoscope of countries involved aim ultimately for a deeper or wider union? A one-size-fits-all template, or a flexi-fit design where individual countries can opt in or out of various components? There are wide differences of opinion at present – both over the shape of economic union desired and also over the nature of political ambitions. The debate has become more urgent in the aftermath of the Great Recession owing to the differential economic fortunes of member states impacting on the euro, disagreements over the role of national *vs* common policies in the union, and the revealed divergent visions of what Europe should be. This has implications for all member countries, and also for other countries outside the EU and currently queuing up to join, such as Iceland, the Balkan states of Croatia, Bosnia Herzegovina, Macedonia, Serbia, and the special case of Turkey.

As a way into this debate we shall be concerned with, firstly, the economics of customs unions and then common markets. Issues surrounding the problems of the euro and monetary union are left for a later chapter. In the meantime the reader will be left to ponder for him- or herself what the political structure for Europe should ideally be and in what direction the union should be heading from its present crossroads.

The economic theory of customs unions

The tighter customs union of a group of trading countries all maintaining a common external tariff (CET) against outsiders raises important economic issues that are distinct from free trade areas (FTAs) and thus warrant separate analysis.

One of the features of an FTA is that member countries practise independent policies with respect to the rest of the world, and this fact can be exploited by outsiders. There is nothing to stop, say, West Indian cane sugar being imported into one low-tariff country (like the UK when it belonged to EFTA) and then being redirected within the association to a higher-tariff partner (say, Switzerland). Importing countries wishing to frustrate this tariff dodging have to apply costly, complex and (frequently) ineffective ways to identify trade origins. This difficulty of trying to impose rules of origin documentation on EFTA trade actually acted as a form of **non-tariff barrier** to all commerce between member countries.

A customs union does not have this problem. There is no way into the sheltered market by breaching the external wall at its lowest point, since all member countries have a common tariff. The EEC was thus able to enjoy much freer trade between all its participants right from its beginnings.

But such internal freedom comes at the cost of creating a potentially far greater problem – a 'fortress Europe' mentality. Locking in trade between member countries of a customs union creates a large market place of pooled economies in which all can share, but this is at the expense of denying free access to other countries, and the potential gains from trade that they may bring. How far beneficial trade is created, on the one hand, and blocked, on the other, is difficult to measure in the real world (how can you know what might have been?), but there are a number of guiding principles. The issue to examine here is *trade creation* versus *trade diversion*.

Trade creation

When countries first join a customs union there is an initial impetus to trade as a result of the removal of barriers between them. If the economies involved are relatively large and diverse, the efficient industries in each will gain from the enlarged market; the less efficient will suffer from the increased competition.

The consumption effect of trade creation will be that each country now benefits from an increased selection of goods and services provided by a wider range of producers, and prices will be driven down in all member countries to the lowest level that prevailed before the union.

The production effect of trade creation is that, as the sales and profits expand in the more efficient producers, so resources from the less-successful businesses will transfer to this better paid employment. (Assuming a customs union, not a common market, the redeployment of resources at this stage takes place *within* each member country, not between them.) Increased competition within the union promotes the eventual dynamic gains of more efficient industrial practices, plus the economies of scale available in a larger market.

Trade diversion

Trade diversion, on the other hand, occurs when one member country previously imported commodities from a low-cost, more efficient third-party producer, but subsequent to the introduction of the customs union now finds these imports shut out by a high external tariff. Consumption must now turn to the purchase of higher-cost alternatives provided by a less-efficient domestic or partner country producer.

The production effect of trade diversion is that resources are now kept employed in protected, inefficient industries rather than being made to search out more productive, more competitive destinations.

It should be appreciated from this analysis, therefore, that not all trade that is generated within a customs union is necessarily beneficial. Some or even much of it may occur in place of what could be more economic trading relationships elsewhere.

For example, an initiative to produce, say, a new super-jumbo jet in a European-wide joint venture is bound to be trumpeted in the press as a great economic benefit by the politicians and industrialists involved. Whatever the media hype, however, it should not obscure the fact that it all depends on the costs involved – it might be wiser for Europeans to purchase American or Asian products and devote

European resources to other employments where their technological edge (i.e. comparative advantage) is stronger.

If closer European integration is the result of erecting trade barriers against the USA and East Asian nations, rather than the outcome of fundamental economic compatibilities, then such integration will profit no one. A customs union that promotes internal growth only by reducing its trade links with the outside world will not produce an efficient reallocation of shared resources in the long run.

So long as common external tariffs are maintained, then whether the overall impact of economic integration is a valid cause for increased prosperity depends on the balance of the beneficial trade-creating effects versus the harmful trade-diverting effects of the union.

If growth in European trade and incomes by itself is no indicator of the benefits of economic integration, what is? Under what circumstances is a given customs union on the whole trade-creating or trade-diverting?

Criteria for a successful customs union

Competing, not complementary economies

If member-country economies prior to union are similar – that is, if they tend to be competing in the same markets at home and abroad – then the eventual customs union will most likely be trade-creating. If the original economies are complementary – for example, one being a primary producer, the other being a manufacturer – then closer integration may be trade-divertingly inefficient.

This at first sight seems confusing. But think of it this way: market *competition always breeds efficiency*, through a process of survival of the fittest. Two competing countries with rival industries, each with slightly different cost structures, will cause the relatively less efficient businesses in both countries to decline, with resources thus switching to the more efficient ones. Note that the initial impact is negative – much publicised unemployment – but in the longer term, the size of the united market has grown for all, so the potential for redeployment must be good. There is a beneficial trade-creating effect: resources are now more efficiently allocated within each country compared with before.

Now consider the other scenario. A customs union with complementary, non-competitive industries will dovetail neatly together at first – one country perhaps producing the raw materials which supply the other – but neither partner now has any competitive impulse to improve. Both nations are protected from foreign rivals by CETs. Domestic consumers and employers who might have preferred to purchase lower-cost foreign produce/inputs have their trade now diverted to less efficient, more costly domestic goods and services.

Low common external tariffs

Protection promotes inefficiency. Trade diversion will therefore be less the lower the general level of CETs. A customs union is a second-best alternative to all-round free trade. The nearer a CU approaches this free trade ideal, the greater the benefits to incomes and growth for all.

With the eastern expansion of the EU, there has been a significant reduction of trade barriers between the Central and East European countries (CEEC) and earlier member countries (the EU15), but, for these new entrants, the adoption of the common external tariff has led to loss of trade with third parties. Indeed, the CET has had to change in regard to farm products – involving a major overhaul to the Common Agricultural Policy since the agricultural sectors in Eastern Europe are so much bigger than in the West. (Poland and Romania alone have 50 per cent of the agricultural area and as many farmers in total as in the whole of the EU15.) The trade-diverting effect of all this has been to extend (less than they wanted) support to East European farmers who benefit from increased sales to the EU, but the CEEC lose access to cheaper external suppliers (see Box 6.1).

Box 6.1   Eastern agriculture: transition and EU accession

In the space of fifteen years, Eastern European nations emerged from a monolithic command structure tied into the old Soviet economy, achieved transition to independent market systems and then negotiated accession to the European Union.

The upheaval has been immense. It involved liberating prices, privatising state-owned agriculture and industry, opening internal and external competition, managing immense redeployment of resources and all the while keeping a lid on inflationary pressures. The original command structures had previously directed all economic organisation, squashed any private enterprise and dictated prices and incomes. Blowing away much of this took the form of a 'big bang' at the end of the 1980s and early 1990s, though dismantling commands and freeing up markets was the easy part – managing all the implications as they ripple through Eastern Europe is the work of lifetimes.

At the outset of the 1990s, eastern agricultural productivity and prices were low. There was much disguised unemployment. (The inheritance from the old Soviet days was 'we pretend to work, and they pretend to pay us'.) These were 'economies of shortage' (a term coined by Hungarian economist Janos Kornai) where producer and consumer choice had been limited to only what the planning commissions decided. With suppressed demand, the initial effect of liberalising prices, therefore, was to cause them to rise rapidly. Between 1988 and 1990 in Poland, for example, food prices increased by 500 per cent – yet input prices in almost all CEEC agriculture increased even faster than output prices, leading to losses and falling farm production.

Privatising state assets and collective farms was most efficient where they were broken up and sold to private companies run by professional managers. Leasehold arrangements on land and capital were a particularly successful transition institution, whilst tangled property rights disputes with pre-communist owners were unravelled.

Nonetheless an initial recession was inevitable for all of Eastern Europe as outputs plummeted; the recovery has since been long drawn-out. Farm productivity improved slowly through the 1990s where the path of transition was kept to. Generally speaking, those nations that took the first steps along the transitional highway (Czech Republic, Poland and Hungary) have made the furthest gains compared with those following later (Bulgaria and Romania). In total, between 1988 and 1998, CEEC food exports to the EU15 doubled; as shortage economies, however, their food imports from the EU increased ten-fold! To compensate there has been rapidly rising investment in the east, both in agriculture and in industry, and economic convergence between the two halves of Europe has proceeded apace.

Echoes of the traditional economic organisation of the east will, however, take many years to overcome. In 1998, in Poland, the agricultural labour force was 19 per cent of the total; in Romania it was 40 per cent – the majority on very small and inefficient family farms. This contrasted with the average for the EU15 at the time of 5.7 per cent (the Netherlands 2.0 per cent; the UK 1.6 per cent). Nonetheless the urge to continue with reforms and to cement them with accession to the EU has been unstoppable. With agriculture this has meant negotiating with that most traditional and unreformed component of the EU – the **Common Agricultural Policy** (CAP).

As mentioned, thanks to the transitional reforms, farm prices and productivity in the CEEC were on a rising trend through the 1990s – but not yet up to the average level of the EU. As eastern and western markets became one in 2004, this brought a modest decrease in prices for the west and a greater increase in prices for the east – the inevitable result being a fall in consumption of agricultural products in the CEEC but a rise in production. Also, since CEEC food prices rose, this meant that their exports outside Europe fell and were instead diverted into the EU.

With CEEC accession, under the old CAP farm support rules, eastern farmers would have been in line for massive direct and indirect payments. The CEECs argued, naturally enough, that their farmers should be given the same favours as all others in the EU. Same club, same rules.

Unfortunately, the eastern enlargement of the EU meant swallowing too large an agricultural sector to be digested by the old CAP body. The impact of subsidies to CEEC farmers would have broken the EU budget and at the same time generated increases in farm outputs that would have led to surplus food mountains. The original economies of shortage, driven by unresponsive Soviet-style commands, would have been converted into economies of wasteful excess, driven by unresponsive CAP commands!

The resulting compromise – a 'transitional' set of supports for CEEC agriculture that limit the levels of farm payments they receive – is clearly unsatisfactory and further changes are inevitable. The challenges facing the CAP are, however, immense – ensuring equity between east and west, between large and small farms and between urban and rural sectors; at the same time reducing volatility of outputs and prices, protecting the environment, and not discriminating excessively against the developing world. Whatever reforms are next introduced (planned for 2015), it is certain that not all will be pleased: the essence of economics is that trade-offs exist and you can't have everything.

Since at least the 1970s one of the ongoing political struggles within the EU has been to try and reduce the agricultural CET, and, although still discriminatory, trade diversion now is less than it would otherwise have been. Negotiations within the EU's agricultural commission and between the EU and the WTO have been lengthy and, at times, bitter. The focus has shifted within the EU away from insisting on protective price supports (which act as trade-excluding tariffs) to providing more income and welfare payments to farmers (which have a somewhat less distorting effect on trade). As a result, the European CET has come down, but there is still substantial trade diversion. The losers continue to be efficient farmers in North America, Australasia and numerous developing countries; and European consumers.

More members

The larger the union, the more countries that can join the free trade zone, the larger and more widespread will be the benefits. Clearly the economic resources that can be reallocated and the trade-creating benefits that can be generated therefrom depend on the geographical size of the union. The gains from specialisation and economies of scale applicable from the union of the Benelux countries (the forerunner to the EU) were minuscule compared with what is now possible within the European Union. All twelve transition/accession economies have seen a rapid increase in trade with the EU15 – at the cost of decreasing commerce with North America and East Asia – but the trade-diverting disadvantage here may lessen as production activities within the enlarged EU are rationalised (see below regarding a common market and the mobility of capital – for example, a manufacturing plant in the west moving east to take advantage of reduced costs). Dynamic comparative advantage may thus evolve to the benefit of all. As European economies further integrate, the potential for bringing together underutilised resources can be exploited and, with this, trade and economic growth both within and without the union will increase.

Little diversity

In order to benefit most effectively from the economies of large-scale production – where costs and prices can be kept down for all – the market should be homogeneous, with little diversity. A large European market is not large if it is fragmented into small product areas where consumer tastes and preferences are diverse and must be separately catered for. The more that participants of a union perceive themselves to be different to other groups, therefore, the less scope there is to profit from a common market.

This important point is very relevant to a continent as culturally varied as Europe. In the Americas, two consumers living 3,000 miles apart speak the same language, live the same lifestyle and respond to the same advertising campaigns. The same is not true in Europe where selling something as mundane as a chocolate bar in northern France requires a totally different psychology to selling it in southern England. Thousands of years of history have bred differences in prejudices that neighbours in the same town in places like the former Yugoslavia, Northern Ireland and Spain still fight, and die, over.

The economic benefits from the European Union are limited, therefore, insofar as the market place remains fragmented in many smaller, distinctively different communities.

Flexible technology

The need to cater for local differences in consumer tastes can, however, be responded to using modern, flexible technology allied to an educated and highly skilled workforce. Manufacturing techniques are becoming more and more sophisticated in custom-designing products at relatively low cost. It used to be 'any colour you want, so long as it's black!' The premium that had to be paid to satisfy individual preference was prohibitively high. This is no longer the case today, thanks to the revolution in digital design and innovation in manufacturing. Small runs of production can be as economic as long runs for an increasing array of sophisticated goods and services. Computerised systems can re-tool assembly lines and switch products in minutes today – a process which used to take months and even years in the past.

The difficulties presented by the fragmentation of markets in culturally diverse unions, therefore, can be considerably reduced by modern technology. The gains from trade are enhanced.

A productive labour force

An increasingly competitive world economy requires labour to be increasingly efficient. If the long-term growth of labour productivity in Europe fails to keep pace with that of labour elsewhere, then keeping business within the EU will ultimately become trade-diverting. One inescapable feature of European labour markets is an **ageing population** and, with it, a falling **participation rate**. These are benefits of past economic success and improved welfare provision which have produced falling birth rates, smaller families and increased indulgence in leisure activities. But a smaller and older working population compared with America and Asia does not mean labour will lose its dynamism over time, however, if educational standards rise in compensation. In that way, you *can* teach old dogs new tricks and European labour productivity will thus continue to improve. Crucial, therefore, is the implementation of an efficient education system that raises skill levels and facilitates occupational and geographical mobility of labour. Equally important is the erosion of social prejudices and official and unofficial regulations that restrict the ability of people to change and improve skills and employments.

Foreign direct investment

High external tariffs – whether erected by individual countries or by customs unions – have prompted in the past much foreign direct investment. Japanese and

American multinational corporations, fearful of being shut out of a fortress Europe, have set up their own factories in Britain, Germany, Spain, etc. to serve as a base from which to sell to all of Europe, without restriction. Certain European industrialists and politicians have on occasions complained about allowing such foreign rivals inside the protective union, but in fact the result is greater gains in efficiency and a reduction in trade diversion. Insofar as CETs can be bypassed by foreign direct investment, then domestic industry cannot be sheltered from international competition. Philips, for example, the giant Dutch consumer electronics producer, has had to drastically shake up its organisation in order to face up to the challenge from Sony and other multinationals in Europe, let alone in the rest of the world; and so long as Europeans continue to buy Nissan cars produced in the north-east of England, then all other motor manufacturers must also revolutionise their production facilities and practices in order to match Japanese efficiency. Wherever incompetence has nowhere to hide, it must be cut out.

The economic theory of common markets

This last point introduces the notion of moving capital across national frontiers. Just such an issue separates a customs union from a common market – where not only goods and services but also labour and capital are free to move among member countries. The impact of this next phase of increasing economic integration means that now resources may be reallocated not only within European nations but also *between* them.

The free flow of people between countries will inevitably be slowed by social and political factors – even if there is a complete matching of skills. A lawyer in Madrid, for example, may not wish to leave family, friends and business contacts in order to work in Milan. The absence of a homogeneous European market makes such mobility rather slow: language and cultural differences impede movement, information exchange is far from perfect, legal systems and labour protection vary. Political sensitivities are even more restrictive – the eastern enlargement of the EU was *not* accompanied by a simultaneous opening of frontiers to labour. The concern about hordes of Eastern Europeans flooding west to sell their labour at prices below those existing in the EU15 was enough for some nations to introduce work permits to limit migration. Labour mobility has still taken place – indeed for those without restrictions, such as the UK, Ireland and Sweden, there have been migrations in and out according to the economic cycle – but for Europe as a whole internal movement has not been excessive: in the first year of eastern accession, 2004–5, labour inflows as a percentage of national workforces varied from 0.2 per cent (Sweden) to 1.5 per cent (Austria) across western Europe (Tamas and Munz, Institute for Futures Studies, Stockholm, 2006).

With financial markets, however, mobility is already here. Large sums of liquid capital flow all over Europe and around the world to take advantage of marginal differences in rates of profit. With economic and monetary union we can expect more and more investment to flow in and out of partner countries. What are the implications of such increased capital mobility?

It is important to emphasise at this point that we are concerned here with long-term *investment capital* – that is, money that flows into a country in order to set up an increase in productive capital, a new factory, for example – and not speculative flows of funds that are simply taking advantage of differential exchange or interest rates in order to make a financial gain. (This latter issue is touched upon in Chapter 8 on currency union.)

There are contrasting views on the issue of mobility of productive capital, and a resort to economic theory is necessary to explain them.

Consider two possible locations for capital investment: one in the heart of Europe, the other in the periphery. One, say, in the lower Rhine valley, the other in the upper Douro in Portugal. It may well be that the opportunities for profitable investment in the Rhineland 'core' are many and widespread; those in the periphery in the Douro are more limited in extent. Be that as it may, assume that the rate of return on investment in the two locations is different: what can we predict will happen?

With no restriction on capital mobility, funds will flow out of the less profitable investment location and into the more profitable one. This has two effects, one in each centre.

As capital moves out of the less profitable site, the supply of investment funds dries up and as a result their increased scarcity begins to drive up rates of return. Conversely, funds moving into the more profitable location begin to satiate demand. Profit rates must fall. So long as any difference in rates persists, funds will move between the two locations until any discrepancy is eroded. The conclusion reached, therefore, is that the mobility of capital between different countries will eventually bring about an equilibrium in profit rates between them.

Actually this theoretical conclusion needs to be amended a little because there are reasons why capital may not be quite as internationally mobile as implied, why differential rates of profit may persist in rival centres. For example, the risk of currency fluctuation may be a disincentive to move funds across borders. Lack of information or uncertainty over cultural differences may similarly impede movement. Nonetheless the analysis can be adjusted to conclude that profit rates in both centres will converge to a differential that accounts for the divergence in risk assessment. Oporto, therefore, may evolve a rate of normal profits that is x per cent above that ruling in Frankfurt to compensate for the perceived higher risk factor.

So far this adjusted analysis supports the general contention that countries have nothing to lose from removing all restrictions on the long-term movement of capital. Donor countries and recipient countries alike benefit from a more efficient, more profitable employment of European resources. Capital moves across frontiers in pursuit of greater profits; capitalists in periphery countries that are exporting their funds stand to earn greater incomes. There may be a fall in labour employment at first in these sites as capital investments such as new manufacturing plant transfer to the core, but, it is alledged, total incomes rise in both countries so winners have more than enough to compensate losers.

There is a powerful argument, however, *against* this conventional view of the positive outcome of free market forces as applied to capital mobility. Criticism focuses particularly on the limited scope of this analysis: it assumes that only one factor (capital) is mobile and that *all other factors remain constant.*

Given this restrictive assumption, the conclusion is valid. But other factors are very likely to change in a Europe of increasing economic integration. In a dynamically changing environment there may be many forces at work that shift the profitability perspective in both capital-donor and capital-recipient countries.

External economies and diseconomies

Consider, firstly, the implications of inward investment to a vibrant and innovative core region. As more capital accumulates here there are a variety of reasons why profit rates may *not* fall.

Certainly, there will be shortages of land, office space, certain labour skills, etc., which force up prices and act as an **external diseconomy** and disincentive for further capital inflow. Social costs of increased traffic congestion, pollution and possible crime may also increase.

But these problems may spark off increased efforts to overcome them. There exist many economic benefits to regional concentration: external economies of increased competition and efficiency, the establishment of service and supportive industry, research and development, innovative technology and the growth of skills. If these benefits from concentration increase at a faster rate than the costs involved, the profit rate will not fall.

Employment opportunities for capital and labour (especially those with entrepreneurial skills) will not decrease; indeed they may act as a continual beacon to drain these resources away from the periphery.

By the same argument, exactly the opposite effects are operating in the periphery (see Figure 6.1).The most mobile, employable resources are moving out of the country. What is left behind are those who are increasingly unemployable, an ageing capital stock, decaying infrastructure, inappropriate skills, out-of-date technologies, and a market place of falling incomes and influence. Profit rates are

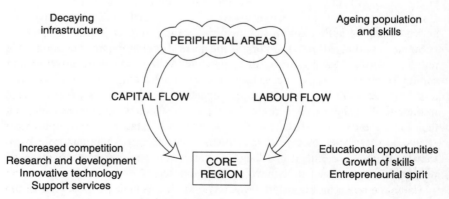

Figure 6.1 The most mobile, employable resources move out of the periphery.

shrinking faster than the attractions of return investment in this depopulating region can reverse.

As an illustration of these themes, British critics point to the problem of industrial decay in certain regions of the UK. Unemployment rates in Northern Ireland, South Wales and north-east England, for example, remain persistently above the national average. That such a phenomenon has lasted for well over half a century, despite repeated central government efforts to reverse the pattern of decline, is evidence that the centripetal forces which drain the peripheries of resources are strong and they are not easily reversed.

Some have predicted that just such an outcome awaits Europe: the unbridled effect of free market forces operating on capital employed in Europe will generate cumulative growth in some countries and cumulative decline in others – but due to the severely proscribed powers of the Brussels bureaucracy, such polarising economic effects will occur without the mitigating effects of sufficient redistributive transfers from a strong central authority. Despite its economic difficulties, Northern Ireland continues to enjoy substantial income support from the UK. The same is not true for poorer areas in a free market Europe.

East and West Europe, northern and Mediterranean states – all have a different economic inheritance, different socio-political cultures and varying stability in institutional underpinnings. Some member states have a long way to go to reach the standards of material well-being of others. Some are successful in embracing rapid change; others experience great difficulty. What future awaits a European Union of mobile resources is impossible to predict with certainty. That incomes as a whole will grow is highly likely, notwithstanding the tendency for periodic slowdowns or recessions. That the distribution of incomes will change is equally likely. But to deduce from this that Europe will polarise into richer and poorer regions, accentuated over time, cannot be safely predicted. The centripetal model – where resources drain into the core region – is one possibility. The alternative scenario is a multipolar Europe, where growth centres arise in a number of regions – each exploiting its own comparative advantage. The immensely rich cultural diversity of Europe might be said to support this argument.

The European experience

It is time now to look in a little more detail at the patchwork quilt of countries that together make up the European Union and examine how far they can be said to form a truly common market (see Table 6.1).

No map or set of statistics by themselves, however, can completely capture the true nature of the heterogeneity of Europe. Centuries of commerce and conflict, nation-building and empire-building have bred regional differences that are impossible to summarise simply. Some parts of the continent have enjoyed stability, independence and freedom from dictatorship or invasion for nearly a thousand years; others have only recently emerged from the horrors of war and ethnic conflict, and hence are still trying to define their nationhood. Certain states have well-established, mature market economic systems with flourishing,

Table 6.1 European nations, selected data.

Country	Area (000 sq km)	Population (millions) (2011)	Pop. density Per sq km	GDP/head (PPP) 2010	% growth GDP 09–10	% GDP invested	Language
Austria	84	8.4	101.1	125	2.1	20.8	German
Belgium	31	10.9	356.0	118	2.2	20.3	Flemish/French
Bulgaria	111	7.5	68.7	43	0.2	23.5	Bulgarian
Cyprus	9.2	0.8	86.5	98	1.0	18.4	Greek/Turkish
Czech Republic	78.9	10.5	135	80	2.3	21.3	Czech
Denmark	43	5.6	127.5	124	1.7	16.6	Danish
Estonia	45.2	1.3	30.9	65	3.1	18.6	Estonian
Finland	305	5.4	17.5	116	3.6	18.8	Finnish
France	544	65.1	101.4	107	1.5	19.3	French
Germany	357	81.8	229.9	118	3.6	17.9	German
Greece	132	11.3	85.9	189	-4.5	14.9	Greek
Hungary	93	10.0	107.9	64	1.2	19.3	Hungarian
Ireland	70	4.5	65.2	125	-1.0	11.3	English
Italy	301	60.6	204	100	1.3	19.5	Italian
Latvia	64.6	2.2	36.4	52	-0.3	18	Latvian
Lithuania	65.3	3.3	53.6	58	1.3	16.1	Lithuanian
Luxembourg	3	0.5	192.5	283	3.5	16.4	French/German
Malta	0.3	0.4	1303.6	83	3.2	16.7	Maltese/English
The Netherlands	34	16.7	487.2	134	1.8	17.7	Dutch
Poland	313	38.2	121.9	62	3.8	19.7	Polish
Portugal	92	10.6	115.3	81	1.3	19.0	Portuguese
Romania	238	21.4	93.6	45	-1.3	22.7	Romanian
Slovakia	49	5.4	110.3	74	4.0	20.3	Slovakian
Slovenia	20.3	2.1	100.4	87	1.2	21.7	Slovenian
Spain	505	46.2	90.8	101	-0.1	22.5	Spanish
Sweden	411	9.4	22.5	123	5.7	17.9	Swedish
United Kingdom	244	62.4	250.8	114	1.4	14.7	English

Source: Eurostat.

outward-looking industrial and financial sectors; others are still adjusting to the transition from peasant agriculture and centrally planned command systems.

The objective of attempting to generate increased prosperity via increased economic integration through all the stages from loose free trade areas to tighter and tighter unions inevitably involves so much more than economic issues. Given the enormous cultural, political and economic diversity of European nations referred to above, it is scarcely surprising that promoting the ever closer union of such disparate and partisan peoples is fraught with difficulty and delay.

Dismantling the barriers

The easy part is always done first. Eliminating tariffs and quotas and constructing the common external tariff for the original six founder countries was achieved within ten years from 1958. The same process has been repeated (more rapidly) with each successive enlargement of the union and has now begun again with the twelve new Eastern European and Mediterranean entrants.

Linking national markets together, however, is not enough. Establishing the four freedoms of unrestricted movement for all goods, services, labour and capital, and creating a level playing field for all competing firms, was (and still is) frustrated by national differences embodied in numerous non-tariff barriers.

A single market which exhibits different prices for the same model of motor car; which restricts the sale of insurance and financial services in certain regions; where certain governments are allowed to grant hefty subsidies to some airlines but not to others, and grant exclusive public service contracts to domestic suppliers only; where its people still need passports and work permits to move around; and where differing technical standards, tax regimes and laws all operate together, is quite obviously not a common market in the sense normally understood by the term. And yet all these differences and more are the product of European institutions – despite the fact that eliminating such differences was the original objective of the Treaty of Rome in 1957, and additionally was the specific goal of the Single European Act, agreed in 1985 – that is, to achieve a progressive reduction in all restrictions according to a timetable terminating in 1992.

In truth, even without tariffs and quotas there is an infinite range of other factors that can impact on and distort trade between neighbour countries and thus act as forms of non-tariff barriers.

State aid

Nationhood is still officially protected within Europe. Many governments still prevent favoured businesses from going under when they suffer from foreign competition since local vote-winning frequently takes precedence over commitment to European ideals. National interests remain inextricably identified with the economic health of certain domestic companies and with the political complexion of certain governments. Lip service to being 'European' is continually being paid in official circles, but the real losers are European taxpayers and consumers who are required, on the one hand, to subsidise the loss-making businesses and, on the other, to continue to pay higher than free market prices for their products. However, wherever the costs of failing industry are easily identified in terms of the loss of earnings to well-defined groups of workers and the political outcry of numerous citizens, and the benefits are measured in terms of a fractional reduction in future prices to faceless billions of consumers, then the government decision to subsidise national political interests rather than European economic integration will continue to frustrate progress towards a common market.

Public procurement

National governments are extremely unlikely to award highly visible contracts to non-national firms instead of to a domestic producer. When the German Ministry of Transport purchases Fiat cars and French agricultural officials serve banquets featuring Welsh lamb and Rioja wines, then the common market will have truly arrived. The public procurement market in Europe is estimated to be very large (approximately 10 per cent of the combined union GNP), yet only a tiny fraction of this is genuinely open to competition from non-national suppliers. According to the EC Commission's Cecchini report (1988), 0.14 per cent of this trade was won by foreign firms – hardly an open market place. The 1992 programme introduced by the Single European Act outlawed the more discriminatory practices, so that public authorities are now obliged to advertise contracts widely and, for a sufficient period of time, to allow non-national firms to compete for orders. However welcome, this cannot prevent, of course, the continuation of national preference in public purchasing.

Taxation

Europe's internal frontiers are now more open than ever before to the passage of transport – customs checks on lorry loads of goods have (at long last) all but disappeared – but corporation tax and value added tax differences remain between member countries, as do varying excise duties on such goods as wine, beers and spirits. There therefore continues much costly paperwork to calculate tax charges and refunds, and this inevitably inhibits and distorts free trade. (The impact of these formalities is naturally greatest for small and medium-sized European firms which do not have large outputs over which to spread these fixed costs.)

Technical differences

Rules on the harmonisation of technical standards, or mutual recognition of partner countries' regulations, have been in place since 1992, but there is still a long way to go before all nations accept EU standards for every good and service produced. Many manufacturing businesses across the continent cite differing technical standards between countries as their biggest single impediment to pan-European sales. Consumer electronics products, for example, have to be equipped with a variety of different plugs if they are to be compatible with domestic electricity supplies in every member country. Specific state controls on banking, insurance and finance and restrictions on foreign participation and joint ventures in Spain, Greece and Portugal are another form of non-tariff barrier to free competition in services.

Language

It is impossible to quantify the impact of differing languages as an impediment to trade, although obviously they are a major barrier. The lack of a common language is probably the single most important non-tariff barrier to commerce and communication across the entire continent, and yet this is – at the same time – the most important distinguishing characteristic of the European Union. What other part of the world demonstrates such linguistic and cultural diversity? Differing languages *are* Europe. Yet the mobility of resources and the international trade in goods and (especially) services is inevitably greatly slowed by language differences. How can you do business with someone if you do not know what they are saying? Europe now has twenty-three official languages and many other dialects. Translation and interpreting costs in EU administration are immense and selling products across the union involves communication problems that businesses in North America are blissfully free from. *The Economist*, for example, noted that a US company selling computer software packages had access to a domestic market of 57 million home users prior to 2004. In Germany, the biggest European market, there were only 11 million users and they use a language that has little further sales potential outside the country. Small wonder, therefore, that international trade in software services is dominated by large US firms which enjoy the advantage of home economies of scale. In Europe, less than a third of this linguistically fragmented market is taken up by European firms: 60 per cent use American software. (Note: despite examples like these, there has never been any suggestion that Europe should attempt to evolve a common language, unlike the increasing momentum towards harmonisation or convergence on other issues.)

Currency

Different currencies have evolved in Europe for much the same reason as different languages. They are the natural outgrowth of people living in different communities, each trading with one another, but distinct from other societies (see the passage on optimum currency areas in Chapter 8). Weights, measures, units of exchange and the language of commerce all evolved together. Agreement on standardisation of weights and measures has been achieved and, even if much remains to be done – as referred to above – great progress has been made. Currency agreement is more problematic, however. That differing currencies are a barrier to trade is evident – though exactly how big a barrier they are is open to controversy. Some would say that sophisticated foreign exchange markets, and particularly the ability to deal in currency futures, eliminate nearly all problems of financing trade. Others would argue exactly the opposite: that such currency markets actually destabilise international trade.

The introduction of a single European currency – the euro – was designed precisely to overcome this non-tariff barrier to trade and bind participating nations even closer together. It represents the next stage in economic integration between countries. There is much controversy involved here and it requires, in addition, greater understanding of the particular economics of money and banking. These topics will be treated in more detail in chapters that follow.

Conclusion

We can conclude here that promoting the closer economic integration of countries involves numerous and complex economic, political and cultural issues. Increasing economic prosperity in customs unions is not automatically assured – there may be much trade diversion involved as well as trade creation – and additionally some regions will benefit more than others.

The heterogeneity of many different countries and cultures continues to fragment the common market of Europe, but at the same time it is precisely this quality that provides the immense resourcefulness of the union.

There are worrying problems for the future: an ageing population combined with a lower participation rate means that in future 75 per cent of the population must be supported by only 25 per cent at work. In order to carry this weight the European labour markets must become more and not less efficient. The forces of globalisation are unlikely to diminish so we must learn to live in a younger and more competitive world economy. Protectionist sentiments from some political leaders and a refusal to reform and move on do not help.

The occupational mobility and adaptability of European lands and peoples will in the long run provide the key to who gains, and by how much, in the process of integration. The more such fractious peoples see their interests in common, the more quickly (as well as closely) will integration be achieved and the greater will be the economic benefits enjoyed. But this process cannot be hurried: after thousands of years of separate development, Europe needs time to resolve all its differences. An economic integration of varying speeds for differing countries is both necessary and inevitable.

Finally, let us finish with a global perspective. What is the impact of increasing European economic integration on the rest of the world?

As mentioned in Chapter 4 above, one reaction of those left outside a common market is to set up rival trading blocs. A desire to emulate the EU's success and a fear of losing out in competition have fuelled the growth of other regional associations such as NAFTA, the Association of South East Asian Nations (ASEAN) and others. The great danger here, however, is that world trade may become dominated by a few, large, rival groups, and – in an atmosphere of mutual distrust – it may become easier to erect common external tariffs than to negotiate a general reduction in protection. If this occurs, then world trade may become greatly distorted over time. There exists much potential for trade diversion, rather

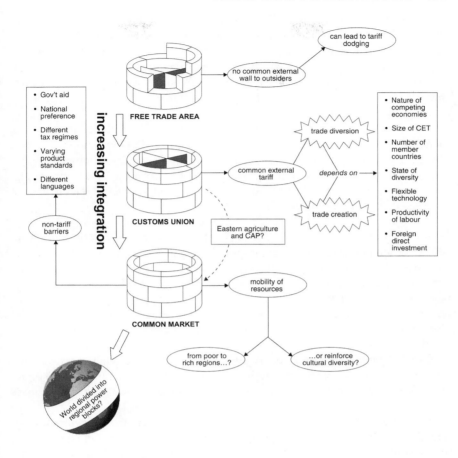

Figure 6.2 The themes of Chapter 6.

than trade creation, but that is an outcome which would benefit no one and is a matter of concern that ought to be in the minds of all governments attempting to set up trade deals. Success in achieving a closer European Union would be a hollow victory if this were to take place in a world divided by mercantilist power blocs.

Key words

Ageing population An ageing population occurs when people live longer, have fewer babies, and thus pensioners and the elderly begin to outnumber children. The average age of the population of a community rises when both birth rates and death rates decline, assuming immigration remains constant. One of the concerns is that, over time, an increasingly large fraction of the population may become dependent on a decreasing fraction of economically active, income-earners.

Common Agricultural Policy The Common Agricultural Policy was the first and the central economic policy of the EEC, set up at its foundation in 1957. Its aims were to stabilise post-war agricultural prices and incomes, to ensure market supplies and to increase general agricultural productivity. Its main feature was to guarantee farm prices at what have evolved as higher than market prices, to subsidise agricultural exports and to support the European farm sector in general. It has successfully met these aims, but at the cost of creating incentives to overproduce, increasing farm sizes, promoting environmentally damaging farm practices, distorting income distribution and causing widespread trade diversion. Reforms just prior to the accession of Eastern European transition economies included moving towards farm quotas instead of price supports, and providing direct income subsidies. The need to reform the reforms, however, has created an ongoing debate and the process is unfinished.

External diseconomies are disadvantages that a business suffers as a result of some outside influence – such as transport difficulties and high rents in the centre of a busy city which force up costs for shops and offices. (Note how this differs from social costs and benefits – these are the effects imposed by a business on its surroundings.) *External economies* are advantages conferred on a business from the environment in which it is operating – for example, an incoming firm that recruits specialised labour from a region that has built up an expertise in certain skills.

Non-tariff barrier Those rules, regulations, customs and other practices and prejudices – aside from imposing tariffs or taxes on cross-border trade – that act to restrict trade and divide a common market into a number of smaller regional ones.

Participation rate The fraction of people economically active in a given population. The smaller the population of working age compared with the number of pensioners or children, the lower the average wages and the greater the attractions of leisure and other non-wage employments (such as child-rearing or being in education), the smaller will be the participation rate. Similarly, in countries where women are expected or compelled to be in the home, the participation rate will be lower.

Questions

1   Distinguish between trade creation and trade diversion. Using these concepts, examine the case for deepening the economic integration of Canada, the USA and Mexico beyond just a free trade area.
2   How might the deployment of resources and the distribution of incomes be affected as a customs union becomes a common market? Who are the winners and losers?
3   Does cultural diversity enrich or impede economic integration and growth? If the EU opts to deepen its integration over time, what might be the social costs involved?

4   How might the EU foster increased agricultural development among its member states without increasing trade diversion?
5   Should the EU focus on deeper integration of its members or wider participation of other countries?

Further reading

El-Agraa, A. M. *The European Union: Economics and Policies*, Cambridge University Press, 2011.

An extensive range of detailed information can be found on the EU website: http://europa. eu.

7 Money, banking and international finance

What power has law where only money rules?

Gaius Petronius (~66 AD)

A banker is a fellow who lends you his umbrella when the sun is shining, but wants it back the minute it begins to rain.

Mark Twain

Introduction

Money is arguably humankind's single most important invention. It has enabled societies all over the world to exchange goods and services, to grow and prosper. Indeed, communities need money in order to function.

Shortly after the dissolution of the Soviet Union, in the winter of 1991/2, many people lost faith in the value of the Russian rouble. As a consequence, the economy disintegrated, living standards collapsed and many people resorted to bartering their belongings in the streets in order to obtain sufficient food. At the time, in the West, people were sympathetic but complacent: it couldn't happen here, could it?

The answer came sixteen years later with the credit crunch of 2007/8 – which was a time when banks all over the globe were unwilling to loan out credit, or money, unless for very short times, at a high price, and only to the most reputable of customers. As a result the developed world was plunged into recession as households could not spend, businesses could not invest, assets lost their value and the dollar devalued.

The usefulness of money is, therefore, easily demonstrated. Without it, people cannot agree to do business and cannot support standards of living far above subsistence level. With money, however, trade can be facilitated and sophisticated lifestyles may develop. Far from being the root of all evil, money is the foundation stone for trade, economic growth and the development of civilisation. It is certainly worthy of serious study.

The functions, forms and qualities of money

The prime *function* of money is to act as a medium of exchange, and any commodity which is held for this purpose – rather than for its own intrinsic value – can thus be defined as money. Money in addition acts to place a price on all goods and services traded, and this includes putting a value on time – the rate of interest on riskless investment indicates how much people are prepared to accept in future compensation for going without their money now. Money should also function as a store of wealth: 'hard' currencies are distinguished from 'soft' ones in that they keep their exchange value for longer – the latter, in other words, are less acceptable as money.

Money at first took many *forms* in the course of its early evolution – salt, corn, sea-shells, etc. – in the many isolated communities where it arose. In all cases, however, in order to function properly as described above, any form of money must possess certain qualities, such as portability, divisibility, scarcity, durability and, most of all, acceptability.

In the last resort, anything which is acceptable in exchange is money. It is this unique characteristic of money that makes it so different from any other commodity in the global economy: it does not matter what is used, so long as it enables exchange to take place. Hence the old saying: 'money is as money does'. And, of course, it is this property which makes it so difficult for any central authority to control it: as soon as one form of money becomes restricted in its use, another form will immediately evolve. We can call this the phenomenon of **endogenous money supply**. That is, the supply of money circulating in an economy cannot be directly controlled by the state for any long periods; it is determined by the popular institutions and practices of the society itself. We shall return to this important principle again and again.

The earliest, most acceptable forms of money that crossed the world were precious metals. Gold, in particular, had all the right qualities, except that it was too scarce. As trade grew, the supply of gold could not keep up. In this way the amount of gold had an inherently restrictive effect on trade (causing gold prices to rise), which created the demand for substitute metals such as silver, and thus the formulation of Gresham's law (named after the Elizabethan financier): that 'bad money drives out good'. (If the official exchange rate between two currencies differs from that which is publicly recognised, traders will hoard the preferred currency and offload the other in market exchanges. The 'bad' money thus changes hands whilst the 'good' disappears into pockets.) In the case of silver, it wasn't such a bad currency. The development of European empires and the rapid opening up of trade in the Age of Discoveries was financed by increased supplies of South American silver and, despite periods of excess supply and unstable prices, it eventually superseded gold as an acceptable currency. Hence the evolution of a pound of sterling silver in the UK as the unit of account – the pound sterling. Equally, in the Spanish empire, the weight of silver passed into the language of money – as the 'peso' and 'plata'.

In time, of course, silver suffered from the same problem as gold and, indeed, all forms of commodity money. Its supply could not perfectly match the rate of growth of world trade. Accordingly a new form of money evolved: paper promises.

A promise to pay – provided it is believed by the recipient – is 'as good as gold'. Better, in fact, since promises are far less costly to produce than precious metals, and so the supply of, firstly, banknotes ('I promise to pay the bearer on demand the sum of . . .') and, secondly, credit, could more closely match the rate of growth of trade.

The catch, of course, is to ensure acceptability. Many banks from the earliest times have therefore had to promote an air of respectability, solidity, stability and all those other terms that are embodied in the architecture of banks and the comportment of their managers. How else would they win the confidence of a community and be entrusted with its savings? How else to inspire traders to accept their promises to pay? As Groucho Marx used to say: 'Integrity? If you can fake that you've got it made . . .'

The modern business of banking

Modern **fractional reserve banking** demonstrates the importance (and profitability) of generating confidence. So long as confidence holds, banks can issue many more promises to pay (liabilities) than they have liquid funds to cover. It does not matter how little in total a bank holds in its reserves, providing it has just enough to satisfy the next claimant who walks in the door. And, of course, the more respectable the institution, the less likely anyone is to challenge its promises. All the more room, then, for the bank to keep creating loans that it will call in at some future date to be repaid with interest. (It profits the banks to increase the indebtedness of the public.)

The only limit to the money supply now is the bankers' sense of self-discipline. As we all know to our cost, history shows they have little. Competitive forces drive commercial bankers to create more and more credit in pursuit of more and more profits. But confidence in banks can evaporate as their liabilities expand too fast, outstripping reserve assets. How can so much credit ever be supported? Empires are being built on sand, and a slight shift somewhere in the system can bring everything crashing down. If all claimants simultaneously run to the bank to withdraw their deposits, there is little there to pay them. Only promises. And if the promises are not believed, there is nothing.

The history of money and banking is thus a history of boom and slump – of the overexpansion of credit, of increasing indebtedness and of bank crashes – recent problems being no different from earlier ones, although they have been bigger and more spectacular of late. Many people around the world, indeed entire nations, have got badly into debt and are now paying the consequences in terms of greatly reduced circumstances. In the late 1980s, some lost fortunes in the collapse of savings-and-loans institutions in North America. Similarly, hundreds of millions of innocent Asians suffered in the late 1990s when bad loans and nervous creditors brought down a succession of banks in Japan, Thailand and South Korea, and prompted crisis and collapse in Indonesia. A decade later and it was the turn of the western developed nations to suffer the biggest financial crash since 1929. All affected have naturally asked: 'Why? What did I do wrong?' And: 'Isn't there someone responsible for protecting us?'

Trying to control what goes on

In each country it is the role of the state-run **central bank** to control national money supplies, to regulate commercial financial operations and to prevent abuses of the system. It is to the Federal Reserve in the USA, the Bank of England and the European Central Bank that hard-hit people in these countries turn to complain. The problem is that world financial practices have evolved too quickly for nationally confined authorities to keep up with them. And successful government moves to improve competition and efficiency in financial markets – making it easier/less costly for dealers to move money from one world centre to another – have inevitably made it more difficult for central banks to control what goes on.

Recent experience in the USA and Europe in administering monetary policy has demonstrated that it is extremely hard to directly control the quantity of money circulating in an open, rapidly evolving, modern, market economy. This is because any central government attempt to regulate bank activity according to one target or definition of money simply drives the market to use other forms of money (as predicted by the argument of endogenous money supplies, described earlier). As mentioned in Chapter 1, 'special investment vehicles' were set up by commercial banks precisely to take certain financial dealings out of the purview of central authorities. A variety of investment banks, accounting firms, multinational enterprises and others expanded their operations, fitting up sellers and buyers of over-the-counter derivatives and other financial paper outside regulated markets. This is all the result of the institutional and technological changes in the financial services industry: many more traders and rarefied forms of money have come into existence around the globe in recent years and have participated in new offshore and onshore money markets with sophisticated telecommunications technology linked worldwide. And, as it has turned out, in serving their own short-term, speculative interests they have actually *subtracted* value (lots of it!) from the world economy.

Faced with embarrassing, partly self-inflicted impotence in controlling their own backyards, monetary authorities in Europe and North America have only the interest rate on their own, central bank funds and '**quantitative easing**' (the supply of their own credit) as instruments to influence the operations of commercial banks and financial traders. Unfortunately, this can be likened to pushing or pulling on a piece of string. If there is plenty of slack in the system it achieves relatively little: if private money-makers want to go in one direction and the central bank wants to go in another, then a long, slack lead between them is of no use.

As different countries lurch from boom to bust, there are those who argue that national economies should disconnect themselves from destabilising world developments by unlinking their currency and their monetary affairs from any fixed international exchange rate system. In contrast, there are others who argue for exactly the opposite course of action – that greater monetary discipline is necessary, requiring stable exchange rates, supra-national regulation and, in the extreme, monetary union.

These are issues that are complex and need careful analysis. The economics of banking, recent changes and their impact on money supplies – both nationally and internationally – are continued in more detail below. The particular arguments for and against monetary union in Europe are considered in the next chapter and the issues relating to international financial crises – which seem to erupt with debilitating regularity every few years – follow later on.

The economics of banking: a simple model

To understand more clearly how the financial world operates, how it is changing and how it affects the lives and livelihood of ordinary people like you and me, we need to simplify the analysis of banking with the use of an elementary model, introducing more complex and realistic qualifications later on, once the basics are understood.

Control of the money supply within a country (assuming for the time being the country can be isolated from international events) lies within the relationship which develops between state authorities and private financial markets. This relationship is never stable in any society – it is in a continual state of evolution – but at its simplest level we can begin this analysis by assuming that there are only two forms of money: cash and credit (transferred by plastic cards).

The institutions of a banking system

Financial market places are where people and institutions buy and sell money – that is, they loan and borrow funds – and in the process determine rates of interest (the price of money) and the money supply (the quantity of funds circulating). Assume that the only traders in this market place are the central bank, several competing commercial banks and numerous private individuals and businesses.

The central bank holds the bank account of the government (it loans and borrows money for the government, amongst others); acts as a banker to all the commercial banks (they all keep their own accounts at the central bank); is responsible for setting the rules and regulations in all financial trade; and is charged with conducting the government's monetary policy within the economy (and internationally).

Commercial banks are *financial intermediaries*, that is they specialise in the business of mediating between those who have surplus money and those who have insufficient. More simply, they accept people's savings and then loan these funds to others who wish to invest. In the process they make money: creating more or less credit as society demands, subject to the effectiveness of central bank intervention. Theoretically, with open competition and access to all relevant information in the money markets, intermediaries will allocate funds only to the most efficient employments. (See Box 7.1.) Private individuals and businesses of all sizes are customers in these financial markets – they are the many people who save and the not-quite-so-many who invest.

Box 7.1   Financial intermediaries and the circular flow of incomes

Remember Chapter 2 and the macroeconomic model of the circular flow of incomes and spending within an economy? So long as injections equal leakages in the circular flow, the aggregate level of demand in the economy will be stable. If injections fall below/rise above withdrawals, then the flow of spending and incomes will fall/rise.

Financial intermediaries play a vital role in equilibrating injections and leakages. Their central economic function is to accept the deposits of savings from those who have excess funds, on the one hand, and recycle these in the form of loans to those who wish to invest funds, on the other. In the process, intermediaries act as an efficient conduit to pool funds from lots of small-scale savers all over the economy, funnelling these resources into those more efficient/profitable enterprises and avoiding those which are less efficient and potentially loss-making. They thus serve an important micro-economic, allocative function – devoting resources to the most productive employments – as well as the essential macroeconomic function of balancing savings (leakages) with investments (injections).

What happens if the aggregate supply of savings/leakages is greater than the demand for funds, i.e. investments/injections? How do intermediaries prevent a recession? In this case, the excess supply of funds in the financial markets will push the price of money (the interest rate) down. When money is cheap, more businesses will borrow and invest, and thus output, employment and spending will all rise. Macroeconomic equilibrium is restored. (You should see that exactly the same logic applies when injections exceed leakages – rising interest rates will choke off excessive, inflationary spending.)

Free financial markets are therefore necessary and sufficient – according to classical theory – to ensure the circular flow of income is balanced, stable and topped up at a level of aggregate demand to maintain full employment. Government intervention is unnecessary. This is a beautiful and persuasive economic model, automatically managed by the price mechanism.

The central bank directly controls the issue of cash (coins and banknotes) within the country. It is held in the hands and homes of private individuals, is deposited in commercial bank reserves and is also kept by these institutions in their cash balances at the central bank.

The creation of money

A country's cash base (defined as M0) is at the heart of its money supply. Commercial banks issue more or less credit to customers (as we shall see) as their cash reserves grow or decline. We can consider how this process takes place first of all in the case of a stable, conservative community where people have no reason to doubt the trustworthiness of their bankers. (Such communities cannot be built quickly – they are the product of lifetimes of responsible financial conduct, where people grow to respect those who hold their money.)

All customers who deposit cash in the banks may come to use debit cards as a safe and easy substitute to transfer funds – especially for large purchases. Most people will not withdraw funds and then transfer this money to someone else. Plastic cards are handed over instead, and the banks involved debit the cash involved from one person's account and then credit it to another's. The cash, therefore, never sees the light of day: it stays in the hands of bankers.

The more trustworthy the community, the fewer cash transactions will be necessary, and the more acceptable will be cards. Thus the form of money changes: commercial bank promises to pay (made via plastic cards) take the place of central bank promises (official banknotes).

Suppose that for every \$1 transaction that takes place in the form of cash in this community, ten times this amount of credit is exchanged via cards. This means that commercial banks can expand the money supply by ten times the value of the cash base. For every \$1 cash deposited by a customer in a bank, therefore, \$10 of credit can be created (by issuing cards to people asking for loans). The banks are confident that at any one time only one in ten customers will ever come in, present their cards and demand cash – so cash reserves are sufficient if they only back 10 per cent of all loans created.

This is the business of banking – to make money (credit) and loan it out at interest. Note that so long as traders accept a bank's credit, it cannot lose. A bank will therefore create more and more money – how much it creates is down to the bank's judgement on the balance between safety and profitability; prudence and security versus risk and greed.

The size of the credit multiplier (ten, in the example above) is a function of the stability and spending habits of the community involved. For politically unstable or economically underdeveloped societies, the credit multiplier may be as low as one – that is, every \$1 loan is backed by \$1 cash, ready to be withdrawn at a moment's notice. Highly sophisticated financial communities, on the other hand, may have very little need for cash. Many billions of transactions may occur daily with an infinitesimally small fraction ever being converted into cash. It is in these circumstances that numerous financial intermediaries have grown up, borrowing and lending all sorts of innovative forms of credit over varying time periods, and – quite clearly – the direct influence of the central bank as the controller of the cash base is greatly diminished.

Control of the money supply

According to textbook theory, the central bank can control money supplies of the commercial banks by varying the economy's cash base through '**open market operations**'. That is, the central bank borrows money from the public through the means of selling bonds and **bills of exchange** in the open market place. This means it sells paper (promises to repay loans at some future date) to private individuals and businesses in exchange for credit. By cashing in this credit the central bank reduces the commercial bank cash reserves. For every $1 reduction in cash reserves, banks must call in $10 worth of loans (assuming the economy maintains a stable 10 per cent reserves/assets ratio). Conversely, by buying back bonds and bills the central bank increases the flow of cash into the commercial banks, which then can increase lending tenfold.

There are other means by which central banks can attempt to control money supplies. Different countries can use one method, or a combination of methods, depending on what suits their practices and institutions best. For example, instead of operating indirectly through open market operations, central banks can directly reduce commercial bank reserves by seizing or freezing a fraction of their deposits – such cash cannot therefore be used to support credit and, again, loans must be called in to a multiplied extent.

Alternatively, central banks can demand a certain reserves/assets ratio by law, and then increase this ratio at times when they wish to restrict money supplies. Thus if banks maintain a 10 per cent ratio of cash to loans and then the central bank insists on a 12.5 per cent ratio, this implies that instead of every $1 cash supporting $10 loans, now it can only cover $8 worth. Twenty per cent of credit circulating in the economy must now be cut back.

Either by reducing banks' cash reserves or by increasing cash ratios, if central banks are successful in curtailing money supplies then they will drive up interest rates in the open market. They may, in fact, decide to operate the other way round: by charging higher base rates on central bank loans (which allegedly underpin the money markets), they may drive all interest rates upward and thus choke off demand (and thereby supply) for credit.

All of these measures have been used to a greater or lesser extent over the years as central banks have struggled to assert their authority and thus regulate monetary policy. (Monetary policy is important because it is one instrument used by governments to manage the macroeconomy. Actually, much controversy has burned between economists as to precisely how important this policy instrument is, relative to other controls. The general consensus now is that money supplies and interest rates do affect such phenomena as rates of inflation and investment, but the relationship is not as close or as predictable as some have argued.)

The difficulty, as we observed earlier, is that there have been an accelerating number of changes recently that have impacted upon banking practices and, as a result, central bank authority and control has for the most part been overtaken by events. Many of the old certainties in this market place have now disappeared.

The global explosion of finance

It was mentioned in Chapter 1 that the growth in global financial assets had accelerated since deregulation in the 1980s, from around 100 per cent to more than 400 per cent of world GDP by 2007. Aside from that **stock** of paper which had accumulated around the time of the financial crisis, by April 2010 the **flow** *of daily trades* in the global foreign exchange markets – buying and selling these paper assets – was valued (according to the Bank of International Settlements) at $3.98 trillion. That is, despite the recession, almost 200 times the value of real goods and services exchanged daily across the world.

The buying and selling that these enormous funds are in exchange for is in paper promises: all sorts of bonds, bills, securities and derivative financial instruments that private money-makers have invented. The forms of credit are so numerous today, and they metamorphose so rapidly, that what counts as money – and what does not – is difficult to define. Some have said that much of this mountain of financial paper is socially worthless – indeed I have argued that it has actually subtracted value. (At the end of 2011, both the US and UK economies – the two countries with the largest financial sectors – have national incomes lower than at the outset of 2009.) But what has driven this great increase in global finance?

Causes

Trade

It first started in the post-war era of capital controls: when central banks restricted the movement of funds in and out of their countries, when exchange rates were fixed between currencies, and each nation could manage its own, independent monetary policy. All trade between different parties, of course, is only possible with an agreed currency and, particularly in the international trade of oil, this was transacted in US dollars. In the Cold War years of the 1960s, the Soviet Union required banking services so that its trade surpluses could be used in the West, but outside the restrictions of the US authorities. The Eurodollar (later Eurocurrency) market grew up, therefore, with banks of varying nationalities operating in London free from the reserve asset requirements and interest rate ceilings demanded either by the Bank of England (because they were not dealing in pounds sterling) or by the Federal Reserve in the USA. Being an 'offshore' market, the banks involved were outside the exchange controls designed to support the (then) world fixed exchange rate system. Their customers were large, private and public enterprises with international interests, dealing in large sums of money (e.g. a minimum transaction of US$1 million). By operating wholesale and free from any restrictions, Euromarket banks had lower costs than their US counterparts, and so could offer better rates of interest to their clients and could profit on small percentage differences. The first lesson of this new industry was thus well learnt: large turnovers, small margins and fleet-footed avoidance of rigid regulation comprised the secret of success.

The accelerating internationalisation of finance gained pace in the 1970s when global recycling of petrodollars became the major preoccupation of bankers (see chapters 5 and 9). Massive balance of payments deficits of western, oil-consuming nations had to be matched by opposite movements of large sums of capital financed through the banks. The reverse side of this same coin was that oil-rich OPEC states with small populations and a limited capacity to quickly spend these fortunes needed international banks to place these funds in interest-bearing deposits. Trade imbalances of any kind require financing – these imbalances were the largest the world had ever seen, and the opportunities for expansion of international finance were a major boost to the industry.

The 1990s' parallel to these events was described in Chapter 1. The trade surpluses in this decade were now due to China's success in exporting manufactures, the related increase in the price of oil and thus again OPEC surpluses, and added to these were those of Japan and Germany – two economies traditionally earning more on exports than they spend on imports. These immense funds were not banked in financial institutions that were offshore but, as a result of deregulation (below), now found their way into the heart of financial districts in all the major centres. Such massive inflows were the seed capital that western bankers were able to multiply many times over in feeding their own backyards.

Technology

Of course moving funds internationally is impossible without bringing financial centres into contact with one another. The enormous growth in global finance needed, and developed with it, the advances in computing and telecommunications technology that brought down the **transactions cost** of trading. Now we take for granted the round-the-clock, 24-hour dealing in a global market place between London, New York, Singapore, Hong Kong and Tokyo (the top five) amongst others. As Tokyo goes to bed, London is waking up, and so New York switches from one set of traders to another. This is nonetheless as revolutionary as steamships and railways opening up the New World which heralded the first era of globalisation in the nineteenth century.

Deregulation

At the end of the 1970s, the stagflationary effects of the oil shocks on western economies heralded the ascendancy of conservative, supply-side economics as espoused by Britain's Margaret Thatcher and Ronald Reagan of the USA. After decades of interventionism, subsidies and controls in all manner of industries, governments in the 1980s seemed to rediscover the dynamism of free markets. Deregulation, privatisation and the liberation of prices became the new orthodoxy. Restrictions on international capital movements were lifted in one country after another, and this allowed the 'genie out of the bottle' – see *Innovation*, below.

Finance used to be compartmentalised such that commercial retail banks catered for the public with lots of small individual current and savings accounts; mortgage companies dealt in long-term house loans; investment banks catered for big business; and a range of other specialist institutions would provide insurance, pension funds, buying and selling of stocks and shares, etc. Now all this was blown apart with multiple takeovers and mergers such that certain big, multinational finance houses could perform all or as many functions as they so chose.

Note that increasing international competition drove deregulation more than anything else. As 'offshore' and foreign banks in London dealt increasingly profitably with large international accounts free of Bank of England controls, then UK domestic banks lobbied the government to allow them unrestricted access to this market also. As the amount of business grew in London, so the same political pressures built up in New York, Tokyo and Frankfurt: central authorities must lighten the load of their controls or risk the loss of business avoiding their shores. Deregulation rapidly became the dominant political economy, therefore, even in countries with allegedly socialist, or interventionist administrations, such as France and Japan.

Innovation

The incentive to innovate came initially from regulatory systems and capital controls which private profit-seekers wished to avoid. If governments resist the tendency towards deregulatory financial policies, then they will attempt to exert more and more restrictions on their particular money markets. This will drive interest rates up and, with such a slippery commodity as money, make it even more profitable for international dealers to try and avoid regulations and move funds around. Controls cannot succeed in such an international environment – the political movement towards deregulation becomes unstoppable.

In the 1980s era of deregulation and liberalisation, there was now no stopping the enterprise and innovative ingenuity of financial markets. Banking moved on from the rather stodgy, conservative role of accepting customer deposits for safekeeping, to the more adventurous, risky but profitable enterprise of designing fancy new paper promises, and selling them on around the world. As profits rose for the sharpest enterprises, so they could grow and take over others. In a period of growth and rapid change, the more innovative the business, the more it succeeds, and the more it seeks to exploit its success. Every change listed here drove along others, all simultaneously.

Risk

The opportunities for financial innovation and profitable **arbitrage** increased as market demand was stimulated. Originally, as mentioned above, it was to finance international trade – the movement of actual goods and services. After the oil price shocks, as exchange rates floated and controls on capital movement were removed, the world entered a more volatile phase where business risk increased – prompting finance houses to develop all sorts of paper products to manage this. Such innovation inevitably led to speculation on commodities, property, and other parties' loans and investments. The **derivatives** market ballooned: by the end of 2006, it was valued at more than $415 trillion (Bank of International Settlements). Traders could buy and sell *future* contracts (that is, agree a price of a commodity for delivery next year), *options* (pay for the option to buy a contract that you may or may not want to take up) and *swaps* (exchanging one contract for another). (See Figure 7.1.)

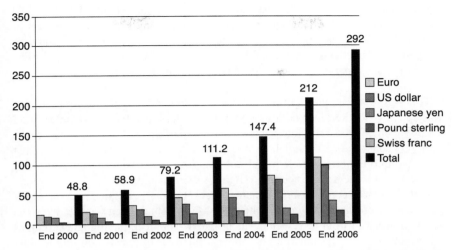

Figure 7.1 Growth of one of the most active derivative products – interest rate swaps – in different currencies, 2000–6 (just prior to the credit crunch). Measured in *trillions* (that is, twelve noughts) of US dollars equivalent.

Source: Bank of International Settlements.

Customisation

One key aspect of the derivatives trade was the meteoric rise of the over-the-counter (OTC) market – that is, designing bespoke contracts to fit each customer on a person-to-person basis outside the regular stock exchanges. An interesting account of financial practice here is given by one trader, writing in May 2008 (just prior to the major credit crunch in September of that year), where he reports on how he started: 'When I marketed and structured derivative solutions, customisation was the key driver – as tailored solutions that better met a client's needs also provided the opportunity to make more money.' He added, with regard to the lack of transparency concerned in these one-off deals: 'Let's face it, banks want as little price discovery as possible because it leads to more generous pricing opportunities.' One other aspect mentioned was that such OTC deals could be arranged on easier terms (i.e. less collateral, fewer guarantees), since they did not have to conform to the stiff regulations that apply to all official stock markets. So that was the way finance was expanding: customised, profitable, less transparent and less secure! He finished: 'But maybe I did 50 transactions a year. This is a very different situation than we have today where tens of thousands of credit derivative transactions and trillions of dollars of notional value get done annually' (Roger's blog, informationarbitrage.com).

Capital asset pricing models

One last important factor in explaining the explosion of finance was the broad acceptance of sophisticated mathematical models that allegedly could price the riskiness and returns on a whole package of derivative instruments. Traders could rapidly punch into their handsets the key variables of a given loan agreement or bundle of securities and quickly define the riskiness and thus price that could be charged to their clients. With confidence in the accuracy of these capital asset pricing models, many more deals could be priced and traded than before.

The significance of all these factors combining, and of information and transaction costs therefore falling, is that the barriers to entry to this industry all but disappeared. Specialist knowledge which used to characterise each segment of relatively conservative financial markets became widely available to any firm that could tap into the relevant global telecommunication network, hire the staff and follow where others were leading. Highly efficient and accessible technology brought increased competition from enterprises formerly unrelated to the industry and, as a result, the trading ethos changed. Many young, keenly entrepreneurial agents now sat in front of screens, watching events unroll, buying and selling as prices moved, making small margins on large numbers of transactions in the blink of an eye. Loyalty to the old firm disappeared – rivalry was intense and successful traders would move from one company to another on the promise of higher rewards. And rewards were based on turnover and quick results, not on developing long-term customer relations, getting to know the ins and outs, strengths and weaknesses, of each client.

Effects

The implication of all these changes for individual countries is that now it is extremely difficult for governments to use monetary policies to control their economies as they so wish. Liberalised markets now mean that central banks cannot control the money supply and the money supply itself can have a very variable impact on an economy. The idea of fine-tuning an economy through regulating the quantity of money or the structure of interest rates is thus hopelessly impractical.

Multiasset markets

How can central banks control the money supply when money itself can no longer be closely defined? In today's financial markets, dealers work with a whole spread of assets of varying liquidity and security from cash through Treasury and commercial bills of exchange, to all manner of different bonds, securities, certificates of deposits, equities, and longer-term advances and mortgages.

Liquidity is the ease with which any of these assets can be converted into cash. Very short-term loans are highly liquid since they will be repaid quickly. Reliable long-term assets can be very liquid also since they may have a high resale value in the **secondary market**. (Government securities with, say, one year to run can be resold immediately to any one of a number of interested buyers.) Less reputable commercial and **'junk' bonds** and longer-term assets may be more difficult to place a present value upon – they are less liquid – but they carry a higher rate of interest as a result.

With so many different financial institutions holding varied portfolios of income-earning financial assets, which particular ones do you include in the money supply? We have seen that as central authorities have restricted the circulation of those assets they have directly under their own control, it has simply prompted the expansion of other financial instruments to take their place. If interest rates on government bills and bonds rise, then a whole chain of substitutions may take place as dealers adjust their holdings of these as opposed to other assets. Prices and interest rates on a host of near and distant alternatives will all shuffle up or down accordingly.

As a result of such diversity, central banks have identified an ever-increasing array of monetary aggregates as the money supply – M1, M2, M3, M3c, M4, etc. – each in turn being used for control purposes, only to be just as quickly abandoned as the authorities found that each did not behave quite as it should have done. Experience has produced **Goodhart's law**: whichever measure seems best to represent the money supply will cease to function as such as soon as the central bank tries to regulate it.

Institutional changes

In addition to the vast, innovative spread of assets held by banks, what actually constitutes a bank now is almost irrelevant. As mentioned, financial markets used to be segmented and specialised. Now domestic and international competition is rife. The **barriers to entry** between different financial sectors have come down and with cross-border restrictions falling, subsidiaries of foreign, international banks have poured into every small financial centre around the world. Many large, national and multinational companies have developed their own financial arms and entered into the competition, and off-balance-sheet and over-the-counter deals have mushroomed outside official money markets.

Dozens of international mergers and acquisitions have occurred over the past four decades involving banks, securities firms and brokerage houses in Europe, the USA and Asia. As a result, which finance house is operating where and dealing in what business is no longer the cosy, predictable affair it used to be. By the same token, this has made the monitoring and control of domestic financial operations by national authorities virtually impossible.

Debt, boom and bust

By loaning out money, and increasing the indebtedness of clients, banks increase their assets and – assuming debtors keep up with their interest payments – the banks' future income rises. As bank balance sheets grow, the size of the financial industry and of the national economy grows. Financial traders are rewarded with commission, their institutions grow in prestige and political influence, and everyone benefits from the merry-go-round. So debt is good. There evolves a tremendous incentive to create increasingly innovative forms of credit, and to push these not only on to the general public but particularly on to other banks (they of course are the ones who love this business). Where investment opportunities in productive enterprise (new plant and machinery) become saturated, where next do financial institutions place their borrowed funds? What better than bricks and mortar, solid houses, elegant city centre office blocks and shopping malls that become temples to booming materialism? With so many funds pouring into these, property prices soar. You can't lose on this, can you? House prices always increase, don't they?

Thus speculative bubbles are formed with the end result described in Chapter 1. If the global expansion of money supplies outruns the world's supply of productive assets, goods and services, then boom turns to bust, with painful consequences for the innocent.

Exchange rate effects

One last effect of the globalisation of finance that we must consider is the effect on exchange rates. With financial sectors operating beyond the reach of central banks, government attempts to influence domestic money supplies and interest rates may have little short-term effect on real economic variables such as consumption, investment and employment, but they may have an immediate impact on the local currency's exchange rate with other monies.

Much depends on how foreign exchange markets interpret the actions of the government in question. A rise in the central bank rate would normally pull in speculative funds from other countries, which would then push up the exchange rate. An attempt by the authorities to increase the price of money, perhaps in order to dampen down spending and inflationary expectations at home, may not then succeed in reducing domestic borrowing and investment if business expectations are positive and the economy is booming. It may, however, put up the exchange rate and thus increase the price of exports and reduce import prices. This may not slow down spending, only stimulate domestic consumption on foreign goods and cause the balance of payments to deteriorate.

With international capital controls deregulated and floating exchange rates that are subject to the volatility of foreign exchange markets, all countries can have an exchange rate policy or a domestic monetary policy, but not both. One policy instrument – the central bank interest rate – cannot be used to serve two contrary objectives. If a country wishes to push up (or down) the rate in the attempt to influence domestic spending, it will have to make do with whatever exchange rate the markets decide. Alternatively, if the authorities wish to influence the exchange rate and either attract or depress demand for their currency, they must put up with whatever is the effect on domestic investment and consumption. Liberalised financial markets, fixed exchange rates and independent money policies are collectively known as 'the impossible triangle', or sometimes 'the policy trilemma'. In the post-war era of the 1950s and 1960s, the element that did not hold was liberalised movement of capital; in the 1970s, it was fixed exchange rates that had to go. From the 1990s up to today, thanks to the globalisation of finance, we have freedom of money movement and floating exchange rates, and the price to be paid is the sacrifice of independent monetary policy.

Conclusion

In a multiasset financial world the clear-cut distinction between a community's base of cash reserves and its total money supply disappears. There is no simple 1:10 credit multiplier relationship; reserve assets are not easily identifiable nor are they completely within the control of the authorities; and – thanks to institutional changes – official banks subject to central bank regulation now represent a diminishing fraction of financial operators.

All the measures referred to above by which central authorities are supposed to influence monetary aggregates – increasing or decreasing commercial bank reserves through open market operations, direct intervention or changing minimum asset requirements – are now only to be found in outdated economics textbooks. These measures cannot work in open, deregulated markets since other highly liquid assets can be quickly substituted for those reserves the central bank calls in, and many non-bank financial operators are out of reach anyway.

In effect, most developed countries since the mid-1980s have opted to pursue an exchange rate policy rather than take any overt monetary stance apart from deregulation. For all the reasons given above, monetary policy is too blunt and unpredictable an instrument to serve the needs of governments. That is, deregulated finance is out of control.

What of the true economic role of financial intermediaries – firstly, the microeconomic function to allocate society's funds efficiently, discriminating between those productive and profitable enterprises, and those that are wasteful? On that score, the funding of sterile construction and speculative derivatives does not impress. Financial markets have failed us. And secondly, what of the macroeconomic function of equating injections and leakages from the circular flow? Clearly unsuccessful also, given that trillions of dollars' worth of assets have leaked from the world economy and we have been plunged into the greatest recession since the 1930s. No full employment equilibrium here.

The fact is that the growth of finance has overtaken the ability of the authorities to control what is going on, and the consequences are serious. Democratic governments and the central bankers they appoint have been rendered powerless by big money institutions – banks that are too big to fail. It used to be thought that, firstly, 'you can't beat the market' and, secondly, 'the market knows best'. (The first quote is associated with Margaret Thatcher who liberalised UK finance in the 1980s; the second quote is associated with the efficient markets hypothesis, the paradigm that dominated in the boom years before it all went bust.) Well, it has been shown that markets do *not* always know what is best. Sometimes they get it so wrong that, not only do they bankrupt themselves, but they put the rest of their nation in hock too as governments are forced into rescuing them. It is not so much that 'you cannot beat the market'; it is more the case that the market beats you . . . and beats you into submission. How we escape from this is left to another chapter.

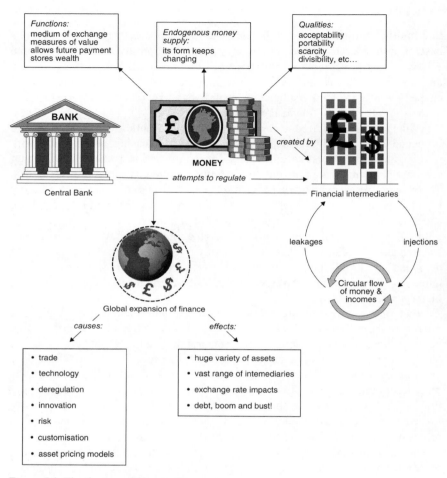

Figure 7.2 The themes of Chapter 7.

Key words

Arbitrage This refers to the exploitation of marginal differences in prices of financial assets between different markets. If the price of a given currency, commodity or bond in Hong Kong or New York is higher than in London, then it pays to buy in the cheaper market and sell in the other. The smallest price differentials can yield significant profits if large volumes are traded. Risks are low since arbitrage implies simultaneous transactions at known prices. Its economic effect is to secure price equivalence between rival centres.

Barriers to entry These are the restrictions imposed on any new enterprise wishing to start up business in a given field. Such barriers may be legal, bureaucratic, financial or economic. Governments may restrict the buying of domestic industrial assets by foreign firms by law, or the process of acquiring all the necessary licences may be exhausting, the costs of insurance or borrowing local funds may be excessive, or the capital equipment necessary to start a business may be highly expensive.

Bills of exchange These originated centuries ago as three-month trade deals. You give me capital on the understanding that it takes me three months to equip a ship, sail out to the South Seas, buy lots of exotic goodies, come back and sell them off at a profit and then pay you back the agreed amount. A bill of exchange is now a promise to pay a given sum in three months' time. The cheaper you buy this bill, therefore, the more you stand to gain. Note that if a private bill, or bond, is guaranteed by a reputable third party (e.g. a well-known bank or business), then you have little risk of loss – the price of this paper is likely to be higher. Such is the case also with **Treasury bills**, which are issued by the government. The riskier the dealer, however, the cheaper they will have to sell their paper – the more profit they have to offer to attract a buyer. (See **junk bonds**.)

Central bank The government's bank, charged with the responsibility to run monetary policy, which includes making loans to and accepting deposits from private, commercial banks and thereby determining the rate of interest on government debt. **Open market operations** was the traditional term used to refer to the central bank's dealings with free market banks and credit institutions to affect the money supply – buying/selling government bonds to increase/decrease the intermediaries' reserves and thus affect their ability to create credit. **Quantitative easing** is its modern, unconventional equivalent used in the current Great Recession: the central bank purchases designated private sector financial assets (*not* government paper), thus flooding the intermediaries with capital . . . the intention being to induce them to lend more.

Derivatives Any tradable paper which derives its market value from that of some underlying asset is a derivative. This would include a promise to buy a certain security at an agreed price at a given date in the future ('futures'), or the option to buy certain shares at a given price within a certain time period ('options'). The enterprise which buys a derivative from a financial institution is in effect paying the seller to take on the risk of a change in economic conditions and prices over the lifetime of the business. For example, a plantation company may be unsure of the income it will earn from sales of a future harvest and thus be unable to make required investments today. An astute bank will offer to sell derivatives on the company's behalf, guaranteeing capital to the plantation, taking on the risk of a commodity price collapse, but making a nice profit if it calculates correctly.

Endogenous money supply This is where the supply of money in a country is not created and directly controlled by the central authorities, but is determined by the actions of private individuals, businesses and banks. The form of money and the nature of credit-creating institutions can change where state attempts to restrict commercial banking activities bite hard, thus leading to the desire to circumvent such controls – an endogenous money supply.

Fractional reserve banking Commercial banks traditionally keep a relatively small sum of liquid funds in reserve in order to meet customer demands for withdrawals. That is, if a bank possesses $5 million in cash deposits from savers, it may decide to create $50 million in credit to loan out to needy investors. The bank's reserve/assets ratio is thus 1:10. That is, it reckons that, of the $50 million of its cheques circulating, no more than one-tenth will be cashed in. Recent ballooning of credit expansion has rendered such reserve/asset ratio calculations obsolete.

Goodhart's law Charles Goodhart, who moved from the Bank of England to the London School of Economics, claimed that any observed statistical correlation between two variables would break down as soon as public authorities attempted to use it for policy-making purposes. This comment is as relevant for central bank attempts to control the money supply by restricting trade in certain reserve assets, as it is for relying on a Phillips curve relationship to control unemployment by opting for a little more inflation. Goodhart's law recognises the fundamental uncertainty of social science.

Junk bonds These are commercial bonds not guaranteed by first-class banks or financial institutions, and they thus carry a lower price and higher risk factor than other market instruments – though they may turn out to be perfectly reputable, despite their name.

Liquidity Forms of wealth that can be quickly turned into cash without loss of value. Banknotes and coins are 100 per cent liquid. Some bonds and short-term loans to reputable clients can quickly be sold off in the markets and thus converted into cash without much loss of face value. If you own a vintage car, some old paintings, certain shares or a loan that now appears 'toxic' or difficult to value, you may have difficulty in finding buyers unless you sell at a discount – these are illiquid assets.

Open market operations See **central bank**.

Quantitative easing See **central bank**.

Secondary markets No one would buy a very long-term promise to pay if it meant that they could not get their money back in emergencies. Ploughing millions into buying shares, bills or bonds would not occur if there were no market place where you could sell them second-hand to other willing customers.

Stock A stock of any commodity or asset exists at a given moment in time, as opposed to a **flow** which is a measure of what is coming in or going out over a certain period.

Transactions cost   This is how much it costs to make a certain trade. If it requires time and effort to find out about asset prices in a neighbouring market, if governments restrict access to foreign currencies or charge a tax on the value of trades, then the cost of doing business may be prohibitively high. Why invest in Country X if the transactions cost involved is higher than in Country Y?

Treasury bills See **bills of exchange**.

Questions

1   How and why have the forms of money changed over history? What are the advantages and disadvantages of such monetary evolution?
2   'Free financial markets are therefore necessary and sufficient . . . to ensure the circular flow of a nation's income is balanced, stable and topped up at a level of aggregate demand to maintain full employment.' Critically assess.
3   Explain how banks can create money many times greater than that which they hold in reserve. What are the risks and rewards of so doing?
4   What has driven the explosive global growth of finance in the twenty-first century? How might this growth have been better used, thus avoiding the boom and bust of recent times?
5   Financial markets are particularly prone to failure. Explain why.

Further reading

Mishkin, F. S. *The Economics of Money, Banking, and Financial Markets*, London: Pearson Education, 2007.
Roubini, N. *Crisis Economics: A Crash Course in the Future of Finance*, Harmondsworth: Penguin, 2011.

8 Exchange rates and currency union

Europe will never be like America. Europe is a product of history. America is a product of philosophy.

Margaret Thatcher

Greed is good.

Philosophy of Gordon Gekko, played by Michael Douglas in the film *Wall Street* (20th Century Fox, 1987).

A team can only climb as fast as its slowest member.

Mountaineering tenet

An exchange rate is the price of one currency in terms of another. Like all prices in free markets, exchange rates are determined by the forces of demand and supply. If, in the foreign exchange (forex) market, there are more dealers wishing to sell euros and buy dollars than the reverse, then the excess supply of euros and the excess demand for dollars will cause the price of dollars to rise and the price of euros to fall.

Such an effect may be due to large numbers of consumers wishing to buy US exports. European importers will exchange euros for dollars in order to stock up on those goods and services in demand.

Consumer demand for goods and services does not tend to change rapidly, day by day, however. Exchange rates that move quickly up and down do not usually do so in response to the volatility of consumer tastes and preferences for imports or exports, therefore. They are more likely determined by sudden switches in the flow of 'hot money' – speculators moving funds from one account, one currency, to another.

All things being equal, a higher rate of interest offered on funds deposited in Wall Street, New York, rather than Frankfurt, Germany, will attract dealers to switch deposits from one centre to another: selling euros, buying dollars, and thus the former falls in price, the latter rises. Such flows will eventually cause exchange rates to settle at equilibrium when dealers are willing to hold existing supplies without rushing to exchange one currency for another; that is – taking all things into consideration – when deposits of all currencies offer the same expected rates of return. This is known as the *interest parity condition*.

Exchange rates appreciate and depreciate when buyers and sellers are anxious to buy or sell their currency holdings. Much then depends on *expectations* – if the riskiness of holding one currency is perceived to increase, then, at the given rate of interest offered on securities denominated in this currency, the markets will be unwilling to take them. A rush to sell will take place. Either the currency will plummet in value or those securities will have to offer a much higher rate of return to tempt dealers to hold on to them. (See Box 8.1.)

Exchange rates between currencies did not always move up and down in a somewhat unpredictable pattern – not for many years up until the oil shocks of the 1970s and the deregulating, liberalising 1980s. Indeed, free-floating exchange rates can be very destabilising for a country's trade in imports and exports. If currencies kept changing value according to the vagaries of forex speculators, then buyers of foreign goods and services would never know just how much money they were committing themselves to spend. How much is a dollar worth today? If

---

Box 8.1   Government securities, debt and rates of return

Government securities can normally be considered riskless. Dealers who buy them are lending money to the government's treasury and they will be paid back with interest when the contracted time is due. Governments of reputable countries will always pay up, it is said, since, firstly, their reputation is at stake and, secondly, they can always resort to increasing taxes to obtain the money they need to pay their creditors.

Massive government borrowing – issuing of bonds, bills and other securities – may, however, cause markets to worry that the build-up of sovereign debt is so great, and perhaps the domestic political scene is so fraught with conflict, that governments may default – that is, fail to pay up on time. It is not unknown for politicians to put local issues and demands first on their list of priorities, before those of international creditors. If that is the expectation, then government securities look a bad bet. Markets will be less willing to buy them/loan money to the government than before.

The role of independent rating agencies (the big three are Standard & Poor's, Moody's and Fitch) can be important here: if they downgrade a government's credit rating, and if dealers follow this advice, then the securities involved will fall in price.

A fall in the price of a downgraded security automatically means it will have to offer a higher rate of return to the buyer. An example: if the government promises to pay you 100 in a year's time, how much would you be willing to pay for that promise now? If the market says 98, then it is putting a rate of return of 2 per cent on that security. If, however, there is an expectation of some risk in a future pay-out, the market will perhaps only offer 92 today. The rate of return has risen to 8 per cent. The price of the bill *falls* from 98 to 92; the return that is thus determined *rises* from 2 to 8.

it is much more expensive than I originally planned, then my purchases may not be possible. My business – if dependent on foreign source materials – may make losses. (Many travel companies go bust for precisely this reason.)

After the trauma of the 1930s depression, when world trade collapsed, the allied powers met in July 1944, just before the end of the Second World War, in Bretton Woods, New Hampshire, to design an orderly return to global commerce. This required an internationally accepted currency. The most prized of all forms of exchange was gold, but not many countries had enough reserves – there was simply insufficient to go round to finance the growth in trade that was hoped for. For the UK and the USA – major trading nations – however, they had for many years used their own currencies to buy foreign assets and so large numbers around the world held reserves of these currencies. A system of fixed exchange rates was thus established where all countries would set their own currencies at a fixed price to dollars (or for some countries, to sterling), which in turn was fixed at a given weight of gold. The world thus traded with effectively a dollar standard system whereby, if any country ran a persistent balance of payments deficit, it would have to cancel the difference in dollars.

Fixed exchange rates can only operate if the demand and supply of different currencies can be kept in line. That therefore requires that, firstly, there is a restriction on speculative buying and selling of exchange and, secondly, there is an international reserve fund to help bail out currencies in temporary difficulty. Therefore strict controls on the movement of capital were enforced at first. (In the immediate aftermath of the war there was an inevitable shortage of dollars since only the USA had the capacity to export while Europe and Japan were frantically rebuilding. In a free market for currencies, the dollar would have soared in price – hence the suspension of a free market.) The **International Monetary Fund** (IMF) was designed at Bretton Woods to be the supporting institution for countries suffering a 'fundamental disequilibrium' in their trade. (The UK found that, at its fixed exchange rate, imports were increasing faster than exports. Selling pounds to buy imports meant that its exchange rate would fall. It could either borrow large sums of dollars from the IMF to give it time to right the imbalance or, under the rules, it could organise a one-off **devaluation** of the pound to re-fix at a lower exchange rate. Eventually, at different times, both measures were tried.)

The Bretton Woods system was outstandingly successful in facilitating a secure international economic environment in which global trade could flourish. Rebuilding after the war, expanding the reach of markets around the world and generating the growth of incomes of all trading nations from 1945 to 1971 was, by any measure, an impressive achievement. (Between 1948 and 1968, the total volume of merchandise exports from non-communist countries grew by an unprecedented 290 per cent.) These were the golden years of globalisation.

All fixed exchange rate systems have the disadvantage, however, that they freeze trading relations between countries at a particular time and if, over a number of years, one country's economy grows at a rate different from that of the other, its currency becomes out of line. Germany and Japan were devastated by the Second World War, for example, and their trading influence was minimal in 1944 when fixed exchange values were determined. After rapid post-war growth, however, the dollar prices of their currencies were, by 1971, grossly undervalued. The dollar was by contrast overvalued. The world had outgrown the Bretton Woods fixed rate system.

Abandoning such a successful exchange rate regime was not easy. Governments typically look upon a high value of their currency as a measure of political prestige and are very reluctant to devalue. The USA, wishing to hold on as the world's reserve currency, first attempted to re-fix all currencies at a lower value to the dollar (December 1971) and then, when that could not hold, gave up and the world resorted to free floating for all exchange rates in March 1973 (see Box 8.2). This was just as well since in October 1973 came the first oil shock (see Chapter 5), the price of oil soared by 400 per cent, and the international buying and selling of currencies thereafter took off into another dimension.

Box 8.2   The advantages and disadvantages of floating exchange rates

Floating exchange rates have distinct advantages:

No conflict between domestic and international objectives. During the 1960s the dollar and the pound became increasingly overvalued as the USA's and UK's **balance of trade** became unbalanced. Imports in both countries were rising faster than exports. With a trade deficit, this meant that they had to deflate the growth of incomes and consumption in order to reduce imports, restore balance and thus keep their exchange rates fixed (especially important since the dollar and the pound sterling were reserve currencies).

With free-floating exchange rates, there is no need to resort to internal deflation to defend an overvalued exchange rate – the currency just sinks in value according to the buying and selling in the forex markets. Similarly, there had been an opposite (admittedly less ruinous) risk faced by Germany and Japan of importing inflation if they tried to prevent an appreciation of their exchange rates. By allowing exchange rates to float down or up, countries could in effect ignore exchange rates and concentrate on domestic policies to secure internal equilibrium free from external constraints.

Central banks could now greatly increase their sovereignty and control over domestic economies. They could restrict domestic money supplies and force up interest rates or increase money and decrease interest rates according to their own estimation of domestic needs, rather than use them to offset fluctuating changes in the exchange rate.

Automatic insulation from external shocks. Sudden changes in external economic conditions – say, heavy selling of a currency due to a war or a financial crisis – would ordinarily push exchange rates down. To maintain a fixed exchange rate system, reserves of foreign currencies would be needed for the central bank concerned to intervene and buy its own currency to defend its exchange rate (calling for more funds from the IMF if necessary). With floating rates there would never again be the requirement to hold a given rate in the face of heavy selling or buying. Excessive shocks have the power to force governments to impose all sorts of unpopular austerity measures to keep their currency stable – which is not necessary if **depreciation** is an option.

Equality of sacrifice. No one country would maintain a reserve currency and thus exercise more authority, or carry more responsibility, than any other in conducting international trade. All currencies could vary in a more or less free market. Under the Bretton Woods agreement it had evolved that the US Federal Reserve was effectively fixing the world money supply, and thus all other central banks had to go along with whatever it decided – buying excess dollars whenever called to do so at the agreed rate. In the end, excessive controls were placed on capital movements between countries to prevent exchange rates being driven outside their permitted bands. At different times, as currency demand and supply changed, so US dollars, sterling, Deutschmarks and yen could not be allowed to be freely interchangeable. Thus restrictions had to be introduced on how much currency people could withdraw and transport overseas. Of course, in reaction to these restrictions, different agents resorted to different strategies to try and circumvent controls. Central banks were thus required to come up with ever more ingenious attempts to prevent the free market from working – an imposition on some currencies and authorities more than on others. Free floating released central banks from this burden, obviated all these requirements to distort and defend the indefensible, and spread the costs and benefits of currency exchange transactions to all buyers and sellers, symmetrically.

A system of completely free-floating exchange rates also has disadvantages:

Lack of discipline. Without the constraint of needing to keep reserves to defend an exchange rate, governments might increase spending or inflate money supplies to satisfy or pacify internal political pressures. For many governments, in many countries, over many years, the lack of any need to keep exchange rates stable has facilitated inflation.

Even with fixed rates, in the case of the USA, the political demands to spend money in the 1960s (e.g. in order to wage a war) prompted inflation, and without the requirement to keep to a fixed exchange rate, we can predict that inflation would have been much greater – as indeed it was after 1973. (See Figure 8.1.)

In the case of the UK, after the breakdown of the Bretton Woods system and the resort to free floating, conflicts between the British Labour government and the trade unions over wage demands were bought off in the late 1970s by granting inflationary wage increases. It was politically easier to buy off the unions and put up with increased inflation than to take the more difficult, and some said necessary, step of breaking trade union power, keeping the money supply down and thus keeping the exchange rate stable. (See Figure 8.2.)

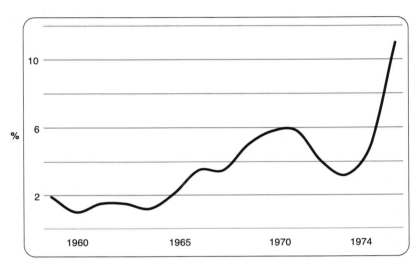

Figure 8.1 US inflation increases as the dollar floats after 1973.

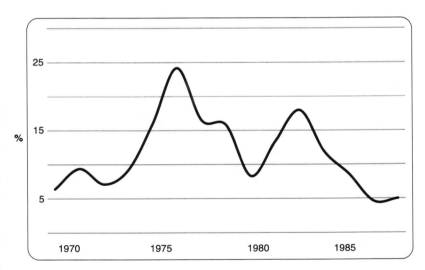

Figure 8.2 UK inflation also increases after 1973.

Excessive volatility. The movement of exchange rates is increasingly affected by rapid inflows and outflows of speculative funds. Financiers buying and selling paper assets across borders have a more immediate effect on exchange rates than does the import and export of goods and services, and the volume of financial transactions now vastly outweighs the movement of goods and services, as we saw earlier. This must mean that with free-floating exchange rates, the movement of the real economy will be at the mercy of volatile movements of exchange rates as a result of speculation. Fluctuating exchange rates mean uncertainty about the international prices that traders and investors in the real economy face. Uncertainty is a serious impediment to trade.

(Supporters of floating rates would argue that the forward exchange markets allow merchants to hedge against exchange rate risk and thus fluctuating prices can be insured against. True. But this is still a transactions cost that traders could well do without and which inhibits trade. Imagine if farmers in Scotland had their own independent currency and had to buy English pounds at variable rates to move, say, Scotch whisky south of the border. Profit expectations – the main influence on long-term investment – could never be certain. Although a hypothetical exercise now, such realities confronted European producers prior to the introduction of the euro and were a major contributory factor, firstly, in fixing exchange rates and, secondly, in unifying the currency; see below.)

Illusion of autonomy. Floating the exchange rate does not mean that central banks can concentrate on domestic equilibrium with total disregard to the international effects of their actions. For example, expansionary economic policies and an increase in imports would drive down exchange rates and increase import prices. This must have an inflationary effect and may drive domestic workers to ask for wage increases. A cost–price spiral results. These impacts on the domestic economy are all the more important the larger the fraction of international trade that features in the domestic economy.

Similarly, a restrictive policy on domestic money supplies, necessary to squeeze down inflation, will increase interest rates and attract hot money from abroad. This will drive up the exchange rate which may cause problems of its own: exports become more difficult to sell. Growth in export incomes will be sluggish, unemployment in this sector may rise. Cries to the government to help affected sectors will be forthcoming.

Not only can international consequences feed back negatively into domestic affairs, but in addition the negative feed back of domestic policy actions to other countries can also be difficult to ignore – see Chapter 9.

Clearly, flexible exchange rates give central authorities more room to move in deciding policy responses to economic shocks – whether internally or externally generated – but that room is anyway limited, especially for any country that is well integrated into the international economy (like the UK, or even more so, the Netherlands).

As a result of both irresistible changes in international economic power relations and the spread of ideas – the free market paradigm – the rule of fixed exchange rates anchored to dollars at a given price of gold gave way to a free-floating system. There remained a role for the IMF, however, since most countries wished to exercise some form of *managed floating* – intervening in forex markets to buy or sell their own currencies if they thought that speculators were going to extremes. The IMF could always be called upon for extra financial support if necessary and suitable guarantees were provided. (See Box 8.3.)

Box 8.3   Managed floating

The demand and supply of dollars is illustrated in Figure 8.3. The demand for dollars DD comes from holders of other currencies (e.g. pounds) wishing to buy; the supply of dollars SS comes from those holding that currency who wish to sell (e.g. to buy pounds). In this example, the price of dollars is listed in terms of pounds.

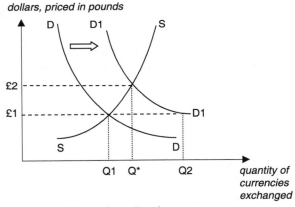

Figure 8.3 Demand for dollars increases.

If, say, owing to a change in expectations over the riskiness of the pound sterling, demand for dollars increases, then DD shifts to DD1 and, at the old price (£1), demand now exceeds supplies. That is, the flow of pounds on to the forex market (Q2) exceeds the flow of dollars (Q1), so the dollar price (measured in pounds sterling) increases or appreciates, from £1 to £2. The equilibrium demand and supply of dollars now equates at Q*. (Note that if the dollar appreciates from US$1 = £1, to US$1 = £2, then at the same time the pound must depreciate such that £1 now equals 50 cents.)

Suppose, however, that the Bank of England wishes to keep the sterling exchange rate constant. It needs to manage the flows of currencies on to the forex markets to offset the increase in market demand for dollars (excess selling of pounds) illustrated above. How does it do this?

The Bank must intervene in the markets, buying pounds – its own currency – and selling dollars out of its reserves in exchange. Thus SS shifts to S1S1. So long as it can do this it can balance the demand and supply with a larger equilibrium quantity traded of Q2 at the old price of £1. See Figure 8.4.

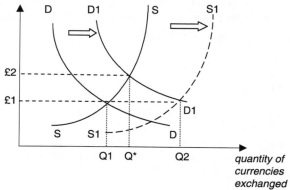

Figure 8.4 The Bank of England sells dollars to maintain the exchange rate.

Note that if the Bank's reserves of dollars become exhausted, it can apply to the IMF (or to the US central bank, the Federal Reserve) and borrow more to tide it over whilst the market demand is excessive, hoping things will calm down soon; it can later buy back dollars and repay what it borrowed. If the market demand for dollars, and the selling of pounds, goes on for a long time, however, the Bank may be forced to stop trying to maintain the old exchange rate of £1, accept the inevitable and allow the dollar to appreciate, the pound to depreciate, and move to the new exchange rate £2.

The uncertainty of floating rates was not welcomed by certain countries in Europe, however, pledged as they were by the 1957 Treaty of Rome to promote 'an ever closer union'. The objective of the common market was to stimulate trade between member countries and, for many (not all), a system of fixed exchange rates was desirable. Indeed, some voices were calling for a currency union.

Different communities, different currencies

Look quickly at the variety of forms of money that have existed through history: commodities, for example, such as salt, goats, corn, precious metals and even cigarettes. The fact that some societies traded with sacks of corn or livestock and others with a variety of different metals seems bizarre to us today, but perhaps this sentiment will be no different to some future European observer who looks back to the twentieth century and sees some communities trading in Deutschmarks, others in francs and others in pesetas. Why cannot Europe bring together its fragmented national markets to form one continent-wide currency bloc for the increased wealth and welfare of all?

Currency areas, like linguistic zones, evolve principally for social, and not economic reasons, and – like languages – the lack of a common currency in a large, populated land mass isolates individual communities and ties them into their own social confines. A currency becomes, therefore, the economic boundary to a social grouping. It is like saying: 'We only trade with these people, not those . . . '

The economic benefits realisable from international trade have driven the move towards European currency union. After two 'hot' world wars and one cold one, political relations between (most) European neighbours are now more harmonious; incomes and consumers' buying power have increased steadily and, thanks to the falling cost of transport and telecommunications exchange, people know of goods and services produced elsewhere, can gain access to them at reasonable prices and – with the globalisation of banking services – can obtain the foreign exchange necessary to make their purchases.

Barriers to international trade have always existed and, at first, it was the natural barriers of mountains, seas, rivers and geographical remoteness that were the most difficult to overcome. It is still costly to transport Mediterranean fruit and vegetables long distances to northern Europe, for example, and Welsh lamb back in return, but continuous transport innovation since the Middle Ages (culminating in the Channel Tunnel and the integrated network of high-speed road and rail links today) has been devoted to overcoming this problem.

The greatest obstacles to trade now are the man-made, nationalist barriers. The intervention of governments has never failed to create more and more complex tariff and non-tariff barriers to reinforce political and social prejudices. It has therefore taken immense efforts on the part of individual political idealists and institutions like the WTO and, within Europe, the European Commission to counter these mercantilist, isolationist tendencies.

Thanks to the EC's success in reducing intra-European restrictions on trade, the single, most important economic barrier to trade that remained within the common market was the lack of a common currency. The Maastricht Treaty, signed in 1991 by all member countries, was centrally concerned with this issue and it laid down strict criteria that European currencies/economies were supposed to fulfil in order to bring about currency union.

Towards currency union

The process of moving from free exchange rates to a currency union is not easy and is crucially dependent on the political will of those member states to ensure their economies converge – that is, to make the sacrifices necessary to bring costs, growth rates and productivity levels in line (see further below).

Technically, this meant introducing the European Exchange Rate Mechanism (ERM), which began its life with *tied floating*. The countries concerned fixed their respective exchange rates to each other within a confined range of values and allowed them to float up and down more or less as a whole – or rather as a flexible 'snake' – against all other world currencies. The system instituted was similar, on a regional scale, to the Bretton Woods system of fixed exchange rates. The anchor currency which evolved, however, was Germany's Deutschmark rather than the US dollar and the system was characterised as a 'crawling peg' – wider bands of currency movement and smaller, more frequent realignments made for a more flexible regime (during the 1980s) that was supposedly more able to accommodate sudden shocks.

To consolidate the next step towards currency union meant moving to *irrevocably fixed exchange rates*, assuring financial markets that there could be no further realignments within the system. This is a difficult feat to achieve. Money markets in an increasingly volatile world must be convinced not only that participating countries are politically committed to the union but also that their economies are not all pulling in different directions. Otherwise, if – for example – economy A is stronger than economy B, then the exchange rate of currency A compared with currency B will rise as dealers trade more in one than the other.

The transition period from declaring fixed exchange rates between partners to actually introducing a new common currency is fraught with difficulty particularly for these reasons, as European experience in the early 1990s proved. Despite well-publicised claims of unshakeable faith in their currencies by various political leaders in Europe, they were unable to prevent the major speculative attacks on the ERM in 1992 and again in 1993 (see Box 8.4).

Box 8.4   Pathology of a currency crisis: Europe, 1992–3

By 1991 the ERM had evolved to become a truly fixed rate system. The Maastricht Treaty had emphasised the importance of currency convergence for all members of the intended union, and it therefore became a sort of virility symbol of governments to achieve this harmony as early as possible. Five criteria had to be met by countries wishing to enter the select monetary integration club: price stability, budget balance, low levels of national debt, equivalent interest rates and fixed exchange rates.

Why were these criteria imposed? Imagine what would happen if one country was borrowing more or deflating more than another. Interest rates in one country would be higher than in the other. With unrestricted financial markets, currencies would flow out of one country and into the other and exchange rates would diverge. How can anyone be persuaded that convergence to a single, common currency is achievable?

But with five, well-published criteria to fulfil, it obviously became easy to compare the success of each European nation in reaching these goals. Newspapers in all member countries published charts grouping those nations closest to meeting these essential targets – the pressure was on all governments to improve their position in the rank-order. A currency that devalued in this rarefied atmosphere would indicate an apparent economic weakness and thus lack of political influence for the nation concerned in the councils of Europe.

Unfortunately, at the same time as this convergence in performance of different member countries was becoming an inescapable political strait-jacket, the external economic forces defining Europe were undergoing radical change.

Countries forming a currency union should not be subject to differential economic experiences. An external and asymmetric shock which impacts on partner countries to contrary effect cannot be accommodated by a common monetary policy. For countries in transition, straining to present a harmonious appearance to financial markets prior to currency union, this is the worst scenario to confront.

Yet this is precisely what happened. The collapse of communism and the unification of East and West Germany in 1990 happened astonishingly quickly – too quickly for the previously divided economies to adjust. East German industry could not compete in the modern western market place. Factories closed and unemployment increased. It says much about their sense of shared political and social identity that West Germans were prepared to pay the increased taxes that were required to support their neighbours. Taxation alone, however, could not pay for all this; government borrowing and spending had to rise. With the German central bank – the Bundesbank – unwilling to increase money supplies (it would have been inflationary), increased government borrowing meant that German interest rates rose.

High interest rates were not an appropriate policy, however, for other countries of Europe which were at this time struggling with recession. The spending boom at the end of the 1980s (prompted by supply-side tax cuts, amongst other things) had led to inflation, increased indebtedness and, consequently, the imposition of deflationary cutbacks. Falling incomes and rising unemployment were the inevitable inheritance at the beginning of the 1990s.

All the elements necessary for a European currency crisis were, by 1992, now in place:

1   The ERM had become a rigidly fixed exchange rate system.
2   EU governments were anxious to prove their anti-inflationary, convergence credentials.
3   As a result of the shock of unification, the Bundesbank had independently set its interest rate at a relatively high level within Germany.
4   Deflation and unemployment were increasingly becoming problems for a number of Germany's partners.
5   Popular support for currency union and the stringent convergence conditions was by no means overwhelming.

It is not difficult to see the incompatibility of these features. In order to ease the widespread recession (which affected the USA, Japan and many other countries too) there was much talk of the need to reduce interest rates. With German intransigence, however, this was impossible without undermining progress to European currency union. Critics, nevertheless, were not slow to point out that US interest rates were far lower than European ones and that the country had entered a period of booming growth.

Pressure to exit the ERM and devalue was greatest on those European states which had most to gain from so doing and where internal political criticism of currency union was known to be strong.

With fixed exchange rates, plus the prediction that they may not stay fixed for very long, you have the perfect scenario for heavy speculation. Sterling fund-holders, for example, have little to lose if they convert all their money into Deutschmarks: if there is no change of currency prices, they can simply buy back later when all the fuss has died down; but if sterling is devalued then they can repurchase far more than they had before. This is not just greedy speculation against a particular country's interests: no responsible manager of insurance or pension funds, for example, can sit idly by if those funds are about to be devalued.

In 1992, the Italian lira was thought to be inflation-prone. In contrast, inflation in the UK was no different from (if not lower than) that in Germany, but the country was suffering from the recession and political support for the pound's membership of the ERM was questionable. Heavy selling of both currencies took place in September of that year and, with the Bundesbank unwilling to supply Deutschmarks, devaluations were inevitable. Additionally, the UK left the Exchange Rate Mechanism entirely (rather than just realign the pound's price at a lower level) and brought its interest rates down.

A year later, it all happened again when the French franc came under attack. Similar to the UK, France's inflation record was not in dispute – it satisfied more of the Maastricht convergence criteria than did Germany – but now it was deep in painful recession and speculators were betting that the country could not go on any longer without taking the medicine of reducing interest rates. This time, speculation embraced not only the French franc but also the Belgian franc, Spanish peseta and the Danish krona. The ERM could not continue in its present form. The narrow band of movement allowed between currency prices was widened from 2.25 per cent to 15 per cent – as good as returning the currencies of Europe to independent, managed floating.

The moral of the story is that any intended currency union requires economic convergence between participating countries and, in this regard, *political idealism should not run ahead of economic realities*. Just as they had brought down the Bretton Woods system before, so economic divergence, political inflexibility and the pegging of government reputations to currency prices caused the ERM to blow apart in the early 1990s. These were two examples of fixed rate systems being untenable in the longer run as economic circumstances change: the warning signs for the establishment of the euro could not have been any clearer. Was anybody listening?

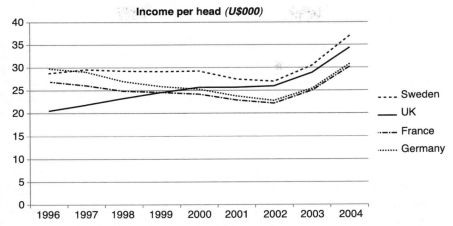

Figure 8.5 National income per capita, 1996–2004 (in thousand US$). Contrast the fortunes of two key European member nations of the euro (Germany and France) with two key European non-members (Sweden and the UK). The pattern for other euro/non-euro nations was even more marked.

Source: World Bank.

The political fall-out from the ERM crisis meant that, although Italy opted to return and remain in harness for adopting the euro, the UK, Denmark and Sweden all decided not to participate in the subsequent manoeuvring to introduce the new currency. What is revealing is that, after recovering from the speculative turmoil of 1993, the three European non-participants all grew faster than the average for the eurozone (see Figure 8.5). The Organisation of Economic Co-operation and Development (an independent, rich nations' forum) reported in July 2005 that, relative to other developed nations, there was in the euro countries 'a lack of resilience' in the face of external shocks (such as the 'dotcom' crisis of 2001–3) and 'a longer-term problem' of slow growth (*Economic Survey of the Euro Area, 2005*, www.oecd.org).

The OECD made some telling criticisms. It mentioned that the eurozone nations exhibited high structural unemployment and were much in need of labour market flexibility; that they were lacking in innovation and the absence of any common market in services was much to blame; and, crucially, 'long-term fiscal sustainability' was 'far from assured in a number of countries'.

Despite the 1990s' ERM currency crisis – that is, the crystal-clear evidence that it is painful, if not actually dangerous, to squeeze disparate economies into a one-size-fits-all currency and common monetary policy – the political will to forge ahead with the euro was unstoppable. The **Stability and Growth Pact** was signed in 1997 by all countries intending to introduce the euro, and pledged them to keep government spending and sovereign debts under control, so that no one country could irresponsibly squander the common money supply. Then the **European Central Bank** (ECB) was established on 1 June 1998 in Frankfurt, Germany, and charged with controlling the new currency and administering the one, unified, pan-continental monetary policy. Finally, the euro came into being on 1 January 1999.

As mentioned above, a currency area is ultimately a social construct: a declaration that 'we wish to trade with these people in the club, and less so with outsiders'. (Note: it must necessarily imply that all members make sacrifices to stay together . . .) But what are the *economic* risks and rewards involved in forming a currency union? And why should any separate country not yet included line up to join the club?

Benefits and costs of a single currency

One direct benefit of a common currency that it is easy to appreciate is the *elimination of transactions costs*. Previously, any trade between euro partners involved paying the cost of exchanging one currency for another. All tourists know this problem – travel from the north of Italy through Austria and into Germany and in half a day you used to lose a considerable sum of money in commission charges when changing cash from lira to schillings and then into Deutschmarks. Monetary union has eliminated this deadweight loss, that is, the significant cost that consumers have to pay and for which they receive nothing.

The indirect benefit of removing transactions costs and *increasing the transparency of European prices* is more difficult to calculate. European consumers are now able to compare prices for the same good from one side of the continent to the other and make their purchases accordingly. Note that price discrimination between different countries is easier to conceal when people use different currencies: it was calculated that during the 1980s, buying a Ford car in the UK was up to 30 per cent more expensive than buying the same model in Belgium, for example. Hiding such differentials is impossible with a common currency. There are still price differences but these are now due to differences in real costs (e.g. transport) rather than to profiteering. There is an undeniable gain in removing the cloak of exchange rates behind which much price discrimination could previously be hidden, though it is difficult to quantify the stimulus that this is now giving to freer European trade and increased consumer welfare.

A common currency *removes any uncertainty over future exchange rate movements*. Cross-frontier investment is impeded by the risk of a change in currency prices. Estimated profits from an investment in another country can be reduced or even wiped out if the currency in which those profits occur unexpectedly devalues. Such exchange rate uncertainty can be partly reduced by hedging in currency futures – paying others to take on this risk – but, again, this cost is another deadweight loss which businesses can well do without. A single currency thus leads to an increase in cross-border investments.

These three benefits are all related: they result from the increased workings of a pan-European price mechanism. Wider, freer trade across the whole continent, it is alleged, will secure a more efficient allocation of combined resources.

The major cost that is ascribed to currency union is the considerable *loss of economic and political sovereignty* involved. With only one pan-European currency, there can be only one monetary policy. National governments opting for the euro have now ceded this instrument of their control, therefore, to the European Central Bank. No member country of the union is free to increase or decrease its money supply, devalue or raise the price of its currency, or adjust the level of interest rates to suit its own particular circumstances. Thus if one European nation grew faster or experienced less inflation than another, and as a consequence was able to sell a surplus of exports to its neighbour, then before European monetary union (EMU) the deficit country could correct the trade balance by choosing either to devalue its currency or to deflate (i.e. reduce) its national income. Both methods restrict a country's ability to purchase foreign goods, but most would agree that the latter option is the more painful. With monetary union, of course, this policy choice is now not available: only deflation is possible.

Further, national governments find that under a common currency they lose fiscal as well as monetary independence. If one government spends more than it raises in taxes, and it can no longer print its own money to cover the difference, then that government must borrow more from the ECB. But no one nation in the union is likely to remain silent if it sees another in its midst taking more than its share of the common currency. The ECB must therefore constrain all governments from running excessive deficits. (What is excessive? That is now something that is supposed to be decided by the union, not by individual governments.)

Loss of sovereignty: only one cost of currency union has been mentioned here, but this is the big one. What is the solution to this problem now there is a single European currency? What policy options do national governments have if they feel that their country is losing out in competition with other European states?

The answer at the national, macroeconomic level is: not a lot! If monetary and fiscal policies are designed to suit a common European market, then differences between member nations obviously cannot be accommodated. The answer, difficult for some to swallow, is that internal, microeconomic flexibility is the only option – and this, as reported by the OECD, is still lacking. That is why the transition period to the euro's eventual introduction in 1999 and also the sovereign debt crisis of 2011/12 (see Chapter 9) have been so destructive. Asymmetries between the different European economies are too obvious for financial markets to ignore – despite pretences to the contrary by political leaders. When individual governments are forced to choose between national interests and a fixed currency, therefore, financiers bet that they will put national interests before European ones. They are not wrong: this remains the Achilles' heel of the euro. Centuries of cultural differences cannot be assumed away by Euro-enthusiasts. The growth of the eurozone since the 1990s has not been plain sailing, and the stresses and strains within the union are an ongoing concern and source of controversy, as we shall see.

This argument leads directly to the following question: how flexible and internationally integrated must a group of economies become before a common currency brings more benefits than costs? What is an **optimal currency area**?

The economics of an optimal currency area

Consider the situation where one country (Country A) experiences an increasing deficit in its trade with another (Country B). Over time, if the unequal demand for these countries' products persists, Country A will move into deepening recession, while B's economy will boom. How can this disequilibrium situation be resolved in a single currency area where the realignment of exchange rates is not an available policy option?

1   Microeconomic, 'supply-side' *flexibility of labour markets* is required. Where wages are flexible and/or labour is geographically and occupationally mobile in and between the two countries concerned, then there is no need for separate currency price movements.

   A slump in demand for A's goods will produce a fall in demand for A's labour. Where wages are flexible (downward), then, it is argued, there will be no unemployment since labour is retained at lower cost. The cost and thus price of A's exports will fall, winning back an increase in demand. The opposite effect operates in the case of Country B. Booming demand bids up the wages of B's labour. As costs and prices rise, so B is not likely to sell as many exports. The trade imbalance between A and B rights itself.

   If wages in both countries are 'sticky' and do not move smoothly in response to changing conditions of demand (they tend not to!), then unemployment will result in A, and overfull employment and perhaps inflation might occur in B. Where labour is mobile, however, A's unemployed workers simply migrate to B, thus removing unemployment in one country and reducing the inflationary pressure in the other.

   If neither condition holds, if wages are sticky and labour is immobile, then differential economic conditions in both countries cannot be alleviated without exchange rate movements. An optimal currency area is thus one which enjoys flexible labour markets.

2   The problem of deficits and surpluses is hardly a matter for concern between large, mostly self-sufficient countries where only a small fraction of goods and services are internationally traded. In contrast, where a group of countries exchange a high fraction of their produce, then they have much to gain from a single currency. Frequent changes in exchange rates between them would trigger far-reaching shocks throughout their economies. Open economies with *a high proportion of tradable goods and services* exchanged between them, therefore, benefit more and suffer less in a currency union. It makes less sense to include those neighbours who are less integrated within the group or have stronger trade links with countries outside the region.

3   Disequilibrium between states involved in a monetary union is likely to be less extreme the more that *economic structures are similar*. World economic events are never stable and who knows what the next shock will be and where it will impact – after the credit crunch, the Great Recession and the sovereign debt crisis? Whatever happens next, it is less likely to put a strain upon a

currency union if the impact has a similar, and not an asymmetric, effect on the countries involved.

How does Europe measure up?

If we apply this analysis to Europe now, we can see how far the countries concerned make up an optimum currency area.

Labour mobility

A number of studies have been undertaken to measure the mobility of labour within the EU compared with other large currency areas. Barry Eichengreen (in *Is Europe an Optimum Currency Area?*, Cambridge, MA: National Bureau of Economic Research, 1991) quotes an OECD study which concluded that geographical mobility in the USA was two to three times higher than that of EU citizens within their own countries. The percentage of population changing their region of residence in 1980 was 6.2 per cent for US citizens changing counties, 3.3 per cent for those changing states. It was 1.1 per cent for English and Welsh citizens changing regions and 1.3 per cent for Germans changing *Lander*.

Eichengreen then tested to see whether the motive for moving was lower in Europe, by comparing regional income differentials. He found that there is greater regional variation in incomes in European nations, which is both evidence of a greater motive for internal migration and a clear illustration of the effect of immobility. He also found that 'regional unemployment rates adjust to one another about 20 per cent more rapidly in the US than national employment rates adjust to one another within the EC'.

If we look at the recent average growth of earnings for different countries and contrast this with their rates of unemployment, then, for flexible labour markets, these data should show opposite trends: growth of average wages and salaries should fall as unemployment (excess labour supply) rises. (See Figure 8.6.) But eurozone countries Germany and France do not illustrate as much labour market flexibility as non-eurozone UK.

Asymmetric shocks

Eichengreen mentions that capital mobility could compensate for the perceived labour immobility. Thus if the rates of current and expected future profits – as reflected in share price movements – are similar around Europe, this would illustrate good capital mobility. Note also that if European industrial structures differ across the continent, they would thus suffer asymmetrically from exogenous shocks, such that profits in one region would rise relative to another.

He looked at two Canadian stock exchanges that specialise in regional businesses – one in French-speaking Montreal, Quebec, another in Anglophone Toronto that lists firms headquartered elsewhere in Canada – and compared these with stock exchanges in Paris, France and Dusseldorf, Germany. He found that, over

(a)

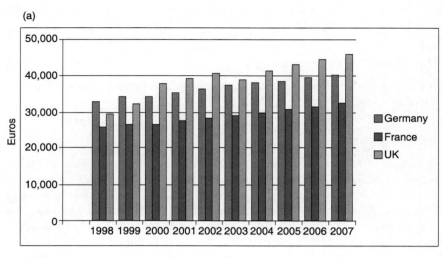

(b)

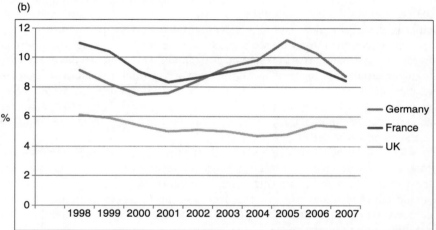

Figure 8.6 (a) Average annual earnings, in euros, for enterprises of more than ten employees, and (b) percentage unemployment, for Germany, France and the UK,
1998–2007. The trends in earnings and unemployment should be opposites – as
unemployment increases in the new millennium in Germany and France, this
should contain earnings growth, but there is little evidence of this shown here.
Labour markets are inflexible, therefore.

Source: Eurostat.

two decades from 1971, share prices in Toronto and Montreal moved much more
closely together (i.e. capital was more mobile) than did those in Paris and Dusseldorf.
The latter were five times more variable than the comparable ratio for Toronto and
Montreal: that is, share prices moved because European capital did not.

A second measure of regional variation is to look at changes in relative prices.
Given exogenous economic shocks, the more real exchange rates react variably

across Europe, then the greater the asymmetry in industrial structure and the stronger the case for maintaining exchange rate variability. European real exchange rates were compared with US regional price differentials over the periods in the 1970s and 1980s. Eichengreen found far greater variability across Europe than between US regions. Importantly, when he repeated the study in 1997, the findings showed little change or convergence in Europe.

Openness to trade

Clearly, smaller European countries have a much higher ratio of trade to GDP than larger, more independent nations. The average of imports and exports to GDP in Europe ranged from 92 per cent in the case of Belgium to 39 per cent for Germany, 32 per cent for France, 31 per cent for the UK and 30 per cent for Italy and Greece. The EU as a whole trades 12 per cent of GDP, compared with 14 per cent in the USA and 11 per cent in Japan (EU data, 2001).

Insofar as trade and integration within a European common market is concerned, some countries are much more tied into the economic fate of their neighbours than others (see Figure 8.7).

Prior to the introduction of the euro, large fractions of the exports of the Netherlands and Belgium were sold to their European partners, so clearly any change in exchange rates between them would significantly affect their export revenues – with knock-on effects for the domestic economy. (This is the **foreign**

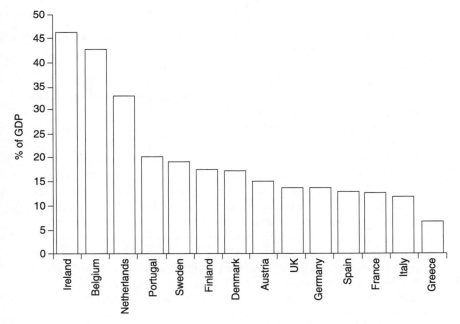

Figure 8.7 Exports to the European Union as a percentage of GDP, 1996.

Source: OECD.

trade multiplier: any change in export demand has a multiplied effect on domestic incomes.) A common currency suits these nations, therefore. (Ireland trades more with the UK which is outside the euro, so it has less to gain than these data seem to imply.)

For countries such as Italy and Greece, however, a far lower proportion of their exports were sold in Europe and so they will feel the constraints of a common currency more than will other countries. Monetary union for these countries will always be problematic until they have loosened their internal markets, reduced structural unemployment and improved the balance of costs and benefits more emphatically in their favour.

Conclusion

Where does all this evidence lead? Clearly some countries in Europe are more suited to forming a currency union than others (see the case for the UK in Box 8.5),

---

Box 8.5   The case of the UK

Gordon Brown, as UK Chancellor of the Exchequer in 1997, set out five criteria that he said would need to be satisfied if Britain was to join the euro. These closely follow the criteria for an optimal currency area, as described above:

1   Convergence. Are business cycles and industrial structures correlated between the eurozone and the UK?
2   Flexibility. Are labour markets sufficiently flexible?
3   Investment. Does capital flow freely between the UK and EU?
4   Symmetry. What impact would joining the eurozone have with regard to UK's specialisation in financial services?
5   Growth, stability and employment: a catch-all criterion for the overall economic impact.

As can be seen, these questions all relate to the flexibility of the UK economy and its liability to suffer asymmetrically from Europe-wide shocks. The reality for the UK is that, although its labour markets are more flexible than most, its economic structure is different from that of many other EU countries. Its agricultural sector is far smaller, it has a strong energy industry and financial services are a major specialism. Changes in food prices, oil price shocks and financial crises would all impact on the UK differently than on other nations on the continent. For example, the UK housing market is more dependent on variable rate mortgages than is the case for many in Europe, and even before the credit crunch, the levels of household indebtedness were greater than the EU average. Gordon Brown's conclusion, repeated many times, was 'the time is not yet right' to join the euro. Many doubt it will ever be!

but many independent economists have consistently declared since the mid-1990s that the continent as a whole does *not* satisfy the criteria for an optimal currency area. The 2005 OECD report quoted above, without mentioning the wisdom of currency union directly, emphasised the lack of convergence of the eurozone just prior to the external shock of the credit crunch that has had such an immense and asymmetric impact on EU member countries.

There are none so deaf as those who won't listen, however. The economic arguments listed above do not count for those whose political idealism (or stubbornness) dictates that the euro must unite Europe with a common currency. Government leaders have closed their ears and eyes to them, but there were always sizeable economic risks predicted for those countries which signed up to join the euro (let alone for those others that are not yet members). They have to live with the consequences.

There is one last qualification that we might emphasise in this conclusion: if Europe suffers adversely from great differences in unemployment consequent upon an exogenous shock, then this may well be ameliorated via the use of an EU structural fund. That is, fiscal transfers from parts of the continent which are wealthy and unaffected could compensate those which are suffering asymmetrically from unemployment (a principle known as 'fiscal federalism', this is indeed something practised in most national economies to offset such differential impacts).

In the case of the USA, fiscal transfers from the centre to individual states in crisis can range from 10 per cent to almost 40 per cent of state expenditures. *There is no such system available in the EU.* The communal European budget in total represents just over 1 per cent of the EU's combined income, and much of that (47 per cent) goes to the Common Agricultural Policy. The structural funds devoted to regional transfers (30 per cent) are mostly designed to support economic development and infrastructure projects in the poorer EU countries; they are not designed to support eurozone countries with a sovereign debt crisis. Despite recent debate over establishing a European Monetary Fund or **European Financial Stability Facility** (like the IMF), the money pot available is still not sizeable enough to help all governments struggling with debt.

We move to consider this concern in more detail in Chapter 9, but the real issue here is *not* the availability of funds. It is rather political, cultural and social. European integration is possible if people want it badly enough. Would north Europeans be prepared to make the sacrifices to help those bordering the Mediterranean? When the two Germanys, East and West, united, the economic differences between the rich market economy and the other, much poorer command economy could be said to have been far greater than those currently between northern and southern Europe – but the sense of shared destiny was far greater also. Where does Europe's destiny lie now, and what are its people prepared to sacrifice for it?

Key words

Balance of trade This is the balance between a country's imports and exports of goods only. It does not include the trade in 'invisible' services, or the movement of currencies or liquid funds on financial or capital accounts.

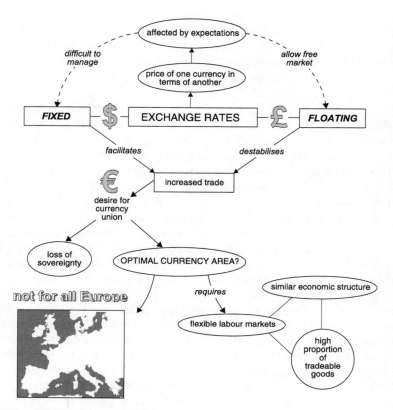

Figure 8.8 The themes of Chapter 8.

Depreciation is a fall in the value of a currency in a floating rate system. **Devaluation** is similarly a fall in a currency's value – though this term implies that the currency does not float but re-fixes at a lower level.

European Central Bank   The ECB is the central bank for Europe's single currency, the euro. The ECB is charged with maintaining the euro's value, that is, keeping inflation to a minimum, and conducting the eurozone's monetary policy by setting the interest rate and regulating the money supply for all seventeen member countries. It is the sole issuer of euro banknotes (it can create as much cash as it deems prudent). As the continent's central bank it may intervene and support the eurozone's main commercial banks if it chooses, but it is *not* within its remit to provide financial support to member *governments*. This has been a major controversy in the sovereign debt crisis.

European Financial Stability Facility Headquartered in Luxembourg, the EFSF is the special fund set up on 9 May 2010 by eurozone member countries to provide short-term financial support for those suffering in the European sovereign debt crisis. The EFSF can issue bonds to those in need, backed by guarantees given by the euro members in proportion to their share in the paid-up capital of the European Central Bank. At the time of writing it is doubtful whether the size of the EFSF's lending capacity (€440 billion) is big enough.

Foreign trade multiplier An injection of increased spending in an economy will lead to a multiplied growth in the circular flow of income (see Chapter 2). Increased spending, for example, can come from foreign customers buying more of a country's exports. Any given impulse of spending raises incomes many times since increased first-round earnings for exporters are then passed on in the form of more spending on business supplies; this increases second-round incomes for a whole range of producers, who then spend this, and so on. The larger the fraction of exports to total production in an economy, the more important the foreign trade multiplier, i.e. the impact of export demand.

International Monetary Fund (IMF) was set up in 1944 to underpin the fixed exchange rate system agreed at Bretton Woods. The IMF would supply short-term loans of foreign exchange to central banks of the developed world if this was required to protect them from a currency crisis. The IMF was established at the same time as its sister organisation, the **World Bank** – which was charged with providing long-term loans to developing countries. Although the Bretton Woods fixed rate system is now history, the IMF has built up a sizeable reputation and expertise, not to mention considerable reserves, which can be called upon in dealing with all sorts of financial crises. (IMF help comes with a price attached, of course.)

Optimal currency area Some relatively small communities have their own currency and set themselves apart from larger neighbours (e.g. the Bahrain dinar which serves a population of 800,000), whereas, in contrast, some extremely large populations share a single unit of exchange (the Chinese yuan, serving a population of 1,331 million). The economics of optimal currency areas considers what is the best size of trading community to be served by a common currency.

Stability and Growth Pact This was a pact signed by all the members of the EU in 1997 to keep their government spending under control – that is, to maintain an annual budget deficit no higher than 3 per cent of GDP and a national debt lower than 60 per cent of GDP. Shortly after it was signed, both Germany and France exceeded these limits but were not subject to any penalty. Later, Greece joined the euro in 2001 without meeting these criteria (see Chapter 9) and most turned a blind eye at the time. Therefore, did the Stability and Growth Pact mean anything? People could be forgiven for thinking that it was just another piece of euro bureaucracy. How things change. The current euro climate is to tie member governments' fiscal hands so tightly that another sovereign debt crisis becomes impossible . . . at the cost of making Keynesian counter-cyclical fiscal policies illegal. The UK at least refuses to sign up to this latest twist in the rules.

Questions

1   Why do so many countries wish to abide by fixed exchange rate systems?
2   'Economic divergence, political inflexibility and the pegging of government reputations to currency prices' cause fixed exchange rate systems to blow apart. How well does this analysis fit the Bretton Woods collapse of the 1970s, the ERM of the 1990s and the euro today?
3   Which countries outside the EU and considering membership (see Chapter 6) should also consider joining the euro? Explain your reasons.
4   'The problem in opting to remain with a floating exchange rate is that there is no compelling discipline imposed on governments to fix the structural weaknesses of their economies.' Discuss.
5   How can countries locked into a fixed exchange rate system, or a common currency, cope with a severe exogenous shock that impacts asymmetrically on the nations involved?

Further reading

De Grauwe, P. *Economics of Monetary Union*, Oxford University Press, 2007.
OECD. *Economic Survey of Euro Area 2010*, available at www.oecd.org/eco/surveys/euroarea.

9 Financial crises, sovereign debt and future reform

> The sound banker, alas, is not one who sees danger and avoids it, but one who when he is ruined, is ruined in a conventional and orthodox way along with his fellows so that no one can really blame him.
>
> John Maynard Keynes, quoted by Robert Skidelsky,
> *Keynes: The Return of the Master*, London: Allen Lane, 2009.

> One way or another, the losses that were built up in recent years will have to be shared between creditors and debtors; in the world economy between creditors in the East and debtors in the West, and within the euro area between creditors in the North and debtors in the South.
>
> Mervyn King, governor of the Bank of England, August 2011.

Introduction

The first, major international debt crisis occurred during the 1980s when a number of developing countries were close to defaulting on the loans they owed to western banks. These banks were so overextended at this time that there was a real danger that a major default would spark a crisis in confidence. If a sufficient quantity of worried depositors had then tried to grab their money and run for cover, any one of a number of banks might have been forced to close, thus triggering a chain reaction of other bank collapses that would have led to a full-blown international financial crisis and quite possibly a 1930s-like worldwide depression.

Fortunately, despite much nervous nail-biting in western financial centres, things never got that bad and certain commentators could look back with satisfaction on those times as a crisis that passed, as a 'battle that was won' (William Cline, *The Economist*, 18 February 1995). The fact that a number of developing countries were still stuck with disabling debt and zero growth was not so important – the overriding concern was to limit the damage done to international banks.

The battle was not won for long, however. In 1994, what started as the Mexican peso crisis quickly rebounded worldwide as nervous international investors tried to liquidate their assets in a number of emerging markets. Then again, in 1997, beginning with the devaluation of the Thai baht, the Asian currency crisis erupted in some of the young and high-performing economies of East Asia – previously thought to be models of successful development – and its effects contributed eventually to the Russian debt debacle in the following year. From this, speculative hedge funds failed on Wall Street, and thus the spectre arose again of the possibility of debt default, worldwide contagion and a catastrophic crash of international finance which would hurt the rich as well as the poor.

Financial crises tend to be ranked in importance according to the threat they pose to the developed world and the banking systems that underpin it. The end of the twentieth century saw a return to a battle against global financial crisis, therefore – and so the big guns of the US Federal Reserve were brought out at the end of 1998 to fight systemic financial collapse yet again. Billions of dollars were secured to bail out fragile Wall Street institutions that, had they folded, would have brought about economic chaos.

You might have thought that with all this evident instability and turmoil in international currency and financial markets, the participants involved would have put in place measures to prevent recurring crises. Not so.

The contrast with the first financial crash of the new millennium, in Argentina in 2001, is quite instructive. Many large depositors saw this problem coming and they had time to take evasive action. Thus, the eventual crunch did not present such a great shock to the international community. The fact that banks in Buenos Aires closed their doors against smaller domestic customers whilst their savings were being devalued inside, causing riots on the streets of the Argentine capital, was, again, not so important. Riots did not occur on the trading floors or in the boardrooms of financial institutions across the world.

The lessons that might have been learned from all these experiences were therefore not taken to heart in the international financial community. Despite Asian and American crises, there was no appetite for an in-depth analysis and radical reform of the international financial system so long as the world economy was maintaining growth through the 'Great Moderation'. This was especially so when the problems could be blamed on immature financial markets in various developing countries. But the warning signs were there nonetheless – with many features appearing in the 1980s and 1990s that were to re-emerge with a vengeance from 2008 on.

Lesson 1

The 1980s' international debt crisis was indirectly caused by *large global trade imbalances*. After the 1970s' oil price hikes, vast petrodollar revenues could not be spent fast enough by the OPEC nations and, since the loss of these incomes had plunged the industrial world into recession, international bankers looked to the resource-rich but capital-scarce developing world to place these funds. With excess funds, rates of interest were low – in real terms, with inflation increasing, actually negative.

Incurring substantial debt is not a problem so long as borrowing is used to finance productive capital and the rates of interest you have to pay do not rise faster than the rates of return on projected investments. Who was watching out for this?

A fundamental weakness in the global market place is that there is no overall regulatory agency responsible for recording and approving international financial affairs. There is no world central bank or government that has the right or opportunity – not then, or today – to see all that is going on with multinational money flows. Neither the United Nations, nor the International Monetary Fund nor the World Bank possesses any such authority. The global economy is thus a truly 'free' market with no all-powerful central administration. Banks and businesses operating across frontiers enjoy all the advantages of freedom from restriction, therefore, but at the cost of having no international policeman to turn to if things go wrong.

With US and UK inflation in the early 1980s, the Reagan/Thatcher reaction was to cut back domestic money supplies, force up interest rates (and thus the price of the dollar and sterling) and 'tough out' the ensuing recession.

Some developing country debtors like South Korea had invested successfully at the time and could pay the rising interest payments on their borrowed dollars. Others in Latin America and Africa could not. From negative interest rates in cheap currencies at the end of the 1970s, indebted countries were now required to pay real rates which had soared to 16 per cent by 1981 in rapidly appreciating foreign exchange. With aid cut off, western export markets in recession, and – in some cases, though not all – domestic investments performing poorly, certain countries declared they could not pay even their interest payments, let alone the capital on the sums they had borrowed earlier. Mexico in August 1982 was the first to publicly admit that anticipated oil revenues would not cover its debts. As this was a country expected to have benefited greatly from the oil bonanza, this sent the international banking world into shock and there was thus a real fear that other, less oil-rich countries, would similarly default, prompting a global financial meltdown. The financial position of other big debtors like Argentina and Brazil soon confirmed these worst fears. Big US and European banks were scared they would go bust and the domino effect would drag the whole world down into a 1930s-type crash.

The conventional banking response to indebted clients is to get them to stop spending and put their finances in order as soon as possible. Additionally, the free market, supply-side paradigm was in the ascendant and so the IMF's 'structural adjustment' for indebted countries involved:

1   balancing government budgets by cutting public spending and raising taxes;
2   liberalising internal markets by privatising and reducing government intervention, and deregulating and freeing prices and (especially) wages;
3   freeing international trade by devaluing domestic currencies, reducing tariffs and protectionist policies, promoting exports and opening up to foreign capital.

With export markets still sluggish, however, the only way that debtor countries could pay their bills was by savagely cutting domestic consumption and invest-ment. For most of the 1980s, therefore, for Latin America and sub-Saharan Africa,

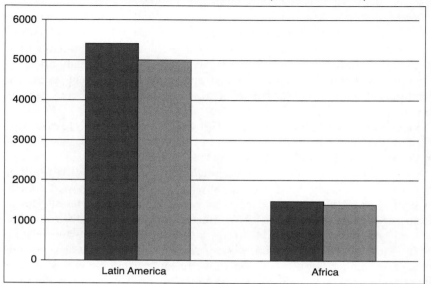

Figure 9.1 The fall in average living standards in Latin America and Africa, 1980–1990 (GDP per capita, in constant 1990 US$).

this was known as 'the lost decade'. The result of conservative, free market policies, for the poorest in particular, was negative growth in living standards (see Figure 9.1).

If incomes are falling for those in debt, they will not be able to pay back what they owe. As this became apparent, so in 1985, US Treasury Secretary James Baker initiated the Baker Plan in which 'structural adjustment' was combined with giving debtors more time. Fifteen highly indebted countries were designated as candidates. Debts were rescheduled, not reduced.

But when the delayed repayment approached, it was clear that for most indebted countries their situation was now even worse than before. Therefore, in 1989 another US Treasury Secretary, Nicholas Brady, launched the Brady Plan, which for the first time conceded that now substantial debt reduction and forgiveness was necessary.

The moral of this tale is that *insisting on austerity and conventional repayment instead of focusing on growth and the debtor's ability to pay means you run the risk of making a bad situation worse, such that debts will never be paid off.*

Lesson 2

Prior to 1997, the East Asian 'tiger' economies were lauded as models of economic success. Countries like South Korea had successfully managed the transition from import substitution to export promotion and, starting from a state of near devastation and poverty after the Korean War in the early 1950s, had sustained one of the highest growth rates in the world – achieving a remarkable tenfold increase in income per capita by the 1990s.

The particular feature of Korea's economic success story since the 1960s had been the remarkably productive relationship between the government and the major industrial groups or *chaebol* – such famous names as Hyundai, Samsung, Daewoo, etc. These businesses are private conglomerate empires, producing a vast array of capital and consumer goods and services, supported by a network of government, commercial and financial contacts. The Korean economy's 'miracle' growth was achieved by a government–business partnership where initial infant industry protectionism was changed into a policy of state-guided funding of the chaebols' export industries. The growth of the Korean economy tracked the growth of these conglomerates, to the extent that in the mid-1990s, 50 per cent of Korean GDP was being produced by the top five chaebol.

One of the puzzles of this miracle growth was always how government–business collusion had proved to be so successful in the Korean model whereas in most other countries it produces corruption, stagnation and distorted development.

In fact the Korean model up until the 1980s was the local institutional response to underdeveloped markets – exploiting Asian values of regulated collusion rather than following the western recipe of active competition – and it made for dynamic growth in conditions of acceptable efficiency, although by the late 1980s the demands for greater market liberalisation were being made more loudly.

However, financial liberalisation took place first *before* any reform of domestic market structures. That is, capital controls were relaxed and international borrowing was facilitated consistent with the (then) worldwide paradigm of liberalising movements in financial markets before breaking up the power of the chaebols and freeing up competition.

The reality was that the chaebols were politically influential, they could see the benefit of getting their hands on almost limitless amounts of international loans, they could press the government to free up capital controls and at the same time win guarantees that these huge Korean businesses would be bailed out in the event of a crisis. Both sides knew that chaebols were *too big to allow them to fail.*

Opening up the sector to international markets released a surge in domestically available credit from foreign banks (see Figure 9.2).

Where was all this money going? It was routed through financial intermediaries – Korean merchant banks and non-bank financial institutions which were directly owned by chaebols and which could *hide their balance sheets* from any outside inspection. These institutions were perceived as having government guarantees, but were essentially unregulated and therefore subject to severe **moral hazard** problems. As rates of return on productive industry began to suffer from diminishing returns, these intermediaries were placing *more and more funds into sterile property* – property whose value was steadily inflating and which promised what Krugman called 'Pangloss values' – that is, high rewards if the best of all possible worlds obtains, but serious losses if not. He notes: 'The overpricing of

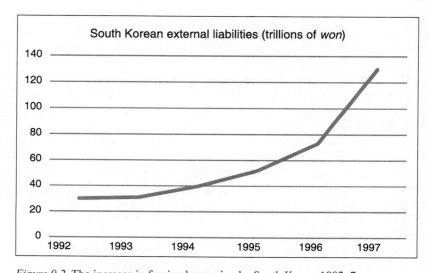

Figure 9.2 The increase in foreign borrowing by South Korea, 1992–7.

Source: F. Mishkin, *The Next Great Globalisation*, Princeton University Press, 2006.

assets was sustained in part by a sort of circular process, in which the proliferation of risky lending drove up the prices of risky assets, making the financial condition of the intermediaries seem sounder than it was.'

Foreign investors went along with this since the Korean miracle over the previous decade had averaged 7 per cent growth and, in Wall Street, the competition to get into East Asia was fierce. Any individual banker who ignored the rush of competitors into the region would be called to task by superiors, or shareholders. The *herding of international bankers*, each desperate not to lose market share to their rivals, thus promoted a limited vision and insignificant risk assessment – and all the time they were piling money into destinations that they could not properly see . . .

Unlike most western industry which had been founded principally on share capital (equity), the boom in Korea and much of East Asia was being built on short-term credit. Financial intermediaries were highly leveraged and here is the moral hazard: local investors were actually *risking relatively little of their own capital*, and if things went wrong they could walk away with limited losses. When the East Asian bubble burst and property prices tumbled (starting in Thailand), panic quickly spread around the region. Debts backed by now worthless assets could not be paid and it was governments (i.e. taxpayers) which had guaranteed banks that had to pay the eventual price.

The contagion that occurred is illustrated in Table 9.1. The fragility of financial sectors and economies built on crony capitalism were exposed. Foreign money that had been so eager to flood into these countries now got out at frightening speed. Net private inflows into the region were US$93 billion in 1996, but this turned into minus US$12 billion in 1997 – a movement of US$105 billion, mostly occurring in the last quarter of 1997. Currencies, stock markets and real economies tumbled.

Table 9.1 The Asian crisis in figures, 1997–8

		1997	1998
Thailand	*GDP in US$*	149.1	111.3
	growth of GNP per capita		– 8.5%
	growth of investment		– 32.0%
South Korea	*GDP in US$*	476.5	320.7
	growth of GNP per capita		– 7.4%
	growth of investment		– 38.6%
Malaysia	*GDP in US$*	100.2	72.5
	growth of GNP per capita		– 9.6%
	growth of investment		– 42.9%
Indonesia	*GDP in US$*	215.7	94.2
	growth of GNP per capita		– 18.0%
	growth of investment		– 44.8%

Source: World Bank.

These are *extreme* movements. The IMF was quickly called upon to help out, but no quick fix could be offered. Conventional rescue programmes were designed to stabilise these economies (providing bail-out loans on condition of cutting back public spending, closing profligate banks, restructuring debts, devaluing currencies and charging penal interest rates), but – as the figures show – severe hardship could not be avoided. As so often, it was the innocent citizens who ended up paying the consequences of irresponsible financial practices.

The severity and contagiousness of the East Asian crisis prompted many calls for reforms at the time and, as noted, remedial action was focused on trying to repair the opaque practices and institutional weaknesses of those countries at the centre of the crisis. A crucial dimension in the Asian crisis was being missed, however, and that was the *institutional weaknesses on the supply side of international finance*. Irresponsible borrowing and asset speculating cannot occur without *irresponsible lending*.

Lesson 3

Adam Smith said that 'there's a great deal of ruin in a nation'. Similarly, Walter Wriston, one-time chief executive of Citibank, is alleged to have said during the 1970s that countries never go bust. The popular idea was that loans to governments are safer than those to commercial enterprise since the former can always levy taxes to raise revenue. The latter may be unable to make profits, may go out of business and, in declaring bankruptcy, leave their creditors with very little.

International banking standards, as echoed in the **Basle accords**, tend to follow this conventional wisdom and rank government bonds as relatively low risk.

In Argentina during the 1990s this country had taken aboard the conservative orthodoxy of privatisations, liberalisation, removal of trade restrictions and greater control of the domestic money supply. The incoming government of Carlos Menem had inherited a devastating hyperinflation, but had countered this by introducing a new currency with the 1991 Convertibility Plan. This tied the peso to the dollar and, in one fell swoop, it eliminated inflation: from 4,000 per cent (!) in 1989 down to single digits by 1992. With confidence returning, the economy achieved a remarkable rebound – growing by 28 per cent between 1990 and 1993. From being an economic basket-case, in a space of just a few years Argentina had turned round and was being lauded in financial markets as a paragon of virtue. With all this evidence that the Menem administration was successful in putting the nation *and* its own fiscal affairs in order, Argentine government bonds thus looked a safe bet.

Banking on its new reputation, public borrowing and spending began to rise. Financial economist Frederick Mishkin notes that from 1993 to 1998 the Argentine economy grew at 'a robust annual average rate' of 4.4 per cent, but as it did so, the ratio of public debt to GDP rose from 29.2 per cent to 41.4 per cent. Not excessively high, but *these debts were building up in the good times . . . a worrying feature should bad times follow.*

And follow they did. The US dollar rose along with the booming US economy at the end of the 1990s and, with the peso pegged to the dollar, it meant that Argentine exports were now more expensive in relation to this country's trading partners. The effect was even more exaggerated as Brazil's currency, the *real*, was at the same time devaluing.

With export earnings falling, recession took hold and, as a result, tax revenues began to fall. Paying interest on past debts in increasingly expensive dollars was now becoming difficult. The budget deficit was widening, necessitating further borrowing . . .

With Argentinian finances looking riskier, for the government to sell bonds and raise funds on the international markets it had to offer an increasingly high rate of return. Having to pay 20 per cent interest on debts was now costing almost 10 per cent of national income. This was a vicious circle – *the sovereign debt trap* – since it implied increasing amounts of public spending, requiring more and more borrowing. No longer able to afford to borrow on the free market, the Argentinian administration had in the end to turn to the IMF for a bail-out package in December 2000, and again a year later. Matters were not helped by international doubts about the reliability of the government's figures. But by then the situation was spiralling out of control. International and domestic creditors rushed to withdraw funds from the country, all banks closed down, the peso traded informally at 50 per cent below its nominal value, and Argentina defaulted on more than US$130 billion in public debts. It was the biggest default in history.

Lending to foreign governments was clearly *not* inherently safer than that to commercial interests. The fault in this popular notion is that, firstly, private customers have to offer collateral – say, their house – to raise funds, so the fear of losing their home tends to ensure they use borrowed funds prudently. And also, should an individual deliberately falsify their accounts in order to raise a loan, they are liable to prosecution: contract law thus enforces security and reduces risks.

But governments have to offer no collateral. Their only incentive to honour debts is the fear of being cut off from future borrowing – and this may not be a sufficient penalty for those administrations with short time horizons in a domestic crisis. In addition, misrepresentation of a country's accounts is easier for national politicians to achieve, since foreign banks cannot force governments to open up all their books, and there is no legal process available to international creditors to prosecute a country's leaders if they suspect a deliberate fraud.

Finally, going through bankruptcy proceedings for any private defaulter is at least a recognised legal process and as such is susceptible to calculated risk assessment. There is no standard process, however, for winding up a government's accounts and renegotiating its debts. Each case is unique; there is no assured outcome for worried bond-holders.

Centuries ago, only governments loaned to other governments and risks were managed by sending gunboats to ensure repayment. The lesson in modern bank lending to sovereign states is that it is *uncertain* – that is, risks are not objectively assessable – and repayment is ultimately unenforceable. *The assumption that sovereign debt is inherently safe and countries never go bust is patently false.*

Lesson 4

Stock markets have a legitimate economic function. They allow investors to pull out their capital from declining enterprises and reallocate it to growing ones. Buying and selling company shares, therefore, is an essential attribute of a healthy market economy – and share prices must inevitably rise and fall in response to such trading.

But such behaviour also allows stock markets to act as casinos. Some of the world's best brains are devoted to (wasted in?) figuring out when to buy certain stocks and when to sell them and thus how to make a fortune out of speculating. Two financial gurus, Robert Merton and Myron Scholes, shared a Nobel Prize in Economics in 1997 for their work on stock market prices. They produced a sure-fire statistical model that demonstrated how to pick winners. This was not just an academic tour-de-force – it was incorporated in Long Term Capital Management (LTCM), the **hedge fund** they helped to found.

Merton and Scholes had found the Holy Grail of finance. Their model told them when to buy into stocks that had hit rock-bottom and how to ride them high and sell when they hit a peak. When everyone else was selling and prices were plummeting, if you could read the right financial indicators, you could pick up hot growth prospects at a bargain when no one else could see it. LTCM was so successful that it made billions for its partners in a year or so – and, of course, with its first-class reputation (other LTCM founders included legendary Wall Street names), more institutions quickly got into the act. Big banks and brokers from all over the USA and Europe were anxious to pile money into LTCM – Chase Manhattan, Merrill Lynch, Union Bank of Switzerland and many more.

The beauty of their model was that it accepted the volatility of human nature and seemed unerringly successful in picking the right moments to buck stock market trends. The key to making money was not in following the herd, but in knowing when to do the exact opposite. All things that go up must come down, and vice versa, and based on precedent and statistical probability, the Merton and Scholes model could spot when.

The problem came when the unprecedented happened. A chain of events which began with the East Asian crisis ended with the Russian debt default of August 1998. The market movements this caused for LTCM were bigger and longer lasting than anything that could have been forecast or imagined. The hedge fund's model told them to keep buying when everyone else was selling, but the predicted recovery never came. LTCM's losses were as spectacular as its previous winnings – only quicker. It lost US$4 billion in five weeks. Worse, it held positions worth US$200 billion in big-named institutions all over the world. As *The Economist* mentioned at the time, if LTCM had been allowed to go bust, the world's markets 'would have gone frantic'.

As it was, Alan Greenspan, chairman of the US Federal Reserve, called a meeting of top New York banks in September 1998 and brokered a deal worth US$3.65billion to keep LTCM afloat. The hedge fund just survived and, along with it, so did the world's financial infrastructure.

As explained in Chapter 3, the dominant paradigm in economics since the 1980s has been rational expectations theory – and the financial market expression of this is the **efficient market hypothesis**. All asset-pricing and micro-forecasting models are based on this. Assuming asset prices are rational and efficient, that is, that they reflect all known data, a range of probabilities is calculated for imaginable future events and, by diversifying portfolios, risks can be reduced in proportion to the number of stocks a hedge fund holds. The key assumption, of course, is that returns on a wide range of unrelated stocks are *uncorrelated*. Similarly, risks are unique to each individual stock – any upside errors calculated on one should be balanced out by downside errors on others.

Mathematical models are seductive, especially those that seem to keep winning. But economist and Keynesian scholar Robert Skidelsky argues that in reality much more of economic life than rational expectations theory accepts falls into the category of being *uncertain* – i.e. incapable of accurate risk assessment. Financial analysts, who are paid to calculate risks and returns, can hardly admit to this and so, according to Keynes, they must fall back on conventions, or rules of thumb, and assume asset prices really *do* reflect all possible future risks. The fact that the financial services industry is highly competitive merely confirms every participant in their conventional judgement. When this accepted view of the future is suddenly challenged by the appearance of an incalculable 'black swan event', a sudden and violent swing in fortunes results. One such event was the Russian rouble collapse that prompted the near-death experience on Wall Street. But the moral of this tale is that *overreliance on mathematical models to capture reality will eventually prove catastrophic.*

2008 and the euro crisis

Many of the above features must seem familiar. They have been played out *al fortissimo* since 2008: global trade imbalances; financial liberalisation; speculative bubbles in property prices; the herding of bankers; irresponsible lending; no world regulator; no effective risk assessment; overreliance on mathematical models; institutions too big to fail; tied currencies; suspect official figures; sovereign debts; insisting on austerity before growth . . .

The first two chapters of this text analysed the credit crunch and Great Recession. Chapters 6 and 8 charted the sustained rise and expansion of the European Union (EU) and the political drive to adopt a common currency (in spite of the lack of economic evidence for this venture). We now need to link the two themes – how the world financial crisis and Great Recession have impacted on the EU and particularly on the future of the euro.

The 2008 crisis demonstrated yet again the myopic attitudes and destabilising effects of international financial markets. The credit crunch involved a flight of capital away from banks and other private institutions and into government bonds and other safe havens. Only later, as increasing numbers of governments found it cheap to borrow, did markets and their rating agencies begin to wonder about the safety of some of these bonds. In a number of countries, of course, faced with a banking system on the brink of collapse, governments were forced to bail out their financial institutions *and* to pump fiscal injections into the circular flow of national incomes to stall the onset of a severe depression. For small countries with internationally connected and massively indebted banks, such as Ireland, the demands on the public purse were excessive. When markets eventually realised this, the banking crisis in this case instantly converted into a sovereign debt crisis – rating agencies downgraded Irish bonds. This only made it more difficult for the Irish government to get out of the hole they had jumped into in order to give their banks a leg-up.

The case of Greece is somewhat different. In 1999, when the euro was first introduced, Greece was left out as it had failed to meet the EU's Maastricht criteria (see Box 8.4). On 1 January 2001, however, by agreeing to a programme of public spending cuts to satisfy these entry requirements, Greece became the twelfth member of the eurozone, enjoying the support of approximately two-thirds of the Greek public. (Of the then EU members, only the UK, Denmark and Sweden remained determinedly outside the eurozone.) As a euro member, Greece benefited from low borrowing costs and the perception that its historic tendency for inflation and excessive public spending would be cured. In effect, Brussels decision-makers turned a blind eye to Greece's actual situation and approved its entry to the euro because it was politically convenient to do so – they wanted to send a signal to other European nations that they too should follow.

Political expediency had outrun economic sense. After an audit commissioned by the incoming Greek government in 2004, *Eurostat* (the EU's statistical authority) revealed that the budgetary statistics on the basis of which Greece joined the eurozone had been 'underreported'. That is (as European Central Bank Chief Economist Otmar Issing later stated), the Greek government had cheated. The 2001 administration claimed its budget deficit was less than 1 per cent of Gross Domestic Product, well within the Maastricht 3 per cent threshold. European Commission reports have since revealed that Greece's budget had not been within the 3 per cent limit in a single year since its accession.

The currency bloc's leaders had been too polite, there was insufficient scrutiny and, as the situation became clearer, there were no sanctions administered for Greek misrepresentation and no real efforts from either side to come to terms with the country's indebtedness.

In reality, the situation revealed the difference in cultures between certain northern European and Mediterranean states. Politics in Greece is dynastic: based on family, friends and influence which can be bought. Enmities and rivalries go back generations and you believe what politicians actually say, or promise, at your peril. Excessive public spending (to buy influence) and inflationary finance (paying back what you owe in devalued currency) is endemic. European banks that bought Greek euro-bonds thinking these were now safe; investors assuming they were implicitly lending to 'Europe'; political leaders thinking that Greece was now enfolded in a corrective union – all were guilty of delusion.

When the credit crunch eventually came in 2008, Greece was reluctant to reveal the extent of its massive budget deficit in the wake of the global crisis. In fact, it had the highest government deficits and the highest public debt to national income ratios in the EU (see Table 9.2).

Somewhat belatedly, rating agencies downgraded Greek government bonds to 'junk' status. Standard & Poor's, for example, cut its debt rating seven times from the end of 2009 to summer 2011 from A grade to CC, the third-lowest rung on its rating scale. This meant that financial markets now charged 20 per cent p.a. interest on lending to Greece (compared with less than 2 per cent for Germany). Such a high rate means that the government cannot afford to borrow (it would not be able to generate enough funds to pay such a high rate of return), and unless the rest of Europe rallies round and gives it sufficient funds, Greece must default on its debts.

The problem is that Europe has a common currency but not a common polity. All important decisions are taken at national level by member countries, and negotiating any way out for Greece is impossible when disagreements abound, as they have.

The conventional view – that Greece must adopt austerity measures and pay off its dues – has condemned the country to deepening recession, nationwide protests and (unless this policy is reversed) no way out for years to come. Rising

Table 9.2 Greek debt statistics, 2009–12.

	2009	*2010*	*2011*[a]	*2012*[a]
Budget deficit as % of GDP		10.5	*9.5*	*9.3*
Public debt as % of GDP	127	143	*158*	*166*

Notes: [a] Forecasts.

Budget deficits are a measure of how much government spending exceeds revenues and thus how much must be covered by borrowing. Borrowing every year must mean the level of government debt rises. Austerity measures that cut back public spending will reduce deficits, as can be seen from the first line, but *any* borrowing requirement must increase the accumulated debt. And if income is falling faster than debts, of course, the debt to income (GDP) ratio will rise.

Source: EU Commission.

unemployment and falling national income mean falling tax revenues and more demands for public spending on welfare programmes. Budget deficits become increasingly difficult to control.

With austerity programmes, there is little chance of Greece ever raising sufficient income to honour its massive and increasing debts (see Table 9.2). So long as Greece retains the euro as its currency, it must drive its internal costs and wages down such that its exports become competitive with other eurozone countries and can thus begin to earn gradually increasing trade revenues – a process that took Germany some fifteen years to achieve when the rest of the world was booming in the 1990s . . .

Fifteen years of austerity with only a vague promise of success? Not popular. One recommendation therefore is for Greece to leave the eurozone, return to its own (devalued) currency and adopt the 'Argentinian solution'. Foreign debts incurred in euros would be an immense burden and, in the Argentinian case, the government refused to pay. As its currency came down, however, the country found it easier to export and grow and return to full employment.

The implications of a unilateral Greek exit from the euro and devaluation, however, would be politically calamitous – and turn hyperactive financial markets to speculate against other eurozone nations with heavy debt burdens: Portugal, Spain, Ireland, Italy, maybe France. The euro might blow apart. (Theoretically, the common currency could eventually be restricted to a much smaller group of nations whose finances are tightly aligned, but cut loose from indebted administrations the new euro would immediately soar in value, making it more difficult for those countries to earn the excessive export revenues that they prize so much!)

The only realistic long-term solution is to adopt policies that allow Greece to return to growth. The country must be given breathing space. This implies rescheduling some debt payments, forgiving others. An *orderly* default. The creditor banks (many French and German) and other private sector bond-holders would have to bear the losses involved, and they in turn would need financial support to avoid a disastrous chain of bank crashes – another credit crunch and international financial crisis.

Moreover, to offset speculation against other nations that markets declare are next in line for default (the candidates mentioned above), a financial support network, or firewall, must also be put in place to stop the contagion spreading from Greece. That is, more money has to be found.

So who pays in the end? The process would have to be financed through the European Central Bank, the European Financial Stability Facility, even some new form of European Monetary Fund. But where do they get *their* money from? Maybe some they will print themselves, but ultimately the buck stops with taxpayers again. In this case, *if the European Union is to mean anything, those who have signed up for it will have to pay for it.* The West German support of East Germany was essential for the successful currency union between these two states in 1990. If the political will of creditor and debtor nations within the euro to support their common currency does not show the same commitment, then it must fail.

International financial reform

The history of banking, as mentioned in Chapter 7, is one of boom and bust. Unfortunately, it seems that each generation of financiers has to learn this for itself – putting everyone else at risk as they do so. Yet as economists Carmen Reinhart and Kenneth Rogoff have emphasised, if we look at financial crises over the very long run (they consider eight centuries), then major default episodes are not at all uncommon: 'typically spaced some years (or decades) apart, creating an illusion that "this time is different" among policymakers and investors'.

The problem is that the social cost of the learning process is immense. Reinhart and Rogoff calculate that major property price collapses average six years in duration; domestic output and employment may slump for longer or shorter, depending on how governments react, and the explosion of public debt that these crises create can cast a very long shadow indeed. 'Lost decades' of depression may yet haunt us again.

One wonders whether there will ever be sufficient and widespread political determination to reform global financial practices. Let us review some of the underlying causes and destabilising market failures which need to be addressed.

Global trade imbalances

A build-up of trade surpluses on one side of the world implies a build-up of trade deficits on the other. The market response to imbalanced trade is a corrective move in currency alignments, but this cannot occur so long as, in the Chinese case, the yuan is rigidly controlled; nor is it possible within Europe given a common currency.

If persistent trade surpluses are just accumulated, rather than spent, then this has a deflationary, recessionary effect on all other nations. The response we have seen to date, of recycling these funds by buying foreign Treasury bills, bonds and other paper assets, has not solved the problem – only fuelled increasing financial innovation and the stimulation of an asset price bubble and bust. A better use of accumulated wealth is *to spend it* on productive capital, at home or abroad, or simply to buy more of other countries' exports.

The short-run incentive, of course, is to carry on accumulating export revenues, continue to get richer and richer at others' expense, ignore the pain this causes countries like Greece, and haughtily recommend that they too put their house in order and become more internationally competitive. This ignores the fact that you cannot demand debtors to pay up and simultaneously restructure their economies overnight, and, even if it were possible, the world cannot have more successful exporters without an equal number of importers.

Perhaps, with no incentive to change present mercantilist attitudes, a deepening recession forced on to others will in the end solve the problem. There is the possibility that increasingly protectionist measures will be levied by deficit nations or, if not, Germany, China, Japan and the OPEC nations will anyway find that the growth in their trade surpluses slows down as the world economy slows.

Distorted incentives

It may be that the world will have to live with global trade imbalances. Germany and Japan have been running trade surpluses since 1945; the OPEC nations since the 1970s; China since the 1980s. These export-oriented economies are not going to restructure any time soon. In consequence, the world will thus have to turn its attention to how to manage short-term capital flows.

The huge demand for financial assets from surplus countries need not provoke a speculative and destabilising boom if bankers are held to pay for their actions. From the sub-prime mortgage crisis in the USA to the worldwide securitisation boom, the global system of financial compensation has rewarded bankers for fitting-up transactions and immunised them from losses. That is, financiers were paid excessive bonuses for innovating complex loans, buying and reselling them, and were not rewarded or held responsible for the outcome of such deals. They were therefore not particularly careful in assessing the quality of the loans they were making; indeed they frequently worked with borrowers to make these debts look more attractive, saleable and profitable for the banks.

Because the profits involved were potentially enormous and the downside losses seemingly limited, 'special purpose vehicles' were created in the securitisation process to leverage huge sums on little capital of their own, and to keep them off their parent banks' balance sheets. The creation of credit could thus multiply exponentially under the radar of the regulators.

Where was the penalty for such irresponsible lending? It was conspicuously absent. Quite the opposite, financial intermediaries and their managers had every incentive to follow the herd and increase the systemic risk because of the competition to retain market share, and the assumption that losses were unlikely and would anyway be socialised – that is, paid for by everyone else.

Inadequate risk management

Whose job was it to check that the explosion of credit was not leading to excessive risk? The free market paradigm states that if there is unsatisfied demand, then, collectively and by 'the invisible hand', risk assessors will emerge to provide this service. Firstly, by the principle of *caveat emptor*, every individual bank must take responsibility for each credit instrument it purchases and every customer to whom it proposes to extend a loan. That is, they should employ competent risk assessors of their own. Secondly, banks can pay a specialised professional credit rating authority to do this job. Thirdly, creditors can take out insurance against loss – a credit default instrument. With such efficient market arrangements, who needs regulators to keep track of what is going on? (Especially if they are one-eyed and kept at a distance from many transactions . . .)

On the first point, an instructive feature in *The Economist* of 7 August 2008 ('Confessions of a Risk Manager') reveals the situation within one global bank. A chief risk assessor contrasts his function of monitoring deals within his organisation to those of front-line traders responsible for setting them up:

In their eyes, we were not earning money for the bank. Worse, we had the power to say no and therefore prevent business from being done. Traders saw us as obstructive and a hindrance to their ability to earn higher bonuses . . .

At the root of it all, however, was – and still is – a deeply ingrained flaw in the decision-making process. In contrast to the law, where two sides make an equal-and-opposite argument that is fairly judged, in banks there is always a bias towards one side of the argument . . . The risk thinking therefore leaned towards giving the benefit of the doubt to the risk-takers. Collective common sense suffered as a result.

The same manager made another revealing comment with regard to the second point above:

We also trusted the rating agencies. It is hard to imagine now but the reputation of outside bond ratings was so high that if the risk department had ever assigned a lower rating, our judgment would have been immediately questioned. It was assumed that the rating agencies simply knew best.

There are three major, international credit rating authorities (CRAs): Standard & Poor's, Moody's and Fitch. The record of their assessment of credit risk is, to say the least, questionable. Indeed, as has been mentioned earlier, there are endemic weaknesses in their operation.

Firstly, there is an inevitable conflict of interest when the banks pay such agencies to approve their deals. The CRAs are private profit-making enterprises, they want to attract business and, as oligopolistic rivals, no one agency wishes to lose out to the others. They are intimately tied into the financial infrastructure (big shareholders of banks also own shares in the CRAs); they possess the same tunnel vision, and are rewarded for positively evaluating their clients' loans/debt packages. This is crony capitalism. Secondly, the mathematical models upon which all risks and rewards are calculated provide fatally false assurance. They are poor substitutes for proper, thoroughgoing investigation of the personal relations and complications in each transaction, but of course they facilitate rapid 'evaluation' and thus expansion of business. Lastly, having seriously damaged their reputation in approving dud packages in the securitisation fiasco, the CRAs have since overreacted in the opposite extreme, have judged country risk excessively, and have thus contributed to the market panic in the eurozone sovereign debt crisis. Hardly impressive objectivity.

The third market safeguard for managing risk is the credit default swap (CDS). This is the financial markets' offering to help insure, say, a worried bond-holder against loss. The idea is that if you lend money to another and become worried that this particular borrower will default, then you can buy a CDS from a third party. They agree to take on this risk and pay you back if the original borrower defaults. Of course, the third party will charge you a price for the CDS it sells you – the price being its measure of the default risk. A neat idea. Markets love it.

The trouble is that any real insurance agent conducts an individual interview with the person to be insured and there is a legal requirement that all known risks are disclosed. Actuarial analysis is employed to calculate the premium and the probability of an insurance claim. None of this is required in a CDS – it is a financial instrument that can be bought and sold like any other paper asset, and (distorted incentives again) it pays the originator to create it and trade it. CDSs were invented in the 1990s, took off in the new millennium, and by the end of 2007, the market value of these traded assets totalled US$62.2 trillion; this slumped to $26.3 trillion by mid-2010. Deals are all privately arranged; there is no full transparency or regulation; prices on each CDS do *not* reflect objective risk, only the speculative demand and supply of the particular paper in question (which is determined by market sentiment). Credit default swaps are not a market solution to risk – they are part of the problem.

Regulatory capture (too big to fail)

Politicians on both sides of the Atlantic were impressed at the growth of the financial sectors on Wall Street, New York, and in the City of London. The Great Moderation, blossoming credit and rising tax revenues seemed to capture all imaginations and most critics. As US economist and Nobel laureate Joe Stiglitz has said, academics can also take some of the blame for selling the theoretical climate in which the free market paradigm ruled. Distrust of big government reigned; greed was good; rule-makers and regulators were kept in check.

Big banking, in contrast, was free to innovate and expand, safe in the knowledge that its business was at the heart of modern capitalism and too important to be allowed to fail. The LTCM hedge fund crisis had shown that.

Too true. Lehman Brothers was not saved (surprise!), but bigger banks, mortgage providers and systemically vital institutions have had their survival guaranteed by governments and taxpayers, who have had no option but to pump money into the financial infrastructure in the hope of staving off depression. Official manipulation of certain governments' figures aside, from Alan Greenspan and Gordon Brown down, central authorities and regulators had been captured by big money-making enterprises and the self-congratulatory bubble which enveloped them all. They could not see or restrain the build-up of the biggest boom and bust in their lifetime. And when the bust came, these banks were simply too big to be allowed to go under. And so the sovereign debt crisis followed.

Recriminations abound. One concern is that the international financial sector still carries immense influence. Mervyn King has said that if key banks are too big to fail, then they are simply too big. The implied threat is that they should all be cut down in size, but given their political and economic muscle, the likelihood that this will happen is slight.

Global action needed

The policy of breaking up large, economically powerful enterprises into smaller, more competitive units, where the failure of one would not necessarily threaten the whole, has its attractions. Any policy aimed at restructuring, regulating or taxing the banking sector in any one country, however, will be doomed to fail if other financial centres in the world do not follow suit. Financial institutions will simply move their operations from high tax/stiffly regulated regimes to less interventionist locations. International capital is the most mobile of all resources. Any attempt at financial reform therefore must be negotiated, agreed and implemented by coordinated global action.

The meeting of G20 leaders in London in April 2009 made the right sort of noises: it set up the Financial Stability Board (FSB) charged with coordinating, at international level, standards and structures to regulate, supervise and reform global financial practices. The substance of the London declaration addressed many important issues, and all those signing up to the recommendations (given below) are supposedly committed to deliver – but of course the details will be open to interpretation and individual country enforcement. That is where the trouble lies. Certainly, if fine ideas are not backed up by sanctions for any and all rule-breakers, then progress on financial reform will stall.

Recommendations

Make capital requirements counter-cyclical and size related. In speculative booms, banks must be made to retain a higher and higher fraction of their own capital on their books – in line with the inflating value of their loans. This not only reduces the credit multiplier but also, when institutions have to risk more of their own capital, they are likely to be more careful. Capital requirements can alterna- tively be reduced in recessions when making credit more available helps stimulate recovery. Also, since not all banks are of equal economic influence, the degree of regulation should vary according to a bank's systemic importance. If certain 'superspreaders', or systemically important financial institutions (SIFIs), are too big to fail, then they in particular should be required to hold even larger capital requirements.

Although the London declaration did not specify this corollary, by the same argument the onus must be placed on governments to practise more Keynesian *counter-cyclical macroeconomic policies*: budget surplus in booms and raising of interest rates as asset prices rise. The old adage holds true: fix the (budget) roof when the sun shines. Boom and bust cycles have *not* been defeated, and public reserves for spending in recession must be built up in the good times. Similarly, keep an eye on asset inflation and, even if the domestic money supply is not entirely under the control of the authorities, a rise in official interest rates still sends an important bubble-bursting signal to the markets. If budget surpluses are made when times are booming, a Keynesian fiscal stimulus – budget deficits – can be afforded in the bad times, that is, if the myopic rules recently introduced in the euro area don't actually forbid this.

Align incentives with long-term value creation. The G20 supported the FSB recommendation that bankers' compensation should be tied to creating real value. Banks should perform their proper economic function of funding *investment* and not be rolling over deals, taking excessive risks and indulging in speculation. This requires, of course, that all countries make efforts to improve transparency, that they monitor transactions, and especially bring over-the-counter deals and off-balance-sheet vehicles back on to the radar and under scrutiny.

Credit rating authorities need to be regulated. These profit-seeking assessors act as though they were judge and jury on countries and corporations alike, but their practice so far has to been to accentuate the boom and bust cycle and not offset it. If risks are to be properly countered, the CRAs should be rewarded when they get things right, penalised when they get things wrong. (One suggestion has been that each CRA should first put some fraction of its earnings into a communal pot. Then regulators should compare every agency's measurement of default risk against the actual ratio of defaults. Those that have the highest success rate take the pot. That should motivate every risk assessor to be as objective as possible!)

Standardise rules and block all loopholes. G20 leaders agreed that all should promote the same high-quality accounting rules; and adopt the same standards in dealing with tax havens, corruption, money laundering and terrorist financing.

Conclusion

World financial crises have increased in number and severity as flows of world liquidity have been liberalised and as the size of the global financial industry has increased.

Somewhat predictably, as new ways of making money are invented, so the temptation will always be to make as much as possible – which means the next crisis will come along when, again, paper promises outrun the supply of real goods and services available and nothing can hold up asset price inflation any longer. Like the cartoon character running off the edge of a cliff – the legs are racing like crazy, but a catastrophic plunge downwards can no longer be forestalled.

Global finance cannot be left to the international free market alone. Transparent operation, unrelenting supervision, prudent regulation and consistent enforcement are needed. In the absence of an international policing authority, every nation will have to act on its own – but in agreement and coordination with all others. This is a very tall order and one must be sceptical of success.

Nonetheless, given the devastating consequences of the 2008 crisis, it is in every nation's interest to make the effort. Two final points need to be emphasised. Firstly, in the rich world, it has to be said that the financial sector has become bloated. Much financial activity has been in the nature of a paper chase of negative social value. The proper function of funding real investment – that is, discriminating between efficient and inefficient employments of capital and creating future goods and services – has become of secondary importance. In the process, the excess earnings of those working in banking and finance have distorted the economies of (particularly) the USA and the UK. This is not only the cause of much social unrest due to the polarisation of incomes – a normative issue; there is also an important positive criticism. More and more resources – prime city-centre land, scarce capital and key skills[1] – are attracted to the financial sector and away from other, more socially and economically beneficial employments. Like the Dutch disease in natural resource extraction (see Chapter 5), it has made much more difficult the development of high-tech domestic and export industries devoted to manufacturing and alternative (non-financial) services. Distorted economies hamstring growth.

Secondly, and especially in the poorer world, financial crises send the wrong signals to those nations that are gaining some success in developing indigenous industry and commerce. The storing of export earnings in foreign assets denies these countries more productive employment of scarce capital. The notion of building up large dollar reserves is, however, perfectly rational if a poor country suspects crisis contagion, panic selling of its own exchange rate and thus the need to use these reserves to smooth out volatile and disruptive currency fluctuation. Government allocation of capital – that is, politicians deciding where to invest scarce funds – is a necessary substitute for financial markets which are undeveloped or missing, but the best solution is for resources to be allocated by a properly regulated banking system. Where the institutions of efficient and

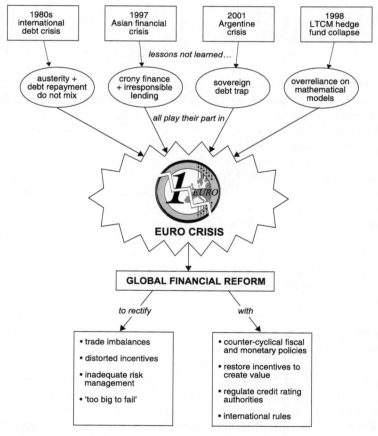

Figure 9.3 The themes of Chapter 9.

economic-growth-enhancing markets are missing, there is an essential role for governments in establishing the required foundations (see Chapter 10). Corrupt, distorted and bloated financial sectors provide an argument, not for the complete overthrow of market systems and their replacement by command practices, but rather for more visible hands to ensure markets operate efficiently.

Key words

Basle accords Banking regulations agreed by a committee of the heads of central banks of the major economies. They include recommendations on how much capital private financial intermediaries should carry in support of their loans, what and how banking supervision should be conducted, the degree of discipline and transparency involved, etc. As financial innovation has accelerated, the risks have multiplied, and the number and seriousness of crises has increased, so the accords have had to be revised – from Basle I (1988) to Basle II (2004) and now Basle III (2010/11). How far individual countries around the world implement these accords, of course, is a matter for each to decide.

Efficient market hypothesis (EMH) This is the theory, derived from rational expectations and New Classical economics, that the prices of financial instruments reflect all available information; the market is perfectly efficient, always at equilibrium and asset prices cannot deviate from their fundamental values. There is thus no remaining easy money to be made by buying some unnoticed, undervalued stock. By the same logic, foolhardy traders who underestimate risks and overprice assets will be compensated for by the far greater number of wiser investors. The assumption that investors are rational, assets are correctly priced and markets are efficient was built into sophisticated pricing models and formulae that allowed traders to evaluate complex loan packages extremely quickly, and increase the volume of their business and the size of their profits. Note that if most dealers are convinced of this hypothesis and that markets are never wrong, then no one will ever go to the trouble of looking for more penetrating information. And this way leads to the speculative booms and busts that the EMH says cannot happen . . .

Hedge funds These are investment funds for the super-rich. They are also known as highly leveraged institutions (HLIs) and attract short-term deposits in order to place them in (hopefully) high-yielding, though volatile, stocks. You hedge your bets if you spread your placements around a number of HLIs. By their nature, however, speculative flows move in and out of these hedge funds very quickly and, additionally, there is the fallacy of composition: sitting in London or New York and switching funds from Hong Kong to Buenos Aires to Kuala Lumpur may make perfect sense to you, but it can provoke a panicky and contagious chain reaction. Huge inflows and outflows of such capital have thus proved to be very destabilising for immature stock markets, and hedge funds have been accused of being at the root of recent financial crises.

Moral hazard If central authorities guarantee to support your business even if investments you make turn out to lose money, then there is no incentive for you to make wise decisions. The authorities are encouraging a morally hazardous, economically inefficient business environment.

Questions

1   Under what circumstances are the IMF's structural adjustment policies appropriate, and when and where are they inappropriate? Explain.
2   Government intervention and allocation of finance can produce wasteful and corrupt lending, yet liberalising private financial markets can lead to boom and bust. How can these opposite evils be avoided?
3   Private money and capital markets have legitimate economic functions, yet they can grow and transform into uncontrollable destroyers of social capital. Explain.
4   Should European financial authorities be able to dictate monetary and fiscal policies to democratic sovereign member governments of the EU? Why or why not?
5   What are the economic consequences of paying bankers and financial traders huge bonuses?

Further reading

Krugman, P. *What Happened in Asia?* available at http://web.mit.edu/krugman/www/DISINTER.html.
Mishkin, F. *The Next Great Globalisation*, Princeton University Press, 2006.
Rajan, R. C. *Fault Lines: How Hidden Fractures Still Threaten the World Economy*, Princeton University Press, 2010.
Reinhart, C. and Rogoff K. *This Time is Different: Eight Centuries of Financial Folly*, Princeton University Press, 2009.

10 Economic development, growth and inequality

It is a reproach to religion and government to suffer so much poverty and excess.

William Penn, 1693

Two nations; between whom there is no intercourse and no sympathy; who are as ignorant of each other's habits, thoughts, and feelings, as if they were dwellers in different zones, or inhabitants of different planets; who are formed by different breeding, are fed by a different food, are ordered by different manners, and are not governed by the same laws.

Benjamin Disraeli, 1804–81

The spectacular gap in incomes that separates the world's rich and poor nations is the central economic fact of our time.

Dani Rodrik, 2003

An inquiry into the nature and causes of the wealth of nations was the very first concern of economics (see Introduction), and we can summarise a number of the issues raised so far in this text and further analyse this most important of questions in this chapter.

As noted in Chapter 1, entrepreneurs and merchants act to mobilise factors of production – labour, capital, land and natural resources – in order to generate the production of goods and services in search of the rewards to be gained from bringing them to market.

Markets bring buyers and sellers together and determine prices – and it is these prices that signal what goods should be produced, how production should be most efficiently organised, and which people/producers should be rewarded by how much.

Markets require flexibility. A shortage of oil, for example, will be signalled by a rise in its price and in the profits earned by producers. This will attract a rush of resources into this industry, the quickest to move earning the most. As consumer demand is eventually sated, so prices and profits will fall, reducing the incentive for a further reallocation of societies' resources. Insofar as prices do *not* fall, this signals that the economy has not yet been flexible enough – further redeployment of resources is still required.

Markets reward technological innovation. Better, more efficient and cost-reducing ways of organising production will grant the innovator a competitive advantage and facilitate increasing economic growth. Chapter 1 documented how market forms of organisation are preferable to rigid command systems in developing technology and spreading its employment in a wide range of applications, and, in world terms, it was noted how the original industrial revolution and economic growth caused countries in Western Europe to outperform other nations around the globe.

Markets have generated inequality. Resources, and nations, that are quickest to move and rapidly respond to price incentives have earned more than those tied to traditional practices. Figure 1.3 contrasts the growth performance of Western Europe with China over the last millennium and the legacy of faster-moving market societies in the West is clearly illustrated. China has taken a couple of centuries to catch on and it is only in the relatively recent past that it has been making up for lost time.

Inequality is one of the defining economic characteristics of the current age. But it is not only inequality between nations but also within them that is of concern. The early chapters of this volume emphasised that markets bring failures as well as successes, and fast-moving financiers in unregulated markets have not only gained excessive incomes and widened inequalities in their own nations, they have also precipitated crises which many innocent bystanders are now paying for.

Financial innovation is a key driver of growth: dangerous if out of control, it is nonetheless a powerful engine which, if harnessed properly, can provide benefits for all. One of the greatest inequalities in the world is between those who know how to make money and those who do not. It is incumbent on society to move the latter so that they are embraced by the former.

What, then, can we say are the main causes of the wealth of nations? It requires control over *factors of production*; a system of economic organisation that ensures their *efficient employment*; the application of *technology* (including financial technology); and finally, the *distribution of the benefits* to all in society.

It is this last point that is politically sensitive. Economists are happy to theorise about the causes of economic growth, they may predict consequences of various income policies, but they can claim no special right to say how the societies' rewards *ought* to be distributed. Who gets what has exercised debate and fomented conflict, terrorism and revolutions over centuries. The division of the world's spoils excites much interest and, given existing international inequalities, there is inevitable concern to understand how to close the gap between rich and poor, and how to empower the disadvantaged and facilitate their increasing economic development.

Measurement

Any inquiry into the nature of development needs first to identify what is meant by the term and how progress in this domain can be measured.

The first and most obvious criterion to consider is the real income enjoyed by the countries studied. The most frequently used measure in this regard is Gross National

Product (GNP) per head of population. It is a crude but fundamental reference point that is relatively easy to obtain and is readily understood. The World Bank, for example, classifies low-income economies as those with an annual GNP per capita of less than US$995; middle-income economies are those with a GNP per capita between US$996 and US$12,195; and high-income economies have a GNP per head of US$12,196 or above per year. (Confusingly, in all its publications now, the World Bank has renamed GNP as GNI – Gross National Income – though its method of calculation is the same. GNP is retained here, however.)

In this example, all incomes are measured in 2009 US dollars – different world currencies being converted into dollars at the ruling market exchange rates. One difficulty with this yardstick is that current exchange rates are not a reliable means to convert dollars into all other monies: according to the imperfections of the exchange markets, they may overvalue some currencies and undervalue others. US$100 can often buy more goods and services in (typically) a poor country than in its richer neighbour. If this is so, then the local currency is undervalued at current exchange rates. GNP figures are thus made more accurate if dollars are converted into other countries' money via exchange rates calculated on a *purchasing power parity* (PPP) basis. That is, exchange rates need to be adjusted such that an identical sample of basic goods and services costs the same in one country as in another. (*The Economist* magazine has used a 'hamburger standard' as a quick approximation of this principle: if five dollars when converted into pesos buys a bigger hamburger in Mexico than in the USA, then the peso is undervalued, Mexico's GNP as measured in US dollars is undervalued, and these figures must be readjusted accordingly.)

Compare the figures in Table 10.1 of GNP *per capita*, measured in current, 2008 US dollars, with GNP *per capita* adjusted to purchasing power parity. Although there are still wide differences between rich and poor nations, the use of PPP figures reduces the gap somewhat. The relative position of economies in this rank-ordering may also be affected (see, for example, Germany).

Table 10.1 GNP per capita, selected countries (in US$ 2008).

	Current	*PPP adjusted*
Norway	84,850	58,810
United States	47,660	47,094
United Kingdom	45,610	35,087
Germany	42,680	35,308
Japan	38,000	34,692
New Zealand	27,320	25,438
Saudi Arabia	16,790	24,726
Russian Federation	9,630	15,258
Colombia	4,640	8,859
China	3,650	7,258
India	1,080	3,337
Congo, Democratic Republic	160	291

Source: World Bank.

Even if adjusted to show national incomes on a purchasing power basis, however, there still remain a number of other criticisms of using GNP per capita to measure development. Many poor people may not be in close contact with the money economy – they may neither sell the product of their work, nor buy many goods or services. Much of what they consume might be provided by themselves or bartered for in unrecorded trade. Subsistence farmers fall into this category. Similarly, many participants in the **informal sector** – such as numerous street sellers, stall-holders and those employed in small workshops – may be more integrated into the modern market economy, but will rarely disclose their output or incomes. Their economic contribution can be estimated by comparing the shortfall between the community's recorded incomes and recorded expenditures, but nonetheless considerable scope for underestimating the true national income of developing countries remains.

The methods used to compile GNP statistics in some countries can be very questionable. If output, expenditure and income data are surveyed with no great professional commitment to the exercise (e.g. by untrained assistants, part-timers, students, etc.), then many inaccuracies will be included as a result of errors and guesswork on the part of investigators, and evasion and fabrication on the part of those surveyed. There may also be deliberate falsification of the results for political purposes.

But even if a country's GNP per capita data were 100 per cent accurate and included all economic activity without exception, it would still not necessarily be the best indicator of development. This is because such data show only a mathematical average income, and averages may conceal very wide income disparities between rich and poor. Plus the whole notion of development implies something more for a country than just a crude measure of monetary wealth. If a nation plunders its stock of mineral resources, desecrates its landscape, pollutes its air, exploits its uneducated workforce and mounts up enormous incomes for a corrupt few, it would 'enjoy' a relatively high GNP per head of population, but would it be developed? For this reason there have been many attempts over the years to define and measure development using a wider range of criteria than just income statistics alone.

A reporter once asked Mahatma Gandhi what he thought of western civilisation; he replied: 'I think it would be a good idea . . .' The notion that material wealth equates with civilisation was challenged.

Development implies that a country's living standards are improving for all; that there is a reduction in poverty and in inequality, and an improvement in general standards of housing, diet, health and education. Apart from such socio-economic indicators, development can also be interpreted as including freedom from oppression and servitude, and freedom to create a greater cultural identity and sense of self-esteem. It implies that the majority of a country's people are actively participating in the development process and that no minority is being persecuted as a means to this end.

Defining development so widely leads to problems of measurement. Freedom House, an independent watchdog organisation, publishes a political freedom index

Table 10.2 Political and civil freedoms, selected countries.

	Political rights	Civil liberties
Norway*	1	1
United States*	1	1
United Kingdom*	1	1
Germany*	1	1
Japan*	1	2
New Zealand*	1	1
Saudi Arabia	7	6
Russian Federation	6	5
Colombia*	3	4
China	7	6
India*	2	3
Congo, Democratic Republic	6	6

Notes: Surveys are carried out annually: 1 represents most free; 7 least free. Note that * indicates a country's status as an electoral democracy. As can be seen, comparing the same countries as in Table 10.1, the rank order for political and civil liberties would differ from that compiled by GNP data alone, however calculated.

Source: Freedom House, 2010.

that would rank some countries relatively lower in development terms than if purely economic criteria were used (see Table 10.2). Criteria such as political rights and civil liberties are employed here.

Critically important though political and civil liberties may be, in confining this study to economics, it can be said that rising average incomes are a necessary but not sufficient condition for development. Increased income may not lead immediately to greater freedoms, or necessarily to the creation of great civilisations, but no sustained development is possible without it. Economic wealth is power, and such power is necessary for the creation of good *or* ill.

In the pursuit of a wider definition of economic development, the United Nations Development Programme uses GNP per capita data calculated on a purchasing power parity basis as a measure of incomes, life expectancy at birth as an indicator of health, and the percentage of adult literacy plus data on educational enrolments as an indicator of education. By weighting these measures together, it comes up with a *Human Development Index* (HDI) on a scale from zero to one.

The nations shown in Table 10.3 can be ranked according to their income per head measured in 2008 US dollars at PPP rates (column 4). Referring to the Human Development Index (column 5), however, the ordering of this selection of countries changes considerably. Contrast the rankings of Chile and Uruguay with that for Saudi Arabia, for example. It is argued that a higher quality of life is better captured by indicators other than crude measures of per capita incomes.

The HDI is not entirely free from criticism, however, because depending on how you weight the three indicators (featured in columns 2, 3 and 4) together you can come up with different results. Compare the findings on New Zealand with the USA, for example: a country which is far richer and with little difference in life

Table 10.3 Development indicators, selected countries.

Rank order of countries		Life expectancy at birth	Mean years of schooling	GNP per capita (PPP 2008 US$)	HDI index 0–1
1	Norway	81.0	12.6	58,810	0.938
2	Australia	81.9	12.0	38,692	0.937
3	New Zealand	80.6	12.5	25,438	0.907
4	United States	79.6	12.4	47,094	0.902
10	Germany	80.2	12.2	35,308	0.885
11	Japan	83.2	11.5	34,692	0.884
21	Hong Kong	82.5	10.0	45,090	0.862
26	United Kingdom	79.8	9.5	35,087	0.849
36	Hungary	73.9	11.7	17,472	0.805
45	Chile	78.8	9.7	13,561	0.783
52	Uruguay	76.7	8.4	13,808	0.765
55	Saudi Arabia	73.3	7.8	24,726	0.752
65	Russian Federation	67.2	8.8	15,258	0.719
79	Colombia	73.4	7.4	8,589	0.689
89	China	73.5	7.5	7,258	0.663
108	Indonesia	71.5	5.7	3,957	0.600
110	South Africa	52.0	8.2	9,812	0.597
119	India	64.4	4.4	3,337	0.519
125	Pakistan	67.2	4.9	2,678	0.490
168	Congo, Democratic Republic	48.0	3.8	291	0.239
169	Zimbabwe	47.0	7.2	176	0.140

Source: UNDP, *Human Development Report 2010.*

expectancy and years of schooling is ranked lower on the HDI. There are grounds to question the methodology used here.

There have been many more attempts than those surveyed above to capture the notion of development in measurable statistics, but there is clearly no single, objective indicator of such a value-laden concept that is without its faults. Since it is differences in incomes that excite most commentators, however, and – as mentioned earlier – it is a popular and frequently published statistic, GNP (or where unavailable, GDP)[1] per capita is used most often in this book as *the* yardstick of development (though its weaknesses mentioned above must always be borne in mind).

Classical theories of trade, growth and development

Adam Smith (1776) wrote that specialisation and exchange are limited only by the extent of the market. His was a treatise in praise of the spread of market organisation that wins converts to this day. His theory was based on the benefits derived from 'the division of labour', the organisational efficiency of competition, and 'the invisible hand' of markets in generating increased productivity and growth. His was an essentially optimistic view of the world economy, and he was witness to the spread of the British Empire and the riches this brought both to the home nation and to some of the colonies which subsequently won independence.

Thomas Malthus, a late contemporary of Smith, drew a different conclusion from his observation of the colonisation of North America. His calculations of the rate of growth of the settlers' population compared with that of their production of food led him to predict an eventual reduction of living standards to subsistence level. His *Essay on the Principle of Population* (1798) asserted that, in the absence of any constraint, every generation would reproduce itself in the space of a lifetime – doubling, say, every twenty to twenty-five years: a geometric or exponential rate of progression. Food supplies, however, he maintained – based on experience with relatively unlimited lands in the colonies – could at best be increased only at a constant rate. Result: food supplies must limit the population to subsistence level. Any one-off improvement in agricultural yields would facilitate a short-term increase in the population which would thus eat up the extra food produced, reducing living standards to poverty again. This doomsday scenario has never left the public imagination (see Chapter 12) and early on earned economics the sobriquet of 'the dismal science'.

Malthusian economics emphasised the principle of diminishing returns to the employment of labour. As more and more of one resource (labour) is employed to another (land), so long as the former is increasing faster than the latter, the returns to each additional input must inevitably fall. Given no change in any other conditions, this is one of the most reliable laws of economics – then as now (see Chapter 1 with regard to the Soviet Union).

David Ricardo further developed this principle in application to capital and industry, and deduced that this would drive down the 'iron law of wages' – a pessimistic prediction, despite his theory of international trade and comparative advantage which pointed the way to increasing trade and growth.

Competition between the European powers drove expansion and conflict between empires through to the nineteenth century and the conclusion of the Napoleonic wars. The first great wave of modern globalisation took place from 1870 to 1914 (see Chapter 4) and was brought about by a fall in transport costs (steamships replacing sail; railways and the telegraph opening up the New World), a reduction in trade barriers (peace and relative stability between the great powers), and faith in the gold standard as a secure international system of finance.

The world economy witnessed a gradual extension of markets that grew wider and wider around their basic centre in Europe. As was entirely consistent with classical economic thinking, colonies and ex-colonies had a comparative advantage in exporting land-intensive primary produce, so western capital was poured into plantations and mines, railways and shipping, all round the world from Argentina to Indonesia, Kenya to the West Indies.

Not only capital but also mass movements of labour took place in a world before passports and visas and at a time when migration was positively encouraged between heavily populated Europe, India and China and the underpopulated lands of the Americas, Africa and Australasia.

Developing countries thus entered the world economy as exporters of primary produce to serve western manufacturers and consumers. Gains from this trade were enjoyed by both parties: the economies of poorer countries were transformed by immigrant capital and labour, and they could thus earn increasing export revenues; meanwhile Europeans enjoyed cheap oil, copper, phosphates, rubber, sugar, tobacco, coffee, tea, etc. The distribution of these benefits – how much the land-rich developing world gained in contrast to Europeans – depended on how efficiently the recipient countries organised their incoming resources and could thus develop their export industries; how beneficial were the terms of trade (whether North American wheat, West Indian sugar and Malaysian rubber and tin could be sold for a high price or a low one – see Chapter 5); and how widespread export earnings were distributed internally. Some countries gained more and thus grew faster than others under this trade regime: Argentina, Australasia and North America were the greatest beneficiaries.

The first phase of globalisation obviously brought economic benefits – world economic growth tripled compared with the previous half-century – but not to all people equally. Mass migrations of labour and capital brought convergent incomes, on average, between the emigrant and immigrant countries, but the rewards of exploiting the new lands were restricted wherever ownership was highly concentrated (Latin America), thus widening inequalities. In contrast, where land was widely settled in family farms (northern North America and Australasia), so too were incomes widely dispersed. In contrast, in Europe, the impact of these changes brought a collapse in the fortunes of the landed aristocracy who could not compete with imports from the New World, whereas it improved the lot of the industrialised worker and factory owner. It must also be emphasised that in those nations receiving much incoming labour and capital, indigenous populations had little choice in determining their destiny – many were wiped out and many of those that were not were forced to take up a role in their nations at the bottom of the social and economic hierarchy.

Specialisation, trade, economic growth – and emerging inequalities – were sustained until the outbreak of the First World War. The huge cost of this conflict for the combatant nations, in human, capital and financial terms, depressed post-war Europe, caused a breakdown in the international gold standard and, after the financial crisis in the USA in 1929, brought about a rise in nationalism, protectionism and a steady decline in world trade. The 1930s' Great Depression was characterised by a collapse of banking, output and incomes for the developed world, and a lack of understanding of how to counter this (until Keynes; see Chapters 2 and 3). It was only the rise of massive public spending in the build-up to the Second World War that eventually restored full employment.

The legacy of war, depression and a world previously dominated by European empires had an immense impact on economic thought, political policies and world relations after 1945.

For the developing world, the experience of the loss of western markets in the inter-war period supported the Prebsich–Singer hypothesis of falling terms of trade, influenced dependency theorists (see Chapter 5) and reinforced the desire of colonised and quasi-colonised nations to gain full independence.

The international market system dominated by the big western nations was distrusted. Governments from Egypt to India, Argentina to Taiwan (then) were empowered to take a more active role in their economies, to channel funds into (especially) public and private enterprise, and generally to protect and promote the diversification of domestic industry and skills away from primary production. Foreign capital was still welcomed in many cases, but restrictions on its use were widespread. Charismatic popular leaders like Nasser in Egypt, Nehru in India, Peron in Argentina, Sukarno in Indonesia and Mao Tse-tung in China came in on this wave of emerging nationalism.

For the developed world, lessons from the mistakes of the 1920s and 1930s, the influence of Keynesian economics, and concern over the industrial and military success and attractions of the socialist command economies prompted efforts to rebuild a stable system of international finance, to grant Marshall aid for Western Europe, and to free up world trade to prompt economic growth.

Theories of economic growth and development

One of the most famous theories to emerge in this era was that of *The Stages of Economic Growth*, by Walt Rostow (Cambridge University Press, 1960). Rostow identified five key steps or stages that all countries must go through to attain development:

1 *the traditional society*, where nearly all employment is in subsistence agriculture and low living standards prevent much saving and investment;
2 *establishing preconditions*, where agricultural productivity rises and an entrepreneurial merchant class emerges;
3 *the take-off*, where increasing investment and growth in a leading sector in the country generates enough momentum to lift the whole economy towards
4 *the drive to maturity*, where success is broadened to include other sectors such that the increased pace of investment and growth becomes self-sustaining; and
5 *the age of high mass consumption* is finally achieved where living standards are increased for all.

Rostow's book contains a simple explanation for continuing poverty (stage 1, above) – a vicious circle where low incomes prevent savings, no savings mean no domestic investment, and no investment means no growth of incomes. In addition, it also provides a formula for success: establishing the preconditions in stage 2 leads on to stage 3, to stage 4 and thus 5.

The Stages of Economic Growth is, however, historical and descriptive (like the above), rather than theoretical and prescriptive. It gives no clear indication of the mechanism of growth and does not predict how such growth will proceed. The different stages involved seemed to follow one another automatically.

A theory of **economic dynamics** was necessary to explain more thoroughly how key variables such as the ratio of savings and investment should interact to produce growth. This was provided in the late 1940s by two economists working independently – Roy Harrod and Evsey Domar – in what has been called the *Harrod–Domar growth model*. Their work, along with Rostow's, inherited the dominant economic philosophy of Keynes with its focus on macroeconomic aggregates, plus it was also witness to the rapid growth of Stalin's Soviet Union which had been built by massive increases in capital investment.

The key to growth in the Harrod–Domar model lay in a country's savings ratio (s) and in its *incremental capital-output ratio* (ICOR, or more simply k). That is, the proportion of national income saved determines a country's flow of funds into investment, and the incremental capital-output ratio determines how much output will grow from this given increase in capital stock (i.e. investment). A country that saves 12 per cent of its income and has a capital-output ratio of 3 can thus have a 'warranted rate of growth' equal to $s/k = 12/3 = 4$ per cent. Meanwhile the 'natural rate of growth' is determined by the rate of increase in the labour force times labour productivity. Put together, the model postulated the 'knife-edge' problem: requiring a delicate balancing act to ensure the warranted rate equalled the natural rate of growth. If the former increased faster than the latter, there would be an excess of unemployed capital; if the latter grew faster, it meant increasing unemployed labour. Following Keynes (see Chapters 2 and 3), an excess of labour (or capital) would not cause a fall in wages (or the rate of profit) that would restore full employment, but would rather result in falling aggregate demand and deepening recession. This model thus gave a role to government in maintaining aggregate equilibrium.

Post-war development thinking was dominated by these ideas. Both Rostow's work and the Harrod–Domar model emphasised the importance of macroeconomic savings and investment ratios. Rostow's book is subtitled *A Non-Communist Manifesto*, and this indicates its genesis in the Cold War era, where the alternative model for developing countries was the evidently successful (at this time) system of massive, state-directed investment under communist central planning.

The Harrod–Domar model can be applied to the developing world in that, if the natural rate exceeds the warranted rate of growth of a country, it gives an explanation for the well-observed phenomenon of disguised or underemployed labour. A more relevant theory specifically designed to model the realities of low-income countries was Sir Arthur Lewis's famous *Economic Development with Unlimited Supplies of Labour* (The Manchester School, 1954). It assumed a dualistic economy – a modern, market, capitalist sector, typically urban and industrial, and a larger, traditional, subsistence sector tied to the land and characterised by classical diminishing returns.

The two sectors are illustrated in Figure 10.1 in Box 10.1 The traditional sector employs the bulk of the population at subsistence level. This notion is derived from the classic economics of Malthus: just enough average product is produced by each family to enable it to survive; any more labour and subsistence earnings fall, and the population, if it has no other source of income, must die off; any less and earnings rise above subsistence and the population grows.

Box 10.1   The Lewis model of unlimited labour supplies

In the Lewis dual economy model in Figure 10.1, the modern sector is illustrated on the left, the traditional sector on the right. At the outset, the former is small, the labour force numbered perhaps in hundreds; whereas labour in the traditional sector may be millions. An increase in the traditional population (beyond Na) may migrate to the city in search of industrial employment. The industrial wage (W) needs to be a fraction, say 30 per cent, above the subsistence average product in the traditional sector (ap) to pay for the cost of relocation – but wages show no tendency to rise since there is an unlimited supply of underemployed and unproductive labour available from the traditional sector. Its migration to the city in search of work carries no opportunity cost: that is, the **marginal product of labour** in the subsistence sector ($MPLt$) is zero.

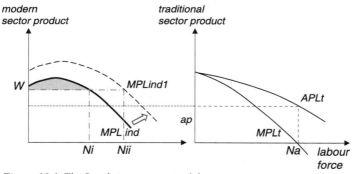

Figure 10.1 The Lewis two sector model.

The demand for labour in the urban, industrial sector depends on its productivity. It rises at first, then falls as illustrated by $MPLind$. The level of employment in the cities at wage W at first is determined at level Ni where the marginal product of labour in industry ($MPLind$) is just equal to the wage (entrepreneurs would not hire labour if it produced less than its wage cost). The total payroll is given by $W.Ni$: that is, the number of workers times their wage. The surplus profit earned above that (shaded) is reinvested back in industry, and the increase in physical capital this produces shifts the marginal product of labour $MPLind$ to $MPLind1$.

Increased urban productivity leads to an increase in the labour force (Nii) but no increase in wages, given the unlimited supply. You should see that the surplus profits now are greater (the area bounded by the $MPLind1$ curve and W) and this induces reinvestment and growth again. The MPLind curve will shift further and further, employing more and more until surplus labour in the traditional sector is eventually eliminated, and then competition for labour between the two sectors will cause wages to rise all round. Living standards rise for everyone: an integrated economy has developed.

So long as there is labour surplus to requirements in the traditional sector, there is no economic loss in redeploying people to the capitalist sector (indeed, this may prevent starvation). Modern industry is guaranteed a cheap labour supply; workers can gain a better wage in urban industrial employment than living at subsistence level elsewhere. The essence of the Lewis model is therefore that growth is achieved by transferring underutilised labour from traditional to modern employments; the profit gained by a more efficient use of society's resources can thus be ploughed back and invested in productive capital – which generates more growth.

Several powerful predictions flow from this analysis:

- Wages *should* be kept low (by western standards) in surplus labour economies – otherwise it will not be employed.
- For growth to proceed, profits must be reinvested in productive industry – not conspicuously consumed, devoted to unproductive prestige projects, or salted away in foreign bank accounts.
- Investment should be appropriate to the economy's resource endowment – that is, poor countries should pursue capital-saving technologies (e.g. transport and telecommunications, fuel-efficiency, recycling, etc.), not labour-saving equipment – otherwise the employment of surplus labour cannot be utilised and earnings will be limited to a highly skilled elite only.
- Inequalities will rise at first and wealth will be concentrated in the modern sector until the traditional sector becomes integrated and involved in the development process.

Note that although the typical interpretation of this model is that cities are the base for modern capitalist industry and peasant agriculture forms the labour-surplus traditional sector, it was not Lewis's intention to promote what has been called 'urban bias' – a policy recommendation of promoting urban industrialisation and ignoring agriculture. It is perfectly possible for farming to be modern, capitalist and a focus for economic growth – though the immediate post-war developing world didn't see it that way at the time.

Lewis, similar to Harrod, Domar, Rostow and others of this era, characterised the problem of developing countries as insufficient savings and investment – in the Lewis model, a problem of a capitalist sector that is too small. Subsequent experience, however, particularly in countries such as India and the old Soviet Union, shows that even with massive injections of capital, because of the rule of diminishing returns, the rewards of investment are disappointing. Check back to Table 1.1 to see the Soviet evidence. (Theoretically this can be illustrated in Figure 10.1 by the shifting out of *MPLind* getting smaller and smaller with each injection of capital, eventually stalling and restricting the level of industrial development and employment.)

Import substituting industrialisation?

Another problem that took some time to emerge was with the implementation of policies designed to promote diversified local industry. Following the arguments of Prebisch and dependency theorists, developing country industries need protection from international competition while they are at their 'infant' stage, until they are fully grown up and can compete on level terms with economically powerful western multinational corporations.

With domestic markets blocked against foreign firms by the use of tariffs and quotas, local demand is turned away from purchasing imports and directed instead to substitute consumer goods produced by emerging infant industries. The development impact can be entirely positive: there is much *learning-by-doing* as new skills, new resources and new products in the country are encouraged.

There is strong theoretical support for import substitution strategies. Almost by definition, the typical less-developed country does not possess perfectly functioning markets that reach across the entire economy. Such market imperfections therefore imply that ruling prices cannot send correct signals to firms and consumers. There may be much latent potential in a country's capacity to supply relatively simple manufactured goods (such as basic clothing, food processing or low-tech machines), for example, but such a comparative advantage may never be developed if local prices, market rates of interest and expected rates of return on investment do not reflect this. In particular, there are underdeveloped or **missing markets** for factors of production. Information for the efficient allocation of capital is lacking; land may be locked up in familial, feudal patterns of ownership; the emergence of entrepreneurs may be obstructed by traditional cultures resistant to change. Limited markets in which an unrepresentative sample of buyers and sellers come together cannot determine prices that allocate society's resources optimally. Profitable investment opportunities may go unrecognised; potentially productive resources may remain undeveloped – especially where substantial **threshold costs** exist. (No one manufacturing enterprise will set up in a poor area if local incomes are too low to promise many sales, but should a number of different businesses set up together, they may generate sufficient external economies: rising incomes and sufficient trade for all – the employees of one firm becoming the customers of others.)

Without protection, price signals from international markets in these circumstances would override national ones. In the absence of controls, with unrestricted access to highly lucrative overseas destinations, a poor country may lose to foreign employments those few resources that are emerging into the money economy. Valued personnel join the 'brain drain'; productive mineral rights are bought up cheaply by multinational companies; accumulated savings go in capital flight to offshore financial centres.

The argument for protection, government intervention and regulation of the domestic economy is therefore justified. With astute government management a network of young industries can grow; management and labour skills can develop; home-grown technology can evolve until the industrial sector is strong and diversified enough to compete with international industry on its own terms – such that continued protection and government allocation of domestic resources becomes redundant.

Government intervention *can* secure such results, but it need not. Sensitively handled strategic trade policies have been productive in some cases (for example, in certain South-East Asian 'flying geese' economies; see Chapter 4), but government failure in this regard is, unfortunately, far more common. Import barriers, protective legislation, hand-outs to local firms, and direct public ownership and control of domestic industry have more often promoted not the growth of infant industries but their increasing dependence.

The absence of foreign competition ensures local businesses can make profits without being strenuously efficient. Worse, entrepreneurs learn that profits are made most quickly not by risk-taking and raising quality standards to win sales in competitive markets, but by rent-seeking: lobbying public officials to get exclusive government contracts; seeking sole rights to import and distribute valued foreign manufactures; promoting laws that increase protection and confer **local monopoly** power.

The domestic economy will thus grow and diversify under protection, but – as incomes increase – amongst the business class that benefits most, there rises a powerful vested interest in the continuation of these detrimental (to the larger economy) policies. Infant industries therefore never grow up.

Where large state-owned industries make up the manufacturing sector, the pressure to maintain import restrictions and centrally allocated investment comes from within the public sector itself (as, for example, in Egypt). Where private industry predominates there may be widespread bribery and corruption of government officials. More subtly, government ministers and top industrialists may graduate from the same restricted elite in society, do business regularly with one another, and thus come to grant each other 'favours' on a reciprocal basis (as, for example, in India).

The price structure of the domestic economy becomes distorted when government intervention is pervasive. Rather than improving the signalling mechanism, it becomes disabling. Tariffs, quotas and foreign exchange restrictions that are designed to shut out imports can lead to an overvalued currency. Governments subsequently come under pressure from the business class to formally fix the exchange rate at a higher than free market level: this enables entrepreneurs to purchase cheap foreign capital inputs, yet their sales remain protected from imported consumer goods. Cheap foreign technology, however, means industry now has an incentive to employ more capital than labour. Capital-intensive industrial techniques are unhelpful in low-income countries with labour surplus: they reinforce divergent dualism.

In India, for example, growth of industrial output between 1950 and 1970 far outstripped the rate of growth of job creation – the overall capital–labour ratio increased threefold. The efficiency of Indian industry did not similarly improve, however. With the allocation of investment directed by government planning and not via financial markets, industrial growth was the outcome of increasing capital inputs rather than the increasing efficiency of each unit. This Indian experience clearly parallels the dismal performance of Soviet capital in Table 1.1. Thus India's incremental capital–output ratio rose from around 4 in the early 1960s to 10.5 in 1975 – a damning indictment of its import substitution strategy. (See Box 10.2.)

Box 10.2   Turning round the 'permit raj'

For more than forty years from independence in 1947, the Indian economy followed the Soviet example of excessive government regulation, planning and autarky. For perhaps the best of motives – to limit the polarisation of wealth and poverty – foreign trade and investment was strictly controlled and domestic entrepreneurs were required to gain government permits to invest in any given industry or region, hire and fire any workforce, and agree to any price of labour or capital. After years of British colonial administration, the Indians had turned instead to being ruled by the 'permit raj'. As a result, growth stagnated. With snail's pace economic progress almost overtaken by population growth, with the government on the verge of bankruptcy and with the glaringly obvious success stories further east in Asia, the subcontinent embarked on a much-belated change of direction in 1991.

With an almost audible sigh of relief pervading the country, regulations were eased, private and foreign investment encouraged, competition fostered, international trade made freer. Economic growth surged through the 1990s (see Figure 10.2) and continues to this day. The situation has turned to such an extent that now western developed nations are becoming increasingly worried by outsourcing to India (see Box 4.2). That is, the intended goal of vibrant infant industry grown to compete globally was achieved *not* by protection but by market liberalisation!

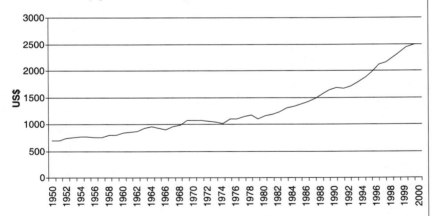

Figure 10.2 Indian real GDP per capita in constant prices, 1950–2000. Note partial reforms had increased incomes in the 1980s, only to run out of steam by the end of the decade. The major break with the past was brought in by the government of Prime Minister Rao in June 1991.

Urban bias

The Lewis model is a rough approximation of the way in which China has achieved rapid economic growth – releasing labour from the land to migrate to the cities and thus fuel urban industrial development – but the urban/rural wage differential is not 30 per cent as postulated in the model but closer to 300 per cent in reality. This poses problems for China in containing rural unrest at the inequalities that have emerged – but at least the country has managed affairs so far as to secure an impressive rise in GNP. This carries with it the potential therefore of distributing more of the gains to those left out in the development process (though whether or not this happens quickly enough to placate the rural poor remains to be seen).

Other countries' management of import substituting industrialisation policies, and the urban bias involved, has not been so successful. Internal markets favouring industrialisation have in many cases suppressed farm prices in order to guarantee cheap food for urban labour forces and have deliberately diverted investment away from agriculture and into industry. Worse, in employing western labour-saving technology, too few urban jobs have been created. When the bulk of the population works and lives on the land, such policies seem distinctly perverse. Promoting urban industrialisation by discriminating against agriculture is bound to cause dislocation and strife. Rural peoples are forced into the cities in search of better wages, only to end up in ghettos and shanty towns excluded from formal sector employment and straining urban public services beyond their limits. Such outcomes have been typical of Latin America.

The urban industrialisation bias in many developing countries was born of a pessimistic belief that traditional agriculture is inherently backward and has little attraction for modern investment. On closer examination, a number of studies have shown this not to be true. Under the right circumstances, traditional agriculture responds well to market incentives and opportunities for profitable investment are not lacking.

Pro-market farm policies have shown that in applying new technologies such as high-yield varieties of staple crops, fertilisers and irrigation – all capital-saving rather than labour-saving techniques – agricultural productivity can be rapidly increased. Where peasant farmers are not discriminated against by government policy-makers and where food prices reflect the real costs involved in their production, then the agricultural sector can become an integrated part of the growing economy rather than a forgotten backwater in increasingly dualistic development.

The neo-classical growth model

The neo-classical growth model, first developed by Robert Solow in 1956, embodies no overt urban bias. The role of flexible market prices, free from any government intervention, is stressed as the prime allocative mechanism. Markets are assumed to be competitive and efficient, and there is no reference to any government intervention. Growth in production is considered as a function of both capital and

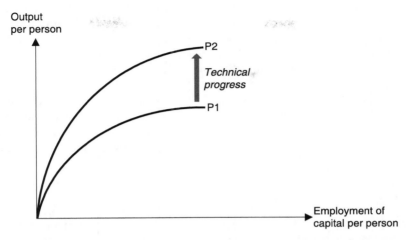

Figure 10.3 Neo-classical growth theory. The diminishing returns on capital employed per head of labour can be shifted by technical progress.

labour inputs, the prices of both are flexible and thus secure full employment, though each factor in isolation is characterised by diminishing returns.

The production function P1 illustrated in Figure 10.3 relates the amount of output per person in an economy to the amount of capital employed per person. As capital per head increases at a constant rate – 0, 10, 20, 30, etc. – output increases rapidly at first but then progressively slows down: 0, 20, 35, 40, 43, etc. As noted, with other factors being constant, the accumulation of capital becomes less and less productive.

Per capita output can only be improved in the long run by a shift upward in the production function. How is this possible? By the invention and application of entirely new productive processes: technical change. Thus the production function shifts from P1 to P2.

Since increasing capital inputs secures steadily decreasing additional outputs, the neo-classical model therefore identifies technical progress as the only means to shift the production function over time. In addition, it should be noted that this model does not discriminate between agriculture and industry in their respective capacities to generate growth through the application of new technology. Both sectors are assumed capable of responding to new products and processes.

Solow's model was an important contribution to the understanding of the processes of economic growth. It predicted that developing countries, with a higher productivity of capital, will grow faster than more developed ones, but as their living standards rise, so growth will slow down. The rate of growth of population also tends to slow down as countries become richer (the demand for children falls as their costs rise faster than their benefits!), and with access to internationally available technology the model predicts that the income per head of poorer countries will eventually catch up and converge with that of the wealthier.

Empirical support for this prediction is provided by evidence from some countries (e.g. in Asia) but not from others (parts of Africa and Latin America). But Solow's most annoying conclusion is that growth is mostly secured by a factor, technical progress, which the model assumes is exogenous – that is, unexplained. Growth is explained by the unexplainable! Where does technical progress come from?

It took another thirty years for Paul Romer to make the next breakthrough in 1986 and devise the endogenous growth model. One reason it took so long was that Romer had to explain away one of the basic tenets of economics – that of the principle of diminishing returns – in order to derive growth paths that would not slow down.

Endogenous growth theory

'Endogenous' growth demonstrates that success breeds success. If a country can get the conditions right, it will find that the only factor of production that is not in short supply is creative enterprise. In fact, although the effort and investment required to make one technological advance may be considerable (say, to build a mobile, cellular phone), the investment required to copy it and apply its use elsewhere is very little. By the same token, once creative imagination is engendered in society, its rewards can be unlimited.

Note, the returns derived by a given company from its investment in one specific innovation may diminish over time – but they can be almost limitless to a wider world which learns to use the idea. Individual companies that developed ballpoint pens, hovercraft, computers, mobile phones, may go broke – but the economic growth these ideas liberate for other companies and countries may have no limit. (See Box 10.3.)

Box 10.3   Living in an exponential world

Sony Corporation claims that technological information doubles every two years: an exponential rate of growth. As information doubles so it creates new products.

For example, how many years did the following technologies take to reach a target audience of 50 million users? Radio: thirty-eight years. TV: thirteen years. The internet: four years. The iPod: three years. Facebook: two years.

In 1984 there were one thousand internet devices. In 1992 there were one million. In 2008 there were one billion.

By the time you read this there will be new technological products and millions of new jobs created that did not exist at the time of writing.

Ideas provoke growth which provoke more ideas and more growth . . .

The reason technical progress occurs and why it is more productive in some countries than in others was referred to in Chapter 1. Recent theorising emphasises the need for investment in human capital – especially in promoting education and unrestricted competition in ideas and their application to industry. But this is not enough. The structure of social relations and the foundations upon which markets are based are found to be of crucial importance – no creativity will be released unless individuals can be assured they can organise production, increase trade and enjoy its rewards free from arbitrary appropriation by princes or pirates. Laws of contract, secure property rights and low transactions costs are essential to facilitate trade and to build an entrepreneurial culture that is willing to undertake the risks involved in technological research.

This is problematic from a developing country point of view. Putting the appropriate business-friendly policies, the microeconomic incentives, in place to reward enterprise at home is difficult enough as it is – especially so when those rewards in technologically leading countries can be so much higher. How can countries emulate innovative cultures such as are found in dynamic science and technology parks, 'silicon glens' and certain private–public partnerships? The fact is that some countries have succeeded at some times in this respect – but others have not. Much research is ongoing on the delicate and fugitive nature of how to institute entrepreneurial and technological success.

New institutional economics

The current Great Recession that began with a banking crisis in 2008 illustrates that getting the balance right between free markets and the appropriate level of central controls is not easy. But markets *need* government. It is in the way that institutions monitor and regulate markets that determines the success or failure of development strategies. Turkish–US development economist Dani Rodrik has said: 'The focus of policy reform in developing countries has moved from getting prices right to getting institutions right' (NBER, June 2008).

Ever wondered why there is much haggling over prices in many developing country souks, bazaars and market places? In the absence of any overarching rule of law, individual traders must engage in repeated bargaining to settle a deal. This is **clientisation**. The essential economic point here is that the transaction costs of doing business in this way are excessive. Since trust in trade is established on a personal basis, then the market cannot develop very far. In contrast, in modern, wealthy market economies there are elaborate systems of monitoring and enforcing contracts which are embodied in law as property rights. It is only because of the existence of these that transactions costs can be reduced and highly complex trading relationships can develop across time and space. People thus have the confidence to deal with others of whom they have no personal knowledge and with whom they have no reciprocal and ongoing exchange relationship.

Nobel Prize-winning development economist and historian Douglass North argues that, *without exception, countries grow slowest where property rights are weak or absent, the rule of law is unreliable and where governments are corrupt.*

North distinguishes between formal (government) and informal (norms of conduct) institutions, and typically the former grow out of the latter. You cannot just graft foreign laws, constitutions and democratic governments on to those who have not grown to value them. He quotes numerous examples from the Roman Empire to the evolution of South and North American societies to support his hypothesis. (See Box 10.4.)

Box 10.4   The informal sector and property rights

In most Latin American cities a large informal sector can be observed that exists alongside the modern market economy. Small-scale, informal business activity such as street vending, the production of clothing, fast food, handicrafts and the provision of a multitude of ingenious services all takes place outside the reach of the law. It is a trade that goes officially unrecognised, untaxed, unregulated and unprotected.

It is nonetheless enterprising. For example, Pepe was the smiling, helpful owner of a small kiosk in Santiago, Chile. He sold food and drink – some of which he made himself, some of which he traded from elsewhere. He could turn his hand to almost any task you requested, and that which he could not fix himself he always knew another who could.

Pepe lived in a place mostly built by his own hand. This is hardly unusual. Informal-sector properties – self-made, semi-permanent residences – have grown up to house small traders and their businesses, and they dot most urban landscapes in all less developed countries. You can find them on almost any plot of unclaimed land – under motorway bridges, alongside rivers and railway lines, behind formal-sector factories and shopping centres, and particularly clustered together in well-recognised suburbs or shantytowns from Mexico City to Buenos Aires, from Recife to Managua.

The output of such informal-sector enterprise can form a large part of a country's Gross Domestic Product and the sector can gainfully employ millions of otherwise destitute people. For example, data from Central America in the mid-1990s showed that the informal sector accounted for between 40 and 60 per cent of total urban employment. Additionally, skills and business acumen are passed on which not only provide the economy with an important resource base but this at almost no cost to the public purse.

Regrettably, however, the informal sector is no springboard for economic development. Shanty towns have been more or less permanent features of too many townscapes for too long. Businesses remain small, vulnerable and technologically primitive, and their owners and employees have not experienced rising per capita incomes over time. So why cannot such a dynamic, enterprising and efficient employer of resources (scarce capital is typically recycled and nothing is wasted in these businesses) act as a spur to the development and growth of the domestic economy as a whole?

The reason why industrial and commercial development seems to become stuck at this low level is tied up with the reason why the informal sector exists in the first place. People have to build their own informal homes and businesses if they cannot get legal title to them. In Lima, for example, a research team headed by economist Hernando de Soto estimated that it cost more than US$1,200 and took ten months to start up a legally recognised small clothing factory. Government officials requested bribes four times to expedite the process. Other researchers found that the bureaucracy required to register a business, which took only three and a half hours in Florida, varied from a month in some places (Chile, Brazil and Bolivia) to two years in others (Guatemala).

In addition to start-up costs, formal-sector enterprise is costly to run. In poor countries with a limited tax base, government revenues are particularly dependent on direct and indirect business taxes (i.e. high rates of corporation tax and VAT). State regulation and bureaucracy are also particularly punitive – minimum wage legislation, social security laws and controls over the hiring and firing of personnel increase labour costs on average by 20 per cent over the cost of informal labour. Where is the incentive, therefore, for the individual entrepreneur to enter the formal sector?

The ease of doing (formal) business – see Table 10.4 – is a key characteristic of countries that have successfully achieved economic growth. There are no surprises in the table between the top ten and bottom ten growthful economies . . . and you can guess which have the largest informal sectors.

The informal sector, though it is easy to enter, may be a developmental dead-end. Where central government cannot provide a stable institutional environment to establish and protect property rights, enforce compliance with contracts and fairly administer the law in civil disputes, the risk of investing in business becomes prohibitive. In modern capitalist market economies, for example, entrepreneurs can raise mortgages on their property, invest the capital so gained, conduct their business and then pocket the profit left over from paying off their creditors. As an informal, legally unrecognised occupier of property in a Latin American city, however, this process cannot even begin. No bank or private creditor will loan money without collateral. And if – at a high price – capital could be found to invest in the first place, who would then guarantee that any business deal agreed outside the law would be fulfilled?

Pepe's enterprise in Santiago came to an abrupt end. After a while the small stock of resources he built up for his kiosk became the target of others envious of his success. With no protection in law he took up arms to defend it himself, but someone was killed in the fight, Pepe was imprisoned and his business collapsed. The moral of the story is that modern economies are built on legally recognised and enforceable property rights, and no informal sector will develop very far without them.

Table 10.4 The ranking of the top ten and bottom ten countries in the world in terms of the ease of doing business. This World Bank index (column 2) averages the country's percentile rankings on nine topics (columns 3 to 11), giving equal weight to each topic. The rankings for all economies are benchmarked to June 2010.

Economy	Ease of Doing Business Rank	Starting a Business	Dealing with Construction Permits	Registering Property	Getting Credit	Protecting Investors	Paying Taxes	Trading Across Borders	Enforcing Contracts	Closing a Business
Singapore	1	4	2	15	6	2	4	1	13	2
Hong Kong	2	6	1	56	2	3	3	2	2	15
New Zealand	3	1	5	3	2	1	26	28	9	16
United Kingdom	4	17	16	22	2	10	16	15	23	7
United States	5	9	27	12	6	5	62	20	8	14
Denmark	6	27	10	30	15	28	13	5	30	5
Canada	7	3	29	37	32	5	10	41	58	3
Norway	8	33	65	8	46	20	18	9	4	4
Ireland	9	11	38	78	15	5	7	23	37	9
Australia	10	2	63	35	6	59	48	29	16	12
Timor-Leste	174	167	128	183	182	132	20	91	183	183
Congo, Dem. Rep.	175	146	81	118	168	154	163	172	172	155
Guinea-Bissau	176	183	103	175	152	132	133	117	139	183
Congo, Rep.	177	176	83	133	138	154	180	180	158	128
São Tomé and Principe	178	177	113	161	176	154	135	92	179	183
Guinea	179	181	171	166	168	173	173	129	130	123
Eritrea	180	180	183	178	176	109	113	165	48	183
Burundi	181	135	175	115	168	154	141	176	171	183
Central African Republic	182	161	148	141	138	132	182	182	173	183
Chad	183	182	101	137	152	154	179	171	164	183

Source: www.doingbusiness.org/rankings.

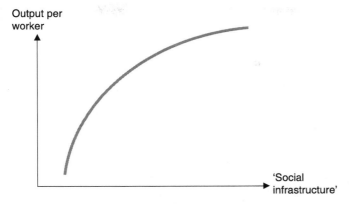

Figure 10.4 A plot of points of 127 countries yields a relationship similar to that shown. Countries such as Zaire (now the Democratic Republic of the Congo), Burundi, Haiti and Rwanda occur at the bottom left corner; the top right is taken up by the USA, Canada, Luxembourg, Hong Kong, Singapore, etc. (Derived from R. E. Hall and C. I. Jones, 'Why do some countries produce so much more output per worker than others?', *Quarterly Journal of Economics*, 1999. They report, 'In just over ten days the average worker in the United States produced as much as an average worker in Niger produced in an entire year . . .').

General laws in economics – applicable everywhere without exception – are rare indeed and North's claim has generated much research and empirical testing. One such survey is illustrated in Figure 10.4. Economists Hall and Jones plot productivity (output per head) on one axis and contrast this with their index of social infrastructure – which measures strength of law and property rights, risk of expropriation, incorruptibility, trustworthiness and freedom from tariffs and trade protection. (Trade restrictions are a form of tax or diversion of funds away from business and promote rent-seeking and corruption.) They find a positive correlation as given above. Note also the overall trend which emphasises that, at first, small improvements of social infrastructure lead to steep increases in productivity . . . an optimistic conclusion!

Very similar results are found by Easterly and Levine (NBER, 2002) who test for the influence of geography, policy and institutions on development across seventy-two countries. The factors they investigate aside from institutional criteria include settler mortality from diseases, access to the sea, mineral and crop resources, ethnic diversity, openness to trade, macroeconomic policies on exchange rates, inflation, etc. Clearly land-locked countries with no coastline may have substantial transactions costs in conducting international trade, and also those nations suffering severe business restrictions will experience difficulties in generating economic growth. However, disadvantageous geography and policies do *not* determine economic destiny. Both can be overcome. The authors conclude that 'endowments and policies have no independent effect once we control for institutions . . . institutional quality seems to be a sufficient statistic for accounting for economic development'. A strong endorsement of the North thesis.

Conclusion

Global income inequalities widened in the nineteenth and twentieth centuries as some countries found the recipe for economic growth, leaving other nations behind. Recent dynamic growth of some developing nations in closing the development gap (the BRIC nations of Brazil, Russia, India and China) has only pointed up another problem: inequalities widening *within* countries as the pathways they have chosen mean some people and some skills have been more in demand than others.

Growth models predict that, by mobilising their own resources and applying technologies from elsewhere, poorer countries can do much to catch up with their richer neighbours. The key to growth is technical progress which can shift **total factor productivity**, leading to the generation of positive externalities and exponential growth. An unrestricted flow of ideas, inspiration and technologies, in turn, is dependent on private enterprise – which requires that the foundations for markets are well established. There is an essential role for government here in allowing room for enterprise to flourish – ensuring the right balance between facilitating growth, promoting research and not excessively distorting incentives.

Economic growth is *not* the natural result of liberalising markets. The unregulated price mechanism takes any underlying institutional structure of an economy as given, and in circumstances of underdeveloped or missing markets, inadequate infrastructure and a grossly unequal distribution of wealth, then implementing neo-classical, liberalising policies can create more problems than it solves.

Free markets are characterised by **positive feedback**: the rich are able to reinvest their surplus income and thereby become richer, while poorer people may be locked into a vicious cycle of poverty, insufficient savings and no growth. Only by government intervention to remodel the economy's institutional foundations can the preconditions for free market growth be established for all.

Putting productive resources at the disposal of local entrepreneurs who have a direct interest in raising outputs and efficiency will not happen through *laissez-faire* – it requires a degree of central command. Whether it is agricultural land reforms, or privatising industry and widening the access to share capital, or reforming the cronyism of many financial markets – it is the same principle. Empower and devolve decision-making to all those with an incentive to create enterprise and productive capital – and then protect them from expropriation. There is no ducking government responsibilities here: if the institutional transformation is botched, then the benefits will accrue not to the wider economy but only to a privileged few who may have little incentive to spread the rewards any wider. (Russia? Wall Street?)

Additionally, the provision of essential public infrastructure is something the free market cannot produce. Road, rail and air transport networks must be provided by governments, as well as education and health services to all. These are essential public goods which confer extensive external benefits to society at large.

Secure property rights and laws of contract to protect trade, to allow the orderly closure of failing business and the transfer of capital to growing ones, are absolutely vital. Legal institutions are the means to build honesty and trust which are in turn crucial business virtues that facilitate long-term investment in the future.

Where the supply of educated entrepreneurs is limited (especially in the earlier stages of development), then co-opting them to the service of the state in ministerial planning commissions has proved successful in Japan, South Korea and Singapore – though whether this is a recipe that will work over long periods of time or outside of East Asia is uncertain.

On closer examination, therefore, those economies that have most successfully achieved rapid growth do not provide unqualified support for neo-classical, *laissez-faire* economics. The direction of strong government has been much in evidence. But, having said this, the direction in which the more successful developers have moved – from Chile in South America, Botswana in Africa to South Korea in Asia – has been increasingly to liberalise markets *once the foundations for growth have been laid*. Ensuring realistic prices operate throughout the economy is the first important policy common to these countries. Four prices in particular deserve mention: the price of agricultural products, the price of labour, the external exchange rate – these are essential to ensure the integration and not the dislocation of the farm sector, the application of appropriate capital-saving and not labour-saving technologies, and the international competitiveness of exports – and interest rates must be correctly priced too: to attract savings, discourage capital flight and to inhibit inflationary expansion of money supplies.

Economic development is not something that can be left to *laissez-faire*, therefore. Sensitive management of a growing economy is something that will always be necessary – firstly, in parenting infant industries; secondly, in providing effective public infrastructure; and, thirdly, in policing fair and competitive goods and financial markets. Resources are allocated between various employments and between a country's present and future needs according to the prices which rule. And these effective signals will only arise if, as Rodrik has said, the correct institutions are firstly established. It is on such foundations ultimately that a successful and flexible market economy is built.

In certain countries, it may be that markets are insufficiently, imperfectly developed. They thus send the wrong signals and, without corrective management, will promote suboptimal, distortionary results. Monopolistic vested interests, a polarised society and a crippled economy can be the outcome. So-called developed nations which thought they had overcome these growth pains are now finding out they are not as developed as they thought. The solution here, however – as it is for all developing nations – is not to suspend the market system but to improve and develop it. The experience of rich and poor nations alike – through their long period of divergence, the more recent period of convergence (for some), and the current time of global recession – teaches us that for growth and development

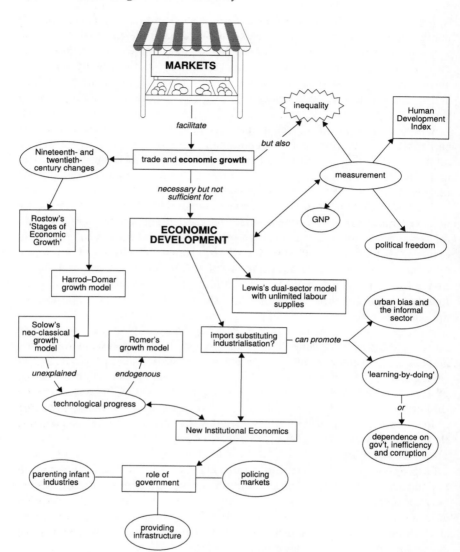

Figure 10.5 The themes of Chapter 10.

we need more, not less, market enterprise . . . and that its supervision can never be relaxed.

Key words

Clientisation The process of negotiating over a deal that establishes reputations and develops a relationship between the market trader and his/her client.

Economic dynamics The study of how an economy moves over time, which typically involves mathematical and computational techniques to see how aggregate variables such as prices, consumption, savings, investment, etc., change and impact on one another.

Informal sector Informal sector businesses are unofficial, unrecognised and unregulated enterprises that may or may not attempt to evade detection; they tend to be small, family-and-friends enterprises, but can extend to large networks of contacts across a country and overseas. Informal sector enterprise ranges from subsistence farmers to urban stall-holders, workshops, repair services and drug-running cartels. Such operations can be very productive, extremely economic in their use of capital, and may offer much employment, albeit at low wages. The informal sector can act as a residual pool of resources for formal sector employment, which shrinks in size as booming conditions mean regular businesses are looking for talent and then takes up the slack in times of recession when formal enterprise is cutting back – though such a straightforward relationship between the two sectors is undoubtedly an oversimplification.

Local monopoly A local trader who faces no competition in the neighbourhood or region.

Marginal product of labour (MPL) The increase in output of an enterprise that is created by the employment of an additional worker. This is a key concept in labour economics since the MPL determines the demand for labour. That is, businesses will demand labour so long as the worker earns enough to cover the going wage rate. As more and more workers are taken on in a business, assuming diminishing return to labour, the MPL falls until the last one employed just produces enough to pay for his wage.

Missing markets Where there may be the need for a good or service but no supplier can be found. With a feudal pattern of ownership, for example, where land is utilised not as a profit-maximising resource but as an indicator of position in the social hierarchy, there will be no market for its purchase and sale. Similarly, there will be a missing market for credit and bank services in the informal sector where registered property rights, collateral or security for loans is not recognised.

Positive feedback Where the smallest change to a system produces a reaction to increase the disturbance, thus causing exponential amplification, and the system rapidly diverges from its starting position. This is in contrast to negative feedback where any disturbance produces a reaction to reduce the movement and return the system to its equilibrium.

Threshold costs The cost of establishing a sustainable enterprise. For industries characterised by substantial economies of scale, such as an iron and steel works, the minimum cost of reaching an efficient size may be enormous. The threshold cost of setting up a car repair shop, hairdressers or a retail store will be much smaller.

Total factor productivity (TFP) The increase in output secured by an enterprise, or an economy, that is due *not* to increasing the quantity of inputs, but to the increased *quality* of those factors employed. Difficult in practice to measure, TFP is usually calculated as the residual improvement that remains unexplained when effects of changes in the quantities of all inputs have been accounted for.

Questions

1   In measuring economic development, the Human Development Index considers only indicators of income per head, health and education. Which other indicators (both negative as well as positive) do you consider are important and what weight would you assign to them?

2   The Harrod–Domar growth model considers that increasing unemployment of either labour or capital would lead to an inevitable recession. Solow's neo-classical model assumes that such circumstances would affect their relative prices, lead to reallocated employment and thus a maintained equilibrium. Which scenario do you consider most realistic?

3   Does the Lewis dual sector model condemn working people in developing countries to permanently low wages? Why or why not?

4   Should developing countries implement import substituting policies or export promoting policies? Or is some combination of the two possible?

5   Which institutions are important to provide a foundation for growth and development and how might a poor country gain such institutions?

Further reading

There are many excellent texts on development economics but there is no agreed consensus on the subject. Here are some favourites of mine:

Collier, P. *The Bottom Billion: Why the Poorest Countries are Failing and What Can Be Done About It*, Oxford University Press, 2007, is a forthright point of view urged by one of the world's leading experts on Africa.

Meier, G. and Rauch, J. *Leading Issues in Economic Development*, Oxford University Press, 2005, is a comprehensive collection of readings.

Rodrik, D. *In Search of Prosperity: Analytic Narratives on Economic Growth*, Princeton University Press, 2003, is an excellent collection of case studies.

Todaro, M. and Smith, S. *Economic Development*, London: Pearson Education, 2009, is a mainstream text.

11 The economics of terrorism

We must examine the costs and benefits of continued armed operations.

M. Al Zahar, a Hamas leader

In Colombia, impersonal norms exist and . . . there is a low law-breaking threshold . . . many consider 'my case an exceptional one' that requires me to break or dodge the law.

Francisco Thoumi, Colombian economist

And Terror like a frost shall halt the flood of thinking.

W. H. Auden

Terrorism is a distressing feature of the modern world economy. It has many facets – ranging from headline-grabbing, high intensity/low frequency incidents such as the attack on the World Trade Center of 11 September 2001; to low intensity/high frequency actions such as recurrent kidnaps, extortion and guerrilla activity in the streets, jungles or mountains of countries around the globe.

Terrorism is not just a modern phenomenon (the original 'reign of terror' was a year-long feature of the French Revolution in 1793–4), but it is worldwide and persistent, with multiple roots and lasting effects. It involves some well-known, international terrorist organisations such as Al-Qaeda; local nationalist or separatist movements such as the IRA, ETA, FARC, Tamil Tigers, Chechnya rebels, Hamas, Hezbollah; and also a host of many other extremist groups less easy to name but nonetheless radical, dedicated and in many cases ruthless.

Terrorism raises many urgent questions and concerns. What makes terrorism different from other violent and criminal activity? What are its causes? Is there any pattern? Why suicide attacks? What are its effects, and how can we prevent it?

A definition

Let us start by trying to define terrorism. Some argue that it is the modern face of warfare – the resort of disaffected parties when pitted against regular armed forces that wield far greater firepower. There is an element of truth in this: if combatants cannot match their opponents' military might, they resort to guerrilla tactics of hiding amongst the native population and practising hit and run tactics. But terrorism embraces a much wider range of activities than this – particularly the resort to what we might call illegal or criminal techniques in terrorising civilians and those who are not participants in any form of regular conflict.

Terrorism is characterised by overtly political or (so-called) religious aims. It seeks to spread fear in the domestic populace beyond those immediately affected. Terrorist practices may involve hostage-taking, hijacking, intimidation, extortion, torture, assassinations, bombings and all forms of extreme violence. It is perpetrated typically by relatively small, radicalised groups who eschew democracy or peaceful means of political dialogue. Finally, terrorism may be local, regional, national or international in scope.

Defining terrorism in this way, and emphasising that political motives are a key characteristic, gives rise to the thought that addressing issues such as democracy and freedom of expression might be the best way to investigate terrorism's root causes. Whilst not denying the relevance of political issues, however, the purpose of this chapter is to assert that *economic* causes and implications are absolutely fundamental to an understanding of the terrorist phenomenon.

Note the importance of this distinction: should terrorism be contested by direct intervention in troubled parts of the world and by attempting to foment political change? Or should we instead be more concerned to alleviate poverty and inequality and to improve economic opportunities? Maybe it is not a case of one or the other but some mix of the two that is most relevant? Clearly, terrorism can be approached from a number of different perspectives – but much recent research shows that an economic approach can be very productive in teasing out some of these answers.

An economic perspective

Economics analyses any human activity as the outcome of rational choice. Terrorists can thus be considered as **utility**-maximisers who weigh up the costs and benefits of alternative actions and proceed accordingly. This certainly sounds a realistic approach to analysing the behaviour of certain separatist organisations whose activities appear well-planned and deadly efficient, but can we assume rationality as a motive for suicide bombers who appear to be fanatical religious zealots? Evidence suggests we can, as will be explained later.

How big a problem is terrorism? It is not always easy to gain access to reliable data, but generally it ought to be emphasised that compared with 'normal' crime, terrorist attacks are extremely rare, and their incidence is random and very variable over time and across countries (see Figures 11.1 and 11.2).

To give an example, in the USA over the fourteen-year period from 1994 to 2008 there were 480 reported terrorist incidents. Contrast these data with the evidence of the US Federal Bureau of Investigation report on crime statistics for the country in only one year: 2006. For the single (admittedly popular) crime of car theft, 1,192,809 motor vehicles were reported stolen – one car was taken every 26 seconds!

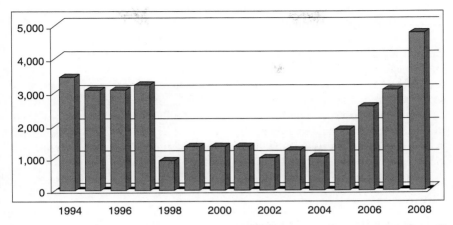

Figure 11.1 Global terrorist incidents over time, 1994–2008. This is a crude measure of the number of attacks reported worldwide, giving no indication of the seriousness of each attack.

Source: Global Terrorism Database, University of Maryland, accessed 23/9/2010.

If terrorism is rare compared with common law-breaking, incidents of *international* terrorism – which tend to be more visible and attract the most publicity – represent an even smaller fraction of overall terrorist activity. Data for the year 2003 from the US National Memorial Institute for the Prevention of Terrorism list 1,536 reports worldwide of domestic terrorism – but only 240 international incidents. (The latter are defined as attacks across borders, or attacks within one country specifically aimed at the persons or property of foreign nationals.) This

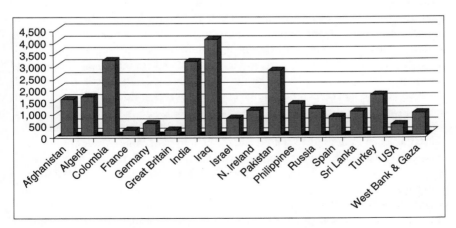

Figure 11.2 Terrorist incidents by country, state or province, 1994–2008.

Source: As Figure 1.1.

proportion is confirmed by data compiled by other researchers over the period 2002–4 which report a similarly low figure of 10–15 per cent.

But whether within or across national borders, and despite their relative scarcity, terrorist incidents when they do occur are profoundly disturbing to the public at large. Fear and concern affects many more than those directly involved. It is precisely this terror invoked by radical violence that most constitutes a threat to social order – and of course is the main reason why terrorists practise their trade.

So what explains such extremism? If we consider that such attacks are practised by disaffected, marginalised groups, what are the underlying causes of such radical activism? This leads us into an investigation of the links between economic conditions and social fractionalisation.

Causes

In poor countries, the lack of transport, communications and socio-economic infrastructure – such as national educational and health provision – can all lead to feelings of separateness or isolation in distant communities and thus promote a lack of identity with the nation-state. A sense of separateness will be even more reinforced if there are geographical barriers such as difficult mountain or jungle terrain as well as different ethnic, linguistic and cultural factors involved.

Countries where terrorism has been prevalent (see Figure 11.2) do seem to feature fractured societies, whether the disaffected minorities are of a political bent (e.g. Marxist FARC in Colombia), or are based on religious differences (Shia vs. Sunni in Iraq; Hindu vs. Muslim in India) or are ethnically based (Kurds in Turkey). All share a resort to violence to express their separateness and to make their discontent known.

What does social research on poor, isolated regions show? Firstly, such communities are characterised by limited economic interchange and social networking beyond the immediate environs: the national government is unable to efficiently provide local justice and law enforcement, rapid and high quality health and education services, unemployment benefits and the like; the modern economy is distant and/or offers few employment opportunities, so individuals must bond together to provide mutual support, protection, food and clothing, health, education and **insurance** against loss. As a result, economic isolation breeds a somewhat introvert culture where members of the community seek guidance from elders and pay little heed to state laws and norms of conduct.

Thus the objectives of peoples whose lives revolve around tightly knit, local communities are not aligned with those of the nation at large. Modern atomistic, competitive market economies emphasise autonomy, egalitarianism, transparency, democracy and accountability – and these norms do not fit at all well with those of poor, hierarchical cultures where loyalty, solidarity and paying tribute to the local patron is prized and continually rewarded. In such contexts, insisting on one's legal entitlement and referring to the overarching rule of the state is considered highly anti-social and is likely to be penalised. A lack of economic development plus social isolation seems to be a potent mix, therefore.

Isolated communities that are not well integrated into the domestic and global economy are unlikely to achieve very positive rates of economic growth – so do poor countries tend to exhibit more terrorist activity?

Some recent research (2010) conducted by two German economists, Krieger and Meierrieks, shows interesting results. Firstly, they argue that the relationship between a country's average income per head and levels of terrorism is theoretically ambiguous: the higher are income levels, the higher the opportunity cost of opting out of society and resorting to radical activism. But similarly, richer countries mean greater state capacity and thus the greater likelihood that any minority disaffection would tend to express itself in guerrilla and terrorist insurgency, rather than open revolt.

Testing for a number of possible causes of terrorism for sixty-five countries between 1975 and 1999, they find – in common with a number of other studies – that the correlation between levels of GDP per head and terrorism is *not* robust. It is not poverty by itself that is a cause of terrorism. Low-income countries are no more prone to generate terrorism than wealthy ones. What they do find, however, is that higher levels of income *inequality* are more associated with terrorist activity. As mentioned above, it is the sense of social exclusion that is an important factor – and in this respect it is wide income inequalities that are relevant, rather than the overall level of income per head of a nation. (Note also that inequality is relevant not only within countries but also between countries: rich countries are more likely targets – though not exclusively – for international terrorists based in poorer nations.)

Poverty and a lack of economic development is certainly a concern where it leads to conditions of lawlessness and, as Africa specialist Paul Collier has demonstrated, this results in an increased probability of political coups and civil war. In the extreme, we can speak of 'failed states' which have no effective control over roaming bands of armed groups and pirates who use violence as a means of earning a living. But this is not terrorism as defined earlier. Indeed, in these circumstances, tightly knit local communities that possess a well-defined sense of identity are the only social units that impose any form of law and order. So how far is social fractionalisation a key determinant?

Poverty, inequality, social exclusion, geographical barriers, ethnic/cultural differences – all these factors may be latent causes of disaffection and terrorism, but there is still something missing. There are plenty of poor, isolated communities – many with an ethnic and linguistic make-up very different to those in the rest of a country's population – but none ever resort to extremist violence against outsiders. There must be other influences at work that promote discontent, drive increasing radicalism, and tip individual and group action over into terrorist protest.

A possible answer comes indirectly from a number of studies that have looked at the relationship between political freedom and terrorism. There is certainly evidence that at both ends of the spectrum terrorism is reduced. That is, in countries with an authoritarian dictatorship where there is little restriction on the power of the state to eliminate political dissent (e.g. North Korea), terrorism does not exist

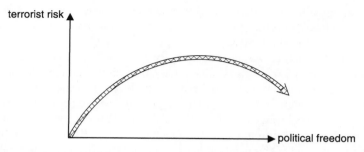

Figure 11.3 Terrorism and political rights.

Source: Derived from Alberto Abadie, 'Poverty, political freedom and the roots of
              terrorism', *American Economic Review*, Vol. 96 No. 2, May 2006.

(or if it does, it is not reported since autocratic regimes also control the media!).
At the opposite extreme, in a liberal democracy where there is freedom of
expression, open access to media and proportional representation in government,
the incidence of terrorism is similarly relatively low (though not zero). The highest
frequency of terrorist attacks occurs, however, in those parts of the world
characterised by intermediate levels of political freedom. (See Figure 11.3.)

An interesting conjecture is that it is not necessarily the *level* of political
freedom itself that is a determining factor, but *the experience of change*. That is,
some form of exogenous shock destabilises a society where previously a precious
balance had been maintained. The negative shock may come about on the economic
front: a sudden slump in fortunes and increased unemployment, or even a
technological breakthrough – such as the discovery of oil reserves – that might
confer riches on a select few. Alternatively the shock may be political regime
change that brings with it a loss of central authority. If either occurs where there
is already-existing economic hardship plus a simmering discontent of dispro-
portionate suffering for a marginalised few, then a resort to terrorism is a possible
response.

A model of terrorism

Bringing all these ideas together is possible in a model developed below and
originally inspired by the theoretical analysis of the illegal cocaine trade by
Colombian economist Francisco Thoumi. This analysis considers the interplay of
norms of conduct of a given society with the perceived costs and benefits of
partaking in terrorism.

Cultural norms

Assume a given group of activists wishing to advance a particular ideological
agenda. The costs and benefits of resorting to terrorism are firstly affected by the
limitations to law enforcement: if capture and punishment is missing, there is not

necessarily any benefit in pursuing your minority political objectives within the law. Majorities (or other minorities with a greater political voice) will otherwise outvote you. Where external constraints are weak, therefore, extremism may pay big rewards. A strong sense of unity in the minority, allied to a vociferous claim for social change, backed by violence and the absence of any inhibiting social institutions, may greatly increase the net benefits from terrorism.

Now apply this notion – where a minority are coldly calculating the gains to be won from extremist violence – to the context of a society with given cultural norms. An immediate objective for the extremists may be to try and effect a marked shift in the local community's norms of conduct. That is, radical groups will work to exploit the sense of difference and separateness of the local community from the nation at large. On the one hand, local solidarity is enhanced by the provision of mutual support and community public services that compensate for state failings. On the other hand, there will be a sustained attempt to generate what has been called **perverse social capital**: converting what might be popular antipathy towards outsiders into actual enmity towards the institutions of the state – the police, armed services, local government officials, even education and health providers who are identified as belonging to a national (i.e. outside) culture and not the local community. This means the promotion of a tolerance of violence done to others outside the group, ideally aided by an acceptance of illegal incomes – from selling drugs, stealing, piracy, kidnapping, simple tax avoidance or money laundering – that can fund improved local amenities and welfare support. (There are few things that will more quickly win over doubting support for your methods from others who may share your sense of isolation and grievance than showing them just how much material benefit they stand to gain if they join your cause.)

We illustrate these and other issues involved in Figure 11.4. The vertical axis measures people's acceptance of state laws – that is, how law-abiding they are –

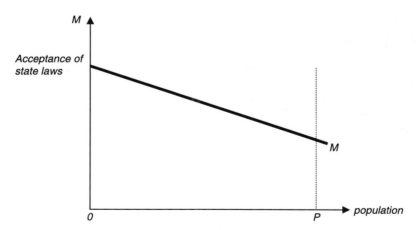

Figure 11.4 The law-abiding tendencies in a homogenous society.

Source: Derived from F. Thoumi, *Illegal Drugs, Economy and Society in the Andes*, Baltimore: Johns Hopkins University Press, 2003.

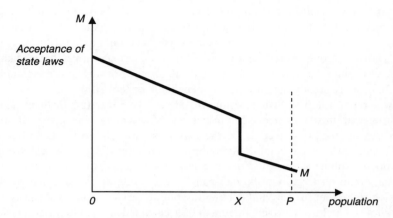

Figure 11.5 Law-abiding tendencies in a split society.

and the horizontal axis measures the number of individuals. 0P is thus the size of the nation's population. Suppose at first we have a homogenous population of a country: one can imagine that we can rank individuals' law-abiding tendencies, falling from high to low from the most honest to the least honest person. Thus the function M – illustrating the norm of lawfulness – ranges from high to low, 0 to P across the entire population.

How would such an objective function change if a marginalised group existed and evolved to become a differentiated and more disruptive entity within the state? The more this group can inculcate a sense of separateness and a rejection of the state's definition of what is lawful, the more this function steps down to illustrate a segmented, fractionalised society. We can thus illustrate – in Figure 11.5 – one section of society *(XP)* possessing different values from others *(0X)*.

Perceived costs and benefits

Whatever the norms of behaviour for different individuals, let us look now at the economic costs and benefits of indulging in terrorist activity. For example, even the most radical and murderously anti-social individual might refrain from any bomb-throwing if he or she estimates that the chances of detection and preventative capture are far greater than the costs of getting all the necessary activists and materials together. Such individuals might go underground and wait, go elsewhere (to less well-defended targets) or disappear altogether if the authorities are well organised and on a state of high alert and if there are high rates of disaffection and desertion from the ranks of supporters.

The direct costs of terrorism can be measured in terms of the resources employed in recruiting others to the cause, in planning and organising attacks, in purchasing materials and stockpiling an arsenal, and paying for the security that ensures the authorities do not find out what is going on. Indirect costs can be measured in terms of what it feels like to live a life 'underground' or on the run, and of the opportunity costs involved – what incomes, livelihood and utility could have been derived from the alternative, non-criminal lifestyle.

There are also direct costs to be calculated with regard to the likelihood of being captured or killed in the pursuit of terrorist goals. The probability of being killed in action is of course 100 per cent for suicide bombers. Given that the precise outcome and thus the ideological 'benefit' of any planned suicide attack must be uncertain, how can possible benefits outweigh the cost in this case?

It is evident, of course, that some terrorists are indeed willing to pay this price, so let us proceed with the logic of this approach – however distasteful it may seem – to see whether it leads us towards some useful conclusions and policy prescriptions. We return to analyse suicide attacks further below.

The benefit from carrying out terrorist activity will firstly be measured in terms of how far a specific attack advances the declared political/ideological objectives of the group concerned. Related to this is how much material damage can be inflicted on the target; how far 'the oxygen of publicity' (as Margaret Thatcher once famously called it) broadcasts the impact; and how far support for the cause can be raised and opposition discouraged. Some may argue that calculating these 'benefits' is entirely subjective and that certain extremists may inflate even the slightest terrorist achievement out of all proportion, but let us continue.

However difficult it is to measure such terrorist 'benefits', we can say with some certainty that, as the effectiveness of governance and the reach of the state increases, the chances of benefits being realised are reduced. Similarly, as the power of central authorities increase, so also the costs of terrorist action – detailed above – similarly increase. In sum, *objective net benefits (benefits minus costs) fall as the power of the state rises.*

For simplicity, assume the net benefit NB of a specific terrorist act is the same across all society. It will rise $(NB3)$ for a state with relatively weak central authority; it will fall for a nation with a stronger and more effective counter-terrorist organisation $(NB1)$. See Figure 11.6.

Note that, for example, any centre-led, counter-terrorist initiative may cause the fraction of society likely to support terrorism to fall from $0Y$ to $0X$ as net benefits fall $NB3$ to $NB2$, but it becomes more difficult to reduce such support when the state attempts to reach out to marginalised, sub-sections of society. A considerable extra investment in state control mechanisms will then be necessary to reduce the people's terrorist sympathies below distance XP.

Conversely, the external constraints on violence may be loosened if, say, a fiscal crisis cuts back the resources devoted to law enforcement, or if the attraction of formal-sector employment and pay is weakened, or if the financial gains from terrorism/drug smuggling/protection rackets/kidnapping, etc. increase. $NB2$ shifts up to $NB3$, or higher, and we can envisage the proportion of criminal activity in society thus becoming critical at greater than YP. Observers speak of a 'failed state' in this case, and terrorism, criminality and corruption become endemic and spiral out of control. Such a scenario may not only affect the objective net benefits in participating in political violence, but will also have a

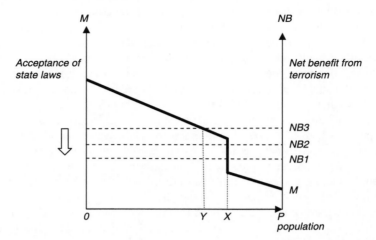

Figure 11.6 The effect on terrorism of increasing state powers in a segmented society. *M* illustrates the value systems of a segmented community. *NB* illustrates the net benefit from a specific terrorist act and this depends on direct costs plus the opportunity cost of non-criminal activity, versus the benefits gained from terrorism, discounted by the likelihood, and penalty, of being caught. As the powers of central authorities rise, net benefits to terrorist activity fall from *NB3* to *NB1*.

steadily widening and corrosive impact on society's values, thus lowering function *M*. You can guess the result of an increase in *NB and* a simultaneous fall in *M*, in Figure 11.6.

This leads us to consider what else might affect society's norms of conduct. Assume for the time being no change in any of the factors influencing the net benefits, described above. What might be the cause of deteriorating attitudes to the state and thus effect a shift down in *M* to *M1*? This brings to mind social upheavals that loosen communal adherence to the old ways of doing things – for example, the rapid influx of immigrants, large-scale internal, rural–urban displacement, or a loss of faith in the central government due to some exogenous natural, social or political shock that impacts on the general culture. Any of these may lead to a shift of accepted norms. A previously containable terrorist threat now becomes dangerously viable (Figure 11.7).

Suicidal extremism

This rational, cost–benefit approach can now be employed to try and understand one of the more disturbing phenomena of modern times – the practice of suicidal terrorism.[1]

Again it must be emphasised that suicide attacks are extremely rare. Though data are not always easy to collect, research shows 367 such attacks worldwide over a twenty-three-year period from 1981 to 2003. The great majority (316)

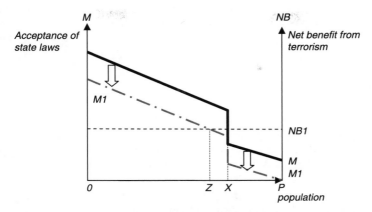

Figure 11.7 The effect of a weakening of society's norms of conduct towards terrorist activity. Negative social change shifts *M* down to *M1*; acceptance of terrorist violence spreads beyond its origins in a marginalised community *XP* to subvert elements of the wider society *ZX*. Now a major institutional or structural change may be necessary to bring back such groups into the social mainstream and thus make an attempt to reverse the damage done.

occurred in the last ten years of this period, however, and the destructiveness per attack also rose. Suicidal terrorism is of growing concern.

Suicide in regular warfare is not new. It was made notorious in Japanese kamikaze attacks on US warships towards the end of the Second World War and US soldiers in the Vietnam War also reported coming up against suicidal adversaries. Such deeds have evoked different reactions according to which side of the conflict the observer stands on – ranging from glorying in the sacrifice of the noble few in the face of overwhelming odds, to shock and lack of understanding at the ultimate price that certain combatants are willing to pay.

In contrast to these 'heroic', last-resort actions of a nation's military, the practice of suicide attacks as a form of terrorism has been associated with the actions of certain (particularly religious) extremists against urban civilians of other religions or cultures. They have been met with almost universal expressions of horror and condemnation.

Dates when suicidal terrorism against civilian targets first occurred are not easy to confirm. However, around the early 1980s the Tamil Tigers – committed separatist fighters based in northern Sri Lanka – pioneered the use of explosive belts packed with shrapnel. The tactic was used as the ultimate weapon to attack generally well-defended targets to which the separatists could not gain access except by passing themselves off as local civilians with their deadly load heavily disguised. About the same time, and it seems for a similar tactical reason, suicide attacks occurred in Lebanon/Israel/Palestine. Suicide bombings have since become particularly associated with Islamic groups such as Hamas and Hezbollah, with the tactic spreading to Iraq, to Afghanistan (the Taliban), and via Al-Qaeda to Europe, North America and elsewhere. Chechen Islamist rebels have also resorted to suicide attacks in their conflict against Russia.

Fanatical or rational?

The question has been asked as to whether suicidal attacks are all the responsibility of fanatical religious extremists – particularly Muslims. The answer is that, firstly, there is *no* strong correlation between religious beliefs and terrorism – which is intuitively understandable since none of the world's major religions preaches hatred or violence and, additionally, the first suicide bombers – the ethnic Tamils – were non-religious. What evidence does show, however, is that it is not religious belief which spawns terrorism; rather it is terrorism which exploits economic and social (sometimes religious) factors to enhance segregation, bind support together and drive individuals to extremes.

Studies of the profile of suicide bombers, particularly in the Middle East, have shown that they are more educated and generally from higher income brackets than the typical recruit to insurgent forces. The employment opportunities of such people are not meagre, indicating a high opportunity cost if such individuals choose the suicidal option. Additionally, for the insurgent organisation involved in promoting this form of attack, the act of suicide strips the group of a highly committed member; plus leaders must explain the individual's loss to the family and the rest of the local community. These are substantial costs.

If suicide terrorism has a high cost, a comparably high benefit is necessary to induce it. Certainly, if advancing the cause of a radicalised minority was easy, such a costly tactic would never be used. Evidence supports this. Where control of the central authorities is weak, in poor countries with rough, unpoliced terrain, extremists can infiltrate civil society without capture and so insurgent violence takes other forms. Suicide attacks are only resorted to when other forms of terrorism are unlikely to succeed. As a terrorist weapon, suicide bombers can be particularly valuable if they are disguised to fit in with the local community, if they are intelligent enough to navigate through a minefield of state defences and can thus get close to their target – typically of high military or propaganda value belonging to a different ethnic, religious or national group. Suicidal terrorism, therefore, is *a tactic of choice* to be used against well-defended, well-organised opponents. It has the added benefit of protecting the terrorist organisation from leaking intelligence since the perpetrators of any successful suicide attack cannot be interrogated.

There is a well-known symmetry between offence and defence: as weapons become more powerful, so too must defensive armour – which only means attackers must become more resourceful over time. We have theorised above that as the power and intelligence of the state grows, then terrorist targets become harder to attack. That implies that if terrorist tactics are to succeed, they must equally become deadlier and ever-harder to detect. Suicide terrorism is thus the resort of cold calculation, not religious fanaticism.

The theory of clubs

Radical terrorist groups display many of the characteristics of a selective club. Consider that sports and social clubs provide services to members that are excludable but **non-rivalrous** up to some point where congestion occurs. In joining a gym or a salsa dancing club, for example, I have to pay for admittance to use the facilities, but my enjoyment of membership is not reduced, and is in fact enhanced, by your inclusion, up to the point when it becomes overcrowded and the gains from joining the club are reduced.

Clubs provide local public goods that the wider society does not offer. Without public provision, costly facilities like gymnasia or dance halls are too expensive to be funded by individuals acting on their own, but they will come into being if sufficient like-minded citizens club together and raise the necessary capital between them. Further, once started, individual costs can be reduced and the benefits increased if the pioneering members can promote the club amongst friends, families and other suitable recruits.

Joining a club means paying the entry price and, typically, the higher the fee the higher the quality of club service it entitles you to. The price involved may not just be monetary, however – in some cases complex initiation rites may be required, especially for the more elitist institutions. In this way, we can begin to see how the theory of clubs can be extended to analyse the behaviour of certain professional associations, regiments, freemasons, public schools, college societies, rugby clubs, religious factions, street gangs and criminal organisations.

Club rules on acceptable codes of behaviour, dress, even diet, will be religiously adhered to if access to valued club goods can be assured. For the same reason, restrictions on members socialising with others outside the group will be accepted, and, in addition, particular standards of dress, hairstyle and coded signalling behaviour will be taken up to enhance solidarity and facilitate easy recognition of co-members. Failure to comply with what is uniform will prompt sanctions and ultimately expulsion from the club.

Sacrifices may be involved in one-off initiation rites, or perhaps required regularly, as proof of ongoing commitment to the club. Forms of self-, or mutual, mutilation are not uncommon (ritual tattoos or piercings for gang members and certain religious castes – e.g. circumcision for Jewish males). The stronger the sacrifice, the greater the demonstration of club support. The costly commitment of many hours of ritualised, rote-learning of holy texts by poor children can be seen as a sacrifice of time by those who are thus unable to work in the fields to help their peasant families.

The ultimate sacrifice is suicide. Why should any club member go that far? Because maybe the provision of local public goods guaranteed by such an act are of significant benefit commensurate with the cost paid. Your participation in a suicide attack is a rational act, it can thus be argued, if by so doing it elevates your family in the hierarchy of the club that as a result loved ones are better provided for, your legacy to the local community is glorified, and you believe it diminishes your enemies and guarantees your entry into paradise.

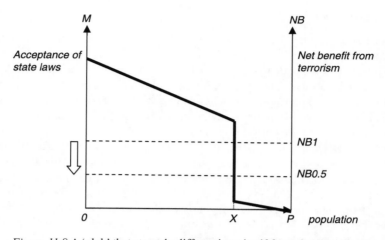

Figure 11.8 A 'club' that strongly differentiates itself from the rest of society. Where suicide and other high costs have to be borne, defection from the ranks of the club is a constant threat to its existence. Hence the need for strongly differentiated sacrifices and norms of conduct that signal commitment and solidarity to the group and reduce the diluting effect of interaction with the outside. Thereby even a significant reduction in net benefits *NB1* to *NB0.5* – say, due to improved policing, or the offer of significant rewards for the capture of guerrilla leaders – has little impact on club membership *XP*.

According to economists Berman and Laitin, the radical groups of Hamas, Hezbollah and the Taliban are each distinctly different, but all originally arose in environments with weak national government provision of public services and all responded by providing local club goods (social support and much-needed income) to their communities. Similarly, suicide attacks did not begin in Chechnya until after Islamic extremists, funded by the Bin Laden network, provided US$1,000 rewards for new suicidal converts and their families were awarded US$100 per month. In addition to suicidal recruits, the fundamentalist leaders also demanded other demonstrations of club membership: compulsory prayers, Arab clothes, a ban on men shaving and women forced out of the labour market. Such sacrifices increase solidarity, whereas outside work in the market economy is an unwelcome distraction with a **negative externality** for the club.

In the Thoumi model, we can illustrate a club with highly committed members in Figure 11.8.

A counter-terrorist strategy

What can be done to counter the threat of terrorism that all the above analysis suggests? If we look at the areas in the world where terrorism arises, what policies should be implemented and strategies employed – both short- and long-term – to reduce this threat?

From Afghanistan to Iraq, from Northern Ireland to Colombia, evidence shows that terrorism feeds on the vacuum where the provision of public services is lacking and where formal market opportunities are limited. Where economic development has lagged behind, particularly in relation to others in the nation who belong to a different ethnic, religious or communal grouping, then there exists a level of disquiet and dissatisfaction that may be exploited. Local support can in these circumstances be bought by a well-organised and radical faction that, based on their own code of honour, can efficiently enforce law and order as they dictate; can provide reliable supplies of foods, medicines and other services such as insurance/compensation; and can seamlessly adapt real local needs and ambitions to their own political ends. Such a rival to national economic and political power is all the more dangerously effective if substantial natural resource rents or foreign aid can be captured and diverted to the terrorists' cause. This has certainly been true of FARC guerrillas in Colombia who, although originally socialist, have resorted to cocaine trafficking, of the Taliban in Afghanistan, who expropriate opium revenues, and the capturing of Noraid from the USA by the IRA.

We can interpret appropriate counter-terrorist policies according to whether they either shift down NB function or shift up M function in the Thoumi model above.

For the short term, efforts to reduce the net benefits of violent terrorism would include investing in greater intelligence-gathering and improving the reach of law and order. Note that focused rather than the indiscriminate use of the armed services is essential if the perpetrators of violence are to be suppressed without antagonising local public opinion. Nothing traumatises local communities more, and thus recruits supporters for armed resistance, than death and injury imposed on innocent bystanders by agents of the state. Instead of shifting down NB, such 'collateral damage' – an emotionless and alienating euphemism – only serves to make matters worse by shifting down the M function.

Efforts to ensure that terrorism is punished wherever possible are a first-order priority to increase the costs of criminal insurgency and to reimpose the authority of the state. Note that proactive and well-informed use of the police and armed forces is necessary to actually go out and capture terrorists; resort to passively beefing-up the defence of terrorist targets is a poor response. Hardening targets in this way only increases the likelihood of suicide attacks or the switching of attacks to softer targets.

Well-executed interception of terrorist sources of revenue – capturing illicit drugs, closing down money-laundering loopholes, infiltrating protection rackets – is another essential requirement to counter insurgency. It starves radical extremists of the resources they need to challenge the state. Successful interdiction of their lines of finance is vital to reduce the benefits of terrorism and thus, again, shift down the NB function. Although an early priority, action to squeeze the funding support to terrorism is a policy that must be maintained over the long term.

Longer-term goals to reduce the benefits of terrorism would include improving access to and rewards from mainstream employment in the formal economy. Subsidising local industry and increasing the provision of jobs will both increase the opportunity cost of terrorism and, importantly, work towards inducing defection from the ranks of the terrorist recruits. Strategies to improve working conditions, economic stability and growth must help reduce the attraction of unlawful activity. Similarly, political certainty and leadership from the centre should emphasise the power of the state and the futility of trying to escape the law, whilst providing the means to exercise a legitimate political voice at grass-roots level should allow a peaceful outlet to extremist sentiments.

The most important and effective long-term objective must be to change the social and economic contexts that fragment society and breed discontent. A sustained attempt must be made to win the 'hearts and minds' of all peoples and thus shift up the M function. This involves efforts to promote a sense of nationhood, to bring marginalised groups back into the social mainstream, to reduce the geographical, cultural and economic barriers, and to value the contributions of minorities.

There are both political and economic factors involved in giving people a vested interest in allying with the state, upholding the law and turning against a separatist culture. Improving transport, communications and public utilities' infrastructure is essential. So is extending the network of state education and health services and being attentive to the social needs of the most disaffected. And clearly, the uniform application of state laws – such that no prince or politician or pauper receives differential treatment – is vital to instil an equal standard for all.

Giving people a political voice, showing them that this counts, matching their concerns and ambitions with others beyond their immediate community – all this helps build a national identity. The role of the media can be very important. Just as 'the oxygen of publicity' can help fuel the fires and spread the impact of terrorism – thereby rewarding the perpetrators – so the same media can support and provide legitimate outlet for local causes, link local to national issues and help generate a sense of inclusiveness and solidarity. Even disaffected insurgents may come to support national sports teams!

None of the above is inexpensive to provide – all require proactive economic investment. There are many up-front costs to prevent the splintering of society. Building networks that tie people together across space and time is the very substance of development economics. This is not an easy solution. If isolation and inequality are at the heart of social exclusion and this is fundamental to the terrorist threat, then the long-term goal must be to reach out and enfold such communities in the national economy. The budgetary demands on the government are no doubt great, but the social and political costs of not financing infrastructural investments may turn out to be even greater.

In conclusion, therefore, we return to the recurring major themes of the world economy: terrorism is another facet of inequality, exogenous shocks and the expression of instability in changing international economic relations.

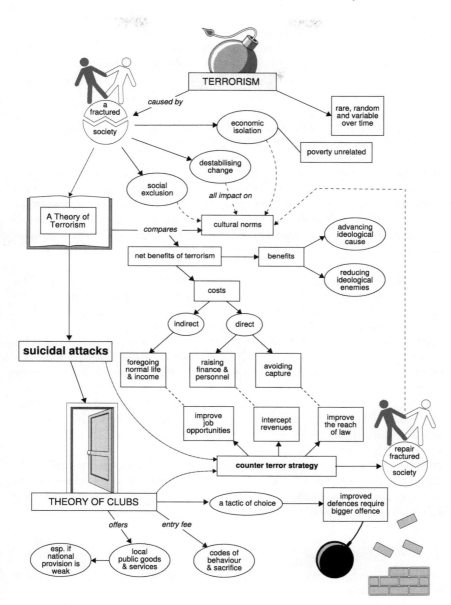

Figure 11.9 The themes of Chapter 11.

Key words

Insurance Generally well understood in a modern market economy: you pay a premium to an insurance company to insure against loss of a car, or a house fire, etc. The company finely calculates the likely risk in deciding the premium to charge you and it will pay compensation if a legitimate claim is made. In a non-money, traditional society your insurance is the goodwill of your neighbours. You pay the premium of supporting the community's objectives when it needs you, in return for being able to call on their support when your house collapses or your family bread-winner is ill or imprisoned.

Negative externality The effect of an outside influence that reduces the resources or lowers the benefits gained by the enterprise in question

Non-rivalrous Public goods at national or local level may be non-rivalrous in consumption: that is, my purchase of such a good or service does not diminish the supply available to you. The benefit I gain from efficient national defences or the police force is not at the expense of my neighbour. Similarly the ability to join and enjoy a local sports club is shared by me and other consumers – in this case, up to some limit where overcrowding occurs.

Perverse social capital The accumulation of skills, contacts, equipment and organisations not to serve the national, public interest, but to subvert it. In the Department of Antioquia, Colombia, for example, the local culture is famous for its hard-working, dedicated and enterprising ethic which has produced a successful and developed formal-sector business environment – yet the same virtues can also be devoted to creating perverse social capital in the form of some murderously efficient cocaine-financed terrorists like the late Pablo Escobar. Indeed, many guerrilla leaders from Che Guevara to Osama Bin Laden come from university-trained elites in their respective societies: there are none so dangerous as those who have gained a good education, resources and a social network . . . and are inspired to terrorise their peace-loving neighbours.

Utility A basic concept in economics otherwise referred to in the measurement of 'satisfaction' or welfare. All economic agents are assumed to be rational and to aim to maximise their 'utility' – that is, pursue courses of action that increase their welfare, however defined.

Questions

1   Distinguish between economic, political and cultural causes of terrorism and illustrate their relevance in examples you know of.
2   How might the objective net benefits from terrorist activity be reduced?
3   What explains how and why a country may accumulate perverse social capital?
4   Explain how the theory of clubs can be used to explain the incidence of suicidal terrorism.
5   Can economic development reduce terrorism?

Further reading

Abadie, A. 'Poverty, political freedom and the roots of terrorism', *American Economic Review*, Vol. 96 No. 2, May 2006.

Berman, E. and Laitin, D. 'Religion, terrorism and public goods: testing the club model', *NBER Working Paper 13725* (January 2008).

Krieger, T. and Meierrieks, D. 'What causes terrorism?', *Public Choice*, Vol. 147, 2010.

Rubio, M. 'Perverse social capital – some evidence from Colombia', *Journal of Economic Issues*, Vol. 31 No. 3, September 1997.

Thoumi, F. *Illegal Drugs, Economy and Society in the Andes*, Johns Hopkins University Press, 2003.

12 Environmental economics
Sustaining spaceship Earth

Black Swan event: 'First, it is an outlier, as it lies outside the realm of regular expectations, because nothing in the past can convincingly point to its possibility. Second, it carries an extreme impact. Third, in spite of its outlier status, human nature makes us concoct explanations for its occurrence after the fact, making it explainable and predictable.'

Nassim Nicholas Taleb, *New York Times*, 22 April 2007

Climate change presents a unique challenge for economics: it is the greatest and widest-ranging market failure ever seen.

The Stern Review: The Economics of Climate Change, presented to the British government, October 2006

Introduction

Predicting the future is uncertain. For example, if you listen to some people, we are all destined to gloom and doom:

- Way back in 1798, Thomas Malthus predicted – on the observation of incompatible trends in population and food growth in the new American colonies – that humankind could not escape everlasting poverty.
- Some hundred years later, at the beginning of the twentieth century, it was predicted that, at existing growth rates of horse-drawn traffic, central London within thirty years would be knee-high in manure and all transport would come sliding (ugh!) to a halt.
- In 1972, D. H. Meadows and others published *The Limits to Growth* in which it was claimed that at existing rates of exploitation the world would run out of oil, other essential minerals and thus the basis for continuing growth by the year 2000.

All these predictions were based on observable growth trends of their time and all have been proved wrong. Why? Because extrapolating existing trends always assumes that things do not change ... and of course they always do.

Like the wedding speeches of Hollywood film stars, economists should bear in mind Sam Goldwyn's maxim: 'Never prophesy; especially about the future . . .'

Experience shows that the price mechanism can provide an effective means to protect the environment. Take the issue of allegedly finite oil reserves. When economies grow, the demand for energy and oil-based products (such as plastics) will grow with them. Increasing demand for scarce supplies will force up prices – at an accelerating rate as stocks are depleted. This will cause consumers to modify their demands and simultaneously make it profitable for producers to seek out alternative energy supplies.

The history of oil prices and outputs shows that, despite the imperfections of this particular market place, increases in prices do call forth greater efforts to search out new oilfields; more efficient and less wasteful technologies to produce oil; increased consumer concern to economise on fuel use; and increased research and development of alternative energy supplies, battery-powered cars, solar-heating panels, etc. Oil prices at the end of the 1990s were lower in real terms than they were twenty years earlier, indicating less relative scarcity, and they can be expected to rise again and fall again in the new millennium as cyclical shortages and surpluses respond to these signals. Although a potentially exhaustible natural asset, oil will continue to be an important energy source long into the twenty-first century.

The most important single reason why certain doom and gloom predictions about the environment have therefore failed to be realised is that the market system employs a remarkably sophisticated and flexible control mechanism – prices – that urges people to change their (environmentally damaging) practices.

The most important single reason, however, that there *is* a growing environmental crisis is that not all natural resources have a market price. Many environmental goods essential for a decent quality of life have no price – they are **free goods** – and are thus being used to excess. There is no market incentive to economise on their use. In the absence of any other regulation, we can predict that those natural assets which have no price (e.g. clean air, including the ozone layer) will be used up and/or polluted the fastest. Other resources (e.g. fossil fuels, whales, hardwoods) possess positive market prices which are too low, reflecting only private costs of production and not their full environmental and social costs (such as the need to clean up oil spillage, conserve rare species, protect unique and fast-disappearing habitats). In these cases, rates of exploitation will be greater than the environment can sustain.

This point needs emphasising. Provision of most goods and services involves costs to the producer, which are internalised in the prices they charge in the market place, and costs to society at large which are external to this process. For example, in an unregulated market system car users will only pay directly for those internal costs such as fuel, depreciation and the loss of time and energy involved in driving. They will not pay for most of the damage inflicted on others by increased pollution, traffic jams, road accidents and the replacement of rural areas by the ugliness of motorised landscapes. These are the external costs imposed on society. And they will continue to rise so long as market prices fail to reflect this important component of real costs.

Adjusting the market mechanism

It is because, in the past, market systems have failed to value natural resources adequately to include all external, environmental costs, that economic growth (especially of the most developed nations) has been seen as being at the expense of the long-term health of the planet. Some critics have argued, therefore, that growth and the capitalist market system that drives it are to blame. But, on the contrary, if we are underpricing our valuable natural assets, then this is an argument for more market operation, not less. (There is plenty of historical evidence from Eastern Europe and the old Soviet Union that the opposite extreme from the free market economy – a command system – is far less environmentally friendly. The nuclear catastrophe that was Chernobyl, for example, polluted half a continent.)

Economic growth need not impoverish the planet. Increased awareness of the interdependence of all living things and the fragility of this relationship is urging the pursuit of **sustainable development** – where we pass on to future generations at least as much environmental wealth as we inherited ourselves.

The analysis of sustainable development requires us to widen and to redefine our understanding of the economic process. For example, in neo-classical theory, economic efficiency is at the heart of the subject. This can be defined in terms of maximising profitability in the production process and maximising utility in consumption – subject in both cases to budget constraints. Thus efficiency is gained in the market economy if producers switch to processes that yield more revenue per dollar spent on inputs and if households switch purchases to commodities yielding more utility per dollar spent on consumption. That is, if you have only a fixed amount of money at your disposal, spending any of this scarce resource on items that yield less reward than others is uneconomic. It is through the measuring-rod of prices that you can determine more efficient, less wasteful allocations of your resources. Producers will decide which are the most cost-effective raw materials and technologies to employ; consumers will decide which combination of goods and services yields most satisfaction.

The problem with the traditional, neo-classical outlook is that it takes no account of the long-term sustainability of this economic process. US economist Kenneth Boulding wrote a path-breaking essay in 1966 in which he argued that the West should stop acting as if it were in a cowboy economy with limitless frontiers and start behaving as if we were all passengers on spaceship Earth, where maintaining its life-support system is of paramount importance.

The signalling price mechanism needs to embrace not only private profit- and utility-maximisation but also environmental sustainability. Standards of living can only be guaranteed in the future if rates of growth of production and consumption do not exceed the environment's capacity to support them.

Readjusting the price mechanism to reflect humankind's multidimensional relationship with the environment is a complex business. Consider the following model:

1 Economic activity begins with primary industry and the creation of resources direct from the environment – mineral extraction, farming and fishing.
2 These resources are processed in secondary or manufacturing industry and converted into finished goods and services which are then distributed to the market place for final consumption.
3 Consumption of goods and services provides utility, which leads to increasing standards of living.

At all stages through this process there is the creation of waste. This occurs in many forms: *1a* in primary production with oil spillages, slag heaps, the burning of agricultural stubble, and the discarding of non-commercial animal and fish products; *2a* in manufacturing and distribution with spent materials, exhaust gases and depreciated capital; *3a* in consumption with the disposal of rubbish and the generation of litter.

As final products yield their utility over time they are all eventually wasted – some more quickly than others. A newspaper becomes waste paper after a day or so; a car passes more slowly over the years into burnt rubber, scrap metal and carbon monoxide. Thanks to the first law of thermodynamics, we can say that the sum of waste products at each stage of the production/consumption process above precisely equals the total value of the original resources:

Resources = Waste = 1a + 2a + 3a

What happens to the waste? Some of it is recycled. This depends on technological abilities and thus the commercial viability of recycling. We can predict that if resources become scarcer and more expensive, and technology cheaper, then the percentage of waste that is recycled back into production will increase. But according to the second law of thermodynamics, we can never approach 100 per cent recyclability since a fraction of energy and matter will always be dissipated in any production process.

Much waste is destined to be dumped back into the environment, therefore. Crucial here is the environment's capacity to assimilate that waste. If waste accumulation exceeds this assimilative capacity then we shall damage the environment. Rivers will become polluted, the air foul and the landscape littered.

This decreases our utility directly since people derive pleasure from the natural world – in leisure pursuits, sightseeing, just sitting in front of the television or reading books about it – and it also further impairs the environment's productivity in generating future resources.

We can thus devise a closed, interactive environmental model (see Figure 12.1) to replace the neo-classical view of economic activity. According to this model, the environment is linked to the economic system in three ways:

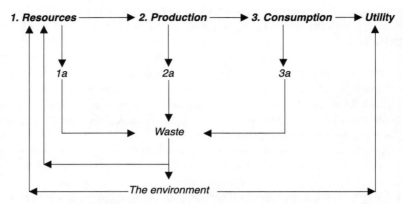

Figure 12.1 The relationship between economic activity and the environment.

- as a supplier of resources;
- as an assimilator of waste; and
- as a provider of aesthetic utility.

Economic growth needs the environment and can only be sustainable in the long run if mechanisms exist to restrict economic activity that is harmful to it and promote such activity that is beneficial. Before looking more closely at policies to adjust the relevant mechanisms, however, we need firstly to consider what we are trying to achieve: which activities are environmentally acceptable and which are not? How exactly do we define sustainable development?

Sustainable development – how much can the Earth take?

The Brundtland Report for the World Commission on Environment and Development (1987) defined this as 'development that meets the needs of the present without compromising the ability of future generations to meet their own needs'.

A number of implications follow from this statement. Firstly, waste generated from the production/consumption process must be kept at a level equal to or below the assimilative capacity of the environment. Secondly, the rate of use or harvest of renewable natural resources such as forest hardwoods, fishing stocks, etc. must be equal to or below the **natural regeneration rate**.

It should be emphasised that these assimilative and regenerative rates are not constant. Atmospheres, seas, rivers and landscapes have a tolerance threshold which can lower over time. Alternatively, such capacities can be augmented by the application of man-made capital: fertilisers improve land productivity; air and water can be cleaned. In any equilibrium between economic activity and the environment, therefore, constant monitoring of rates of assimilation and regeneration is necessary, and waste disposal and harvesting rates should be adjusted accordingly. Analysis of what constitutes an acceptable harvest rate of renewable resources is explored in more detail below.

A third consideration is exhaustible resources. Differentiating between these and renewable resources is easy enough in theory, but in practice the margin between them is blurred. Mineral resources such as oil and coal are the product of geological processes over millions of years and are clearly exhaustible and non-regenerative in human time horizons. But what about native habitats like wetlands or tropical rainforests? Forests can be harvested and are renewable, but to what extent is the extraction of hardwoods, even at tolerably slow rates, destructive of a unique natural habitat? A precious ecological balance can easily be disturbed and thus permanently impaired. There are grounds for treating certain such habitats as exhaustible resources.

It is important to emphasise, however, that *all economic activity is to some extent dependent on the use of exhaustible resources.* The evolution of humankind and civilisation has been fuelled by them. If sustainable development is defined as maintaining the same physical stock of Earth's resources into the future, it therefore means exploiting no further non-renewable assets. But this means no more economic development is possible today, nor – by the same argument – will it be possible tomorrow.

Clearly this is too excessive a requirement. It is hardly consistent with 'meeting the needs of the present'. Exhaustible resources are indeed environmentally irreplaceable, but they are irreplaceable also as supporters of *human* environments. Coal and oil provide essential energy; land is used for housing; forests are cleared for agriculture. Each economic act destructive of the environment yields benefits as well as costs.

Insisting on maintaining a constant natural capital stock into the future ignores, furthermore, the possibility of substituting renewable for exhaustible resources; man-made capital for natural capital.

Consider an example: I am reminded that Roman roads through the English Lake District follow the mountain ridges. Why is this? Why do they not follow the valley bottoms like modern roads? The Romans built their routes on the mountain tops – at considerable expense we can only guess – because it was even more difficult to navigate the valley bottoms which were then carpeted with thick forests. (Exactly the same economic practices were followed more than a thousand years later by the early settlers in New England, USA.) Native forests are an exhaustible resource. They have been replaced almost in their entirety in the UK by town and village, farmland and open moor. The former are undoubtedly an irretrievable loss, but the latter are not without attraction, as any visitor to the Lake District will confirm. In the meantime, the exploitation of native forests throughout the UK helped transform the country into the world's first modern, industrial economy.

The important conclusion from this example is that, as exhaustible resources are depleted, their reduced stock can to a considerable extent be compensated for by increases in renewable resources and man-made capital.

Finally, technological progress is directly concerned with obtaining more from less – economising on the use of our natural inheritance. Engines are increasingly fuel-efficient in our cars, homes and power stations. Energy can be generated far more cheaply from clean gas than from coal, and far more efficiently than from burning the wood and charcoal that led to much of Britain's deforestation in the past. Today, countries use far fewer exhaustible resources to produce one unit of GNP than they did a century ago and they will no doubt use far less in the future than they do now.

All these considerations indicate that preserving the existing physical stock of natural resources for future generations is neither practicable nor appropriate. Sustainable development must always involve some consumption of exhaustible resources alongside continuing technical progress and increasing substitution of other assets.

The relevant questions to ask are, therefore, what rates of exploitation of natural resources are acceptable? How much do we want to raise GNP now as compared with in the future? At what environmental cost? Or conversely, how much do we want to conserve the planet? At what cost to our current versus future needs?

Before analysing these issues related to the rates of exploitation of renewable and non-renewable resources, there are a number of reasons for proceeding with extreme caution when attempting to value natural assets:

- *Irreversibility.* There is the possibility of doing irreversible damage to the planet – for example, the destruction of habitat, extinction of species, desertification and climate change. If we make a mistake, very often we do not know how to reverse it. The costs involved here are large and stretch over all time. They involve not only what is lost but also the forgone opportunity of what might have been.
- *Uncertainty.* The distinctive feature of natural environments is the wealth of interconnected detail – such that a small change in a fragile ecological equilibrium can have myriad unpredictable outcomes over space and time. Our scientific knowledge is limited and the natural world reminds us that it will ever be so. We are uncertain as to the role of the ocean currents in climate determination; we cannot safely predict all the environmental effects of constructing dams and redirecting waterways; it is impossible to trace the final destinations of all waste materials disposed. The borderline between sustainable economic practices and tipping the balance over into cumulative environmental degradation can in practice be difficult to detect until too late. And note that the unpredictability of outcomes can impact on areas far removed from the scene of the original activity: smoke from British chimneys kills fish in Scandinavian lakes; Syrian dams deplete Iraqi waterways; northern hemisphere pollution punches holes in Antarctic ozone layers.
- *Increasing public concern.* Over time, as nations develop and incomes, education and public consciousness improve, so demands for environmental protection and conservation increase. The controversial fact here is that environmental degradation is only a cost if people care about it. And wealthier nations care more in the sense that they are willing to pay more for conservation. (See later on evaluation techniques.) The costs of exploiting

natural assets are greater in rich countries than in poor ones (cutting down the forests may be a matter of survival in Brazil today as it was in Britain of yesteryear), and, with increasing economic growth, will be greater for future generations than for those today.

Summing up, the combination of irreversibility and uncertainty, with effects spilling out locally, globally and intergenerationally, all urge us to err on the side of caution when calculating the costs of environmental exploitation.

Depletion of exhaustible resources

Supplies of exhaustible resources such as mineral deposits are *not* fixed; they become available to the market as a result of a three-stage commercial process:

1 *Exploration and discovery.* Considerable effort and investment are devoted to the search for and identification of profitably recoverable deposits. Despite enormous technological advances, there is an irreducible element of chance here.
2 *Development.* This is the thorough investigation and preparation for extraction of an identified source. Once the relevant capital equipment is in place, there then remains:
3 *Production and distribution.* The exploitation of reserves involves ongoing investment in extraction and transport techniques in order to guarantee the required depletion rate to satisfy market demand.

The speed at which such reserves can be made ready for market and the speed at which they are then consumed by society are both related to the price of the natural resource in question. These rates of depletion/consumption are of paramount importance – too quick and future generations will inherit less and less; too slow and current generations may be paying too high a cost of sacrifice. (If the price of energy is too high, many people may be denied heating and transport. In the extreme, some may die of hypothermia, or inability to reach emergency services in time. These are clear examples of where current generations and thus unborn future generations are paying too high a price.) The issues involved here are thus of **intergenerational equity** and an optimal depletion rate – that is, the rate of resource extraction that is 'best' for society.

There are ethical and economic considerations here. What level of irreplaceable resources is it fair to leave for our children and their children, far into the future, and how do we price future compared with present needs? Neo-classical economic theory has much to say on these points. In a perfect market the price of an exhaustible resource indicates its relative scarcity *and* its environmental importance. Moreover, the optimal depletion rate for any such resource is that where its price is induced to rise at a rate of growth equal to the rate of growth of all prices, that is, the market rate of interest.

Economist Harold Hotelling deduced in 1931 that the choice between exploiting a known oil resource or leaving it the ground for later depends on comparing the current market price of oil with what its revenue could earn if invested in a bank at the going rate of interest. If oil prices are rising faster than the rate of interest, then better to leave it in the ground than sell now and bank it. There is every incentive to delay drilling while the oil asset is steadily increasing in value. If current oil supplies are plentiful and prices are flat, however, then rates of return on alternative investments in the market place will offer a better reward. The owner maximises benefits by selling now and thus investing the oil revenues for a better return elsewhere.

If current resource exploitation increases, then that which remains for the future is depleted – sooner or later prices will be forced to rise; conversely, if exploitation ceases and supplies are conserved for future generations, then prices will at some time come down and thus prompt renewed extraction. The optimum rate of depletion for any exhaustible natural asset thus evolves as that where the rate of growth of prices and revenues just equals the market rate of interest.

The problem with this, of course, is that neo-classical theory *assumes perfect markets* – both of natural resources and of money/capital – such that all private, social and environmental costs are captured in the ruling prices and rates of return. This is not the case. Natural resources are likely to be underpriced, as already explained, and financial markets – as has been demonstrated throughout earlier chapters – are volatile, unreliable and unable to price future uncertainty. Relying on market-determined 'optimum' depletion rates may lead to excessive depletion. See Box 12.1.

Box 12.1   Discounting the future

How much would you be prepared to loan out today for the risk-free promise of 100 in a year's time? Suppose you say 96. That is putting a price on time. In financial markets, the rate of interest on a risk-free asset such as a Treasury bill determines just such a price. If money markets are less optimistic about the future they will determine a higher rate – say 6 per cent. The higher the rate, the greater the premium the market places upon current consumption; the less willing it is to forgo the use of resources today.

Such thinking informs neo-classical economics about how to price the environment. The higher the market rate, the more it discounts the availability of resources to future generations. It thus expresses *the rate of time preference* – how much the present is preferred to the future.

Note, however, that western financial markets may exhibit rates of time preference that are very different from those of people living and working elsewhere. For peoples and societies with uncertain futures – for example, very poor people, or criminals and poachers, or people living in fast-growing economies where alternative investment opportunities offer high rates of return – then there is likely to be a higher premium placed on present rather than future benefits. Alternatively, for an increasing number of people in wealthier societies, there is demonstrable concern that financial markets have time horizons that are far too short and that bankers and their ilk place a greater preference on current rewards than they do on preserving the planet.

Choosing the right discount rate to price natural resources – both exhaustible and renewable – is not something that can easily be taken for granted as neo-classical theory assumes, therefore. Very difficult and debatable value judgements are in fact incorporated in all models that environmentalists, scientists and social scientists use to analyse natural resource exploitation. See *The Stern Review* (2007).

Harvest of renewable resources

Farming, fishing and forestry represent use of renewable resources. Sustainable harvesting of the land and seas can thus be determined in relation to the rates of regeneration involved. If the seas are fished, for example, at a catch rate equal to the rate of growth of the existing fish stocks, clearly this resource can be left at a constant size for the future. Growth rates for renewable resources differ for each one involved. Cattle reproduce faster than blue whales; pine forests faster than tropical hardwoods. Growth rates for a given resource also differ according to its stock size or population density.

This latter point needs further elaboration. Take the case of elephant herds in certain parts of Africa – there is a critical minimum size (*cms*) below which reproduction rates are insufficient to guarantee survival. Above this, however, the herd grows first at an increasing rate – where the natural habitat is underpopulated and can thus support higher densities – then the growth rate slows, declines and finally reaches zero where the environment supports the maximum carrying capacity (*mcc*). The herd cannot grow beyond this size because death rates rise above birth rates as food supplies become insufficient.

Figure 12.2 plots the stock size of a given renewable resource against its natural regeneration rate. Given no interference from humankind, the natural equilibrium population is at the maximum carrying capacity. If for some short-lived reason (say, a year of good climate and improved food supplies) stocks should grow beyond this point, deaths will eventually exceed births and the stock must shrink. Conversely, if the population is reduced, births would outnumber deaths and growth would resume. The regeneration rate of the resource is the key concept since this indicates the environmentally sustainable harvest rate. As illustrated, the rate of growth of any renewable resource varies with its stock size, the maximum sustainable yield possible being indicated at *msy*.

The actual harvest rate that will be practised by those exploiting this resource depends on the costs and revenues involved. Generally speaking, the cost of exploiting a renewable resource will rise as the stock size shrinks. In fishing the open seas, for example, harvesting costs may rise prohibitively for some species

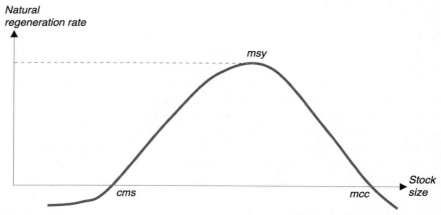

Figure 12.2 How the rate of regeneration of a species varies with its population/stock size.

as their numbers are reduced, the possible locations which they might inhabit are diverse and their market price is relatively low. For large, easy to hunt species such as African rhino and elephant, however, costs of poaching may be low, the gain from sales of rhino horn or ivory may be high, and thus stock sizes in these cases may be driven below their critical minimum size (*cms*) where extinction becomes a real threat.

To conclude the analysis of renewable resources, we return to a consideration of interest rates. How much foresters want to fell virgin hardwoods and hunters prefer to exploit scarce species such as whales, rhino or tigers now rather than at some time in the future depends on their rate of time preference, or discount rate. Where access to the resource in question is open (like virgin forests, or the high seas) or impossible to police (like some very large African game parks), where harvesters' discount rates are high and where the private costs of depletion are relatively low, then species extinction is at serious risk. Harvesting will inevitably take place at a rate faster than the environment can sustain.

Public policy

Confining economic activity to sustainable limits must be the goal of all those interested in conserving the environment. The market economy must be adjusted such that all commodities and economic practices are priced in accordance to the full (i.e. external + internal) costs incurred in their production.

If those overexploiting exhaustible and renewable resources had to pay the price of the damage they inflicted on the environment, they would conserve more. If polluters had to pay for their thoughtless disregard of others, they would think more and pollute less. Inevitably, as industry's costs rise they would pass on some fraction of this to consumers in the form of higher prices, but this is how it should be: more environmentally damaging produce would be more expensive and consumers would thus buy less of them.

What are the ways that can be used to internalise in market prices all external, environmental costs that societies suffer? Firstly, it has been argued that a free market society based on private property rights can for many natural assets achieve sustainable development. Property holders have a vested interest in protecting their resource and they can through the courts of law force polluters, poachers and all violators to pay for any encroachment they cause.

The classic case was given by Ronald Coase ('The problem of social cost', *Journal of Law and Economics*, Vol. 3, 1960) in which he described sparks from a passing steam train setting fire to a farmer's field. The farmer can sue for compensation and in so doing external costs (to the farmer) are internalised to the producer (the railway company). Profits of the enterprise hence fall and this will prompt a cutback in economic activity and/or more careful conservationist practice. Alternatively, instead of cleaning up its act, the railway producer can opt to purchase the property rights of all offended parties. Either way, costs and benefits are adjusted through the free market to internalise the externalities involved. Equilibrium is secured in this case without recourse to government intervention, other than in the institution of property rights in the first place.

This equilibrium, however, is subject to two conditions: (1) it requires that the resource in question is capable of exclusive private ownership; and (2) it assumes that transactions costs are not prohibitive.

1   As has already been observed, many vital resources have open access (e.g. whales, clean air) so no proprietor can prevent others' exploitation. True, for some common properties, e.g. fishing in a remote beauty spot, negotiated agreement between self-enlightened users can be possible, but there is always the temptation for one party to cheat (the free-rider problem). The larger the resource, however – such as a national park – the less exclusive it can be and the huge number of users precludes any effective free market agreement. Government controls become necessary.

2   Even where property rights are enshrined and enforceable in law, the transaction cost of suing for damages (especially where the transgressor is a big, powerful enterprise and the transgressed are many, small, non-organised property holders) may simply be too great an obstacle to overcome. An unscrupulous profit-maximiser may exploit its power, pay minimal lip-service to environmental causes and get away with it. Multinational mining companies working in developing countries have at times been accused of such practice.

Despite this, environmental pressure groups such as Friends of the Earth, WWF, Greenpeace, etc., *are* effective in the unregulated free market. Well-publicised campaigns against environmentally damaging operators, be they private or public enterprises, do succeed at times (e.g. against BP in the Deepwater Horizon explosion, fire and oil spill in the Gulf of Mexico, 2010). There is some evidence, therefore, that sustainable economic activity can be controlled through the free market.

One-off successes are not enough, however, to permanently safeguard the environment from exploitation and degradation. Comprehensive adjustment of the price mechanism is not attainable by such an ad hoc approach. Government regulation of the market system is, in the end, indispensable.

The Stern Review

One of the most comprehensive, widely discussed and inevitably controversial attempts to price the environment and propose measures to offset degradation was the 2006 *Stern Review: The Economics of Climate Change.*

The report was commissioned by the UK government, compiled by independent economists taking into account the widest available range of scientific evidence at the time, and was based on a calculation of significant known risks, acceptance of unknowns and consideration of the ethics of intergenerational responsibility.

It concluded that 'business as usual' was not an option. Average global temperatures over the next century in such a 'do nothing' scenario are projected to rise by 2–3 degrees Celsius (though quite possibly more), which would bring flood risk to one-sixth of the world's population, declining crop yields, widespread hunger and disease, 15–40 per cent species extinction and further future unpredictable shifts in weather patterns. The impact of climate change would not be evenly distributed – carbon emissions are greatest from the developed world (see Figure 12.3), but the poorest and most vulnerable countries would suffer earliest and most – and, given the irreversibility of environmental effects beyond a certain threshold, when the damages first appear it would be then too late and too costly to reverse the process. The report recommended strong early action to reduce CO_2 emissions which should be viewed as an investment: 'a cost incurred now and in the coming few decades

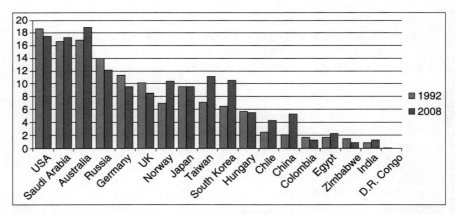

Figure 12.3 CO_2 emissions (in metric tons) per capita, selected countries, 1992 and 2008. Note that the developed world has a generally higher per capita rate, but the different picture between 1992 and 2008 shows that some countries are containing their emissions better than others. (All countries except the Democratic Republic of Congo witnessed positive economic growth over the period.)

Sources: US International Energy Agency; UN data.

to avoid the risks of very severe consequences in the future'. The cost of investing in the planet was put at 1 per cent of GDP per year for the next ten to twenty years, but the cost of doing nothing would be a loss of between 5 and 20 per cent world GDP per year in generations to come.

Critical responses have varied from accusations of exaggerating the dangers on the one hand to being far too cautious on the other. A key issue is the use of a discount rate to calculate future costs and benefits, especially since there are so many uncertainties about future consumption patterns, technological changes and long-term environmental effects. Certainly the *Stern Review* incorporated a lower discount rate – 1.4 per cent – which places a higher value on future impacts than most other economic studies of the time (e.g. environmental economist W. Nordhaus used a discount rate closer to 3 per cent).

This is defensible. Given that there is some evidence that climate change is now happening faster than estimated by Stern, that the economics profession was in general unable to foresee the black swan event of the 2008 financial crisis, and that the myopic policy reaction to increased sovereign debts has been for western governments to *reduce* public spending and intervention in the market place, I would argue that there is every reason for environmentalists to be worried about the future. The case for acting to reduce global carbon emissions is even stronger now than it was.

Policy instruments

There are a number of public policy instruments that can be employed to protect the environment. One extreme is to dispense with any adjustment of market prices and go straight for *direct controls*. Legislation can be passed to outlaw certain harmful practices. This can certainly be effective, and for some situations it may be the most efficient means of government intervention – for example, where clearly identifiable behaviour is considered harmful and must be prohibited, and where prompt and substantial changes are called for. This might include an outright ban on hunting/fishing of threatened species. With regard to climate change, one of the most cost-effective means of reducing carbon emissions would be to effect a change in housing regulations – making it mandatory to provide a minimum standard of insulation and to install energy-efficient lighting and heating systems in all new construction. (Conversion of *existing* buildings might be encouraged by subsidies, see below.)

Direct controls, nonetheless, are too inefficient a mechanism to employ in many cases. Public regulatory agencies must firstly set up laws that are responsive to changing environmental circumstances, and must catch private operators who break these laws, compile evidence to prosecute them, bring cases to court and then succeed in gaining effective penalties. The transaction costs of devoting resources to this end may be more wasteful in some instances than allowing the accused to get away with it in the first place.

Taxation can do the same job of environmental control, in most cases more dependably, effectively and economically than legislation. A carbon tax levied on the emission of exhaust gases, for example, will limit over-rapid exploitation of fossil fuels and thus promote research and development of alternatives. Although not costless – it requires a technology applicable to energy-consuming equipment from car engines to thermal power stations, as well as a bureaucracy of tax inspectors – it is an automatic system that penalises carbon-users on a rising scale appropriate to their environmental impact. An appropriate and globally consistent tax on transport fuels, for example, is currently missing – US taxes are lower than European levels, and within Europe taxes vary considerably – but nonetheless consumers and thus producers have still reacted to increasing fuel duties. This is one of the reasons why new aircraft are 70 per cent more fuel-efficient than forty years ago and 20 per cent better than ten years ago. With more coordinated international action such progress can be accelerated.

The Stern report mentions that many low-carbon technologies are at present more expensive than fossil fuel alternatives, but experience shows that the costs of production fall with scale and with learning from experience. This is a case where there is a clear public interest in providing *subsidies* in research and development of a diverse portfolio of environmentally beneficial technologies applicable to industry, agriculture and transport. Stern argues that 'there are likely to be high returns to a doubling of investments in this area to around US$20 billion per annum globally', and in power generation – which makes up the largest source of global greenhouse gas emissions, see Figure 12.4 – the existing incentives should be increased by two to five times.

Subsidies are appropriate to encourage all conservation and recycling activities that have external benefits not recorded in unregulated market prices. If it is justifiable to tax the production of environmentally damaging practices, by the

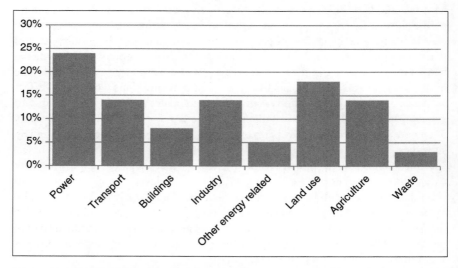

Figure 12.4 World distribution of greenhouse gas emissions in 2000, according to source.

Source: *The Stern Review.*

same argument subsidies should be awarded to bring down the market prices of those products and processes with a high net social benefit and which deserve patronage.

Pollution permits are a novel way of internalising external costs and making the polluter pay. One of the most successful of these is the EU Emissions Trading Scheme which is specifically designed to reduce the EU's carbon emissions, but the idea is applicable to many forms of harmful practice. A regulatory agency decides on the acceptable level of pollution (or, say, access to a specific natural resource) to be allowed. A batch of permits is issued authorising just that given amount and these permits are then offered for sale on the open market. Prices are determined by demand and supply. The more cars that want to pollute a certain commuter route, the more factories which wish to belch out smoke, the more walkers who want to tramp over a certain mountain, the more they have to pay. Higher prices will shift demand to lower-use days and locations.

What price the planet?

Each of the policy instruments above has its advantages and disadvantages; some are suited to some applications, others to others. All, however, share the need to evaluate environmental resources accurately and to adjust market prices accordingly.

The whole notion of calculating just how much certain resources are worth, and the extent of any damage that might be done to them, of course, is fraught with difficulty. How can you measure the costs involved when they are controversial, uncertain and in some cases irreversible? How much is a beautiful view worth? What price clean air, or peace and quiet? What is the environmental cost of burying nuclear waste? But however difficult such questions may be to answer, something must be done. This issue is just too important to leave to uneducated guesswork or to the influence of powerful vested interests. Some rational, scientific means of measuring the impact of humankind's activity on the planet is essential if we are to amend the price mechanism, reduce environmental degradation and promote sustainable development.

Two basic techniques can be identified in assigning monetary values to environmental resources. One involves measuring various costs as indirectly recorded through existing market places; the other involves questionnaires asking respondents what values they assign to, or are willing to pay for, specific resources.

Market surveys

Private property has a market value related to the benefits enjoyed from its use. A significant part of the utility derived from any piece of land is directly related to environmental quality. Thus degradation of a certain locality will result in a measurable fall in property values.

Statistical surveys of a large cross-section of diverse properties at any one time can help isolate the change in valuation attributable to specific environmental degradation. Properties, of course, vary in price for a variety of reasons: the size and state of repair of the property itself, closeness to facilities, etc. After taking into account all these variables, however, the impact of, say, noise and air pollution is calculable. Markets can thus place an approximate value on clean air, and on peace and quiet, in given locations therefore.

By the same process, reductions in farming, forestry and fishing yields can be traceable to the impact of pollutants; the social costs of traffic congestion can be measured in terms of the loss of time and thus outputs of city dwellers; injuries and deaths can similarly be costed (note that insurance companies put a price on people's health and life all the time).

There is an important distinction here, however. There is a difference between someone's or something's exchange value and their/its intrinsic worth. In a market society some people/items have a greater exchange value than others – the death or injury of an average managing director represents a greater loss to the market place than that of the average student. (Terrorists know this: they can demand higher ransom demands if they capture top oil company executives – which is why businesses employ bodyguards in Bogota and international bankers do not visit Somalia.)

The notion of intrinsic value is nonetheless important. The fact that the market places a high value on some businessperson but a much lower one on the salmon he is trying to kill or the stream that he may be dirtying is at the heart of the environmental movement's criticism of the market system. Some fanatical 'Greens' have even argued that businesspeople should hunt each other rather than wild geese, deer or fish, since there is nowhere a shortage of the former, whereas the latter cannot defend themselves and are in danger of dying out in some places. This is a rejection of the market values placed on the resources in question. Some natural assets have a higher intrinsic worth than is recognised by the money economy, it is argued. Market survey procedures as outlined above are thus insufficient to capture how far an increasing number of people value the environment. Other techniques are necessary.

Questionnaires

Economics now recognises that the value of a specific resource includes:

- that which is revealed through existing markets by those directly or indirectly involved (e.g. the value of clean rivers to anglers, walkers and research biologists who splash in them);
- the value placed on the asset by those who might one day be involved and who thus wish to retain the option of using it untainted at some time in the future;
- the value placed on a resource by people who never intend to use it directly but appreciate it for its own intrinsic worth, or existence. (You may live in the centre of Africa, the USA or India and never intend to sail the oceans, but you might nonetheless insist that whales have a right to swim in them undisturbed.)

The total economic value (TEV) of a resource therefore equals:

TEV = actual use value + option value + existence value

It is possible to gain empirical estimates of these values by using questionnaires: asking people to record their willingness to pay for environmental conservation and/or their willingness to accept compensation for its loss.

Construction of the relevant questionnaires is inevitably difficult. They contain biases for a number of reasons: respondents may conceal their true preferences (this is the free-rider problem met elsewhere); they may be influenced in their willingness to pay by the surveyor/nature of the questions asked; respondents may be willing to pay more in one form (e.g. taxes) than in others (e.g. entry fees); and they may value gains and losses asymmetrically. That is, people may be prepared to pay more to prevent further degradation than to secure environmental gains. For all these reasons, therefore, studies come up with different evaluations for the same resource, depending on how the questionnaire is designed.

Research in this area is still relatively new but, despite the difficulties involved, this questionnaire technique – the contingent valuation method (CVM) – remains an important and in many cases the only method of estimating important but elusive option and existence values.

Examples of CVM studies reveal interesting valuations. For the Grand Canyon, USA – quoted by Pearce and Turner – existence values were measured as sixty-six times more important than user values. People valued this resource highly for its own intrinsic worth, not because they wanted direct access to it for themselves. (This is undoubtedly because of this resource's uniqueness as a national asset.) In Norway, respondents were asked how much they were prepared to pay to stop acid rain. The study came up with 400 krona per person, or 2.5 billion krona in total. This was broken down into 1 billion user value and 1.5 billion existence value, although the willingness-to-pay technique here is almost certainly an underestimate. This is because most Norwegians view acid rain as a problem of imported pollution (from British and German sources, at least) and thus presumably would argue that other nations apart from themselves should pay to clear it up.

Conclusion

When financial crises occur, recession takes hold, people fear for their jobs and worry about rising prices – and long-term concerns about the health of the planet tend to recede from consciousness.

But recent western experience of living for the moment, and discounting the effect of a growing dislocation between what real value was actually being produced in contrast to the explosion of spending that accompanied it, brought about the biggest shock to the world economy since the 1930s.

A similar dislocation between the pace of exploitation and pollution of natural resources and what the global environment can ultimately sustain has been evident for some years now.

An inability of the rich world to take a long view has led to a 'black swan event' of damaging proportions to many innocent bystanders. Are we condemned to repeat the experience on an even greater scale?

Some would say yes. The author of the text 'The Black Swan' quoted at the head of this chapter, Nassim Nicholas Taleb, has argued that: 'we never learn that we never learn'.

The planet belongs to all of us. There are ethical considerations involved where certain people's consumption and production habits impose excessive costs on others at a different time and place. Yet economic analysis reveals that continued growth in living standards for all people is consistent with environmental sustainability *providing we invest in corrective safeguards and strategies early enough*, sufficient to reduce present and projected future levels of global pollution.

The Stern Review stated that, by 2050, global carbon emissions must be brought down to 'more than 80 per cent below the absolute level of . . . annual emissions' current in 2006. To attain this goal without sacrificing economic growth, McKinsey consultants estimate that this requires a transformation in carbon efficiency between 2008 and 2050 comparable to the change in labour productivity that took 130 years to achieve after the industrial revolution. This is a major challenge – to raise our heads above immediate economic preoccupations and devote our energies to more distant but even greater concerns. This *is* possible – human ingenuity is the one resource the planet is not short of – but free markets that significantly discount the future will not do this unaided.

Global problems require global solutions. The first step is for all nations to agree that there is an environmental crisis in the making that awaits us if we continue with 'business as usual'. Loss of habitat, melting of glaciers, extinction of species, rising levels of pollution are evident to all those who have eyes to see.

Building and sustaining international action to forestall an environmental crunch is now an urgent priority – a clear perspective on global goals and individual national targets to achieve sustainability being the first essential step.

Many countries, organisations and individuals have already started to act, but better coordination is necessary and the sum total of present efforts is small relative to the size of the task referred to above. And the scale of investment required to safeguard our futures raises all the classic problems of a global public good. At every level – countries, public agencies, private companies, households and individuals – each participant has a private incentive to claim they are doing their bit but to conceal their actions and free ride on the efforts of others.

International agreement is needed on targets, on the distribution of responsibilities, on the need for transparency and on the support to be offered to disadvantaged parties. Since energy consumption is increasing rapidly in some fast-growing countries (see Figure 12.3) and significant replacement of capital stock is imminent in other, more mature nations, then the investments made in the next decade or two could lock the world into a disastrous high-emissions pathway . . . or alternatively provide the opportunity to make major progress towards a sustainable future.

Reaching an equitable distribution of environmental policies across different nations will not be easy. Stern argues that 'there is no single formula that captures all dimensions of equity, but calculations based on income, historic responsibility and per capita emissions' all point to the richer countries taking up more of the global bill for action. He states that creating a broadly similar carbon price signal around the world is an urgent priority which would inform taxation policies, trading schemes and direct action to push markets in the right direction. With regard to the last, international coordination of regulations and product standards, reduction of trade barriers on low-carbon goods and services, agreement on curbing deforestation, preserving diminishing stocks and creating more carbon sinks, are all forms of very cost-effective direct action to reduce emissions.

Resource-rich but income-poor nations in Africa and elsewhere have immediate development needs, high discount rates and thus the most incentive to plunder their natural endowments. They have contributed little to the historic build-up of planetary pollution, but are likely to be hit hardest and earliest by climate change and the associated increased frequency of natural disasters. The international community thus has an obligation to wean them off further environmental degradation and to finance their adaption to a more sustainable path to progress. Bluntly, if we in other parts of the world value Amazonian and African rainforests, then we have to pay those that live there to look after them.

If the rich world is not able to set the example, reduce its own rate of planetary plunder and carry the cost of changing its ways, then there is little chance that others less able to afford it will do so. Malthus's predictions of population growth in 1798 were eventually proved wrong. Planet Earth has supported a much greater increase in our numbers at a higher standard of living than he thought possible. But whether the planet can continue to sustain our continuing economic growth and exploitation of the environment depends on whether or not we can continue to adjust and adapt the market economic system we have devised to provide for us.

Whatever the eventual mechanisms, a political way forward should be found to confront the economics of the environment. For what is certain is that, if we do not pay the full price of plundering our natural inheritance today, then our inheritors will bear the brunt of these costs in their future.

Key words

Free goods Those goods provided to us that involve no economic sacrifice in their production and consumption – sunlight, the air we breathe, a sparkling mountain stream. Free goods have no market price; in contrast, economic goods and services are all those that are the product of scarce resources and, even if they are subsidised or given away free, they are costly to supply.

Intergenerational equity Exhaustible resources can be used today or in the future: by ourselves or by our children. If we choose to consume them now we raise our standard of living, which our children will benefit from, but they will be denied future supplies of natural capital. Conversely, if we choose not to consume known supplies of exhaustible resources today there will be undoubtedly more available for future generations, although they will not inherit such a high standard

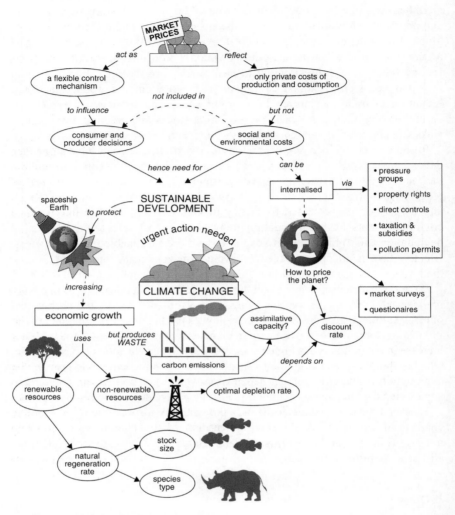

Figure 12.5 The themes of Chapter 12.

of material wealth. The issue of whether to have jam today or jam tomorrow thus depends on how we value present versus future costs and benefits, and how we wish to spread them between ourselves and our heirs. An equitable decision distributes the costs and benefits 'fairly' between the generations.

Natural regeneration rate The rate at which a renewable resource regenerates itself in its undisturbed state. This will depend on the size of the resource in question in relation to its environment: a given animal population, for example, will have a critical minimal size – below which its reproduction rate falls lower than its death rate and thus it will eventually die out – and at the opposite extreme a maximum carrying capacity where (typically) food supplies cease to be sufficient and thus death rates again rise above birth rates and the stock size falls again.

Sustainable development Easy enough to define in general terms – 'meeting the needs of the present without compromising future generations' – but very difficult in practice to measure. People's valuation of specific environmental assets is inevitably subjective, and may vary from one day to the next as tastes change. And whose tastes are we talking about? Next problem: if valuing the environment today is difficult enough, how about attempting to value the future? The choice of a suitable discount rate to put a figure on future, as opposed to present-day, environmental assets is even more controversial, as the text above discusses. No one said economics was easy. In the end, the solution adopted is to be as objective, transparent and rigorous as possible in our calculations, make explicit all assumptions and areas of difficulty involved, and outline the conclusions, and policy choices involved, that flow from the analysis.

Questions

1 Why have past predictions of resource depletion been badly mistaken? Is the *Stern Review* any different? Why or why not?
2 How can discount rates be used to determine the rate of exploitation of non-renewable resources? What are the economic implications of too high a discount rate; too low a discount rate?
3 How might awarding property rights be used to protect excessive harvesting of (a) North Atlantic fish stocks; (b) African tropical rainforest?
4 There are many measures that might be introduced to reduce the world's carbon emissions and they differ according to which country is concerned. Explain. Which measures would be most cost-effective and easiest to introduce in *your* country?
5 How would you measure the value of clean air in the town where you live? Is it worth preserving? At what price?

Further reading

Field, B. C. and Field, M. *Environmental Economics: An Introduction*, 5th edn, New York: McGraw Hill, 2009.

Pearce, D. W. and Turner, R. K. *Economics of Natural Resources and the Environment*, Hemel Hempstead: Harvester Wheatsheaf, 1990.

Stern, N. *The Economics of Climate Change: The Stern Review*, Cambridge University Press, 2007.

13 Conclusion

What future awaits us in the twenty-first century and beyond?

'The time has come,' the Walrus said, 'To talk of many things: of shoes, and ships, and sealing-wax; of cabbages, and kings . . .'

Lewis Carroll, from *Alice's Adventures in Wonderland.*

Having endured an unexpectedly tumultuous entry into the new millennium, perhaps it might be wise to look forward a little more carefully to what might await the world economy around the next corner of its evolution. What have we learnt, if anything, from the experiences surveyed in the foregoing, and which themes touched upon might offer insight to what may lie ahead?

Trade joins all our destinies and not in ways we always expect. The global financial crisis which started unravelling in 2007 still has a long way to go before its impact is overshadowed by other events. Sovereign, corporate and individual debts will constrain the economic activity of those affected for many years. The emphasis is now on cutting back spending, putting financial affairs in order and trying to repair reputations. The principle should be to devote more resources to productive, rather than speculative, enterprise . . . but when aggregate demand and business confidence are low in a recession, it is difficult for the private sector to identify both where future investment is to be devoted and from where capital is to be raised. Theoretically speaking, when the private sector stalls, Keynesian economics dictates that the public sector must step forward and take up the slack – but having exhausted public funds and run up sovereign debts there is no further stimulus that is possible from this source. As a result, the engines that powered the Great Moderation – North American and European spending – have run out of fuel.

Some have predicted that the axis of the world economy must shift east. Certainly, if present trends continue, the Asian consumer market will be twice the size of that in the USA by the year 2020. However, so long as China, India, Japan and oil producers amongst others rely on exporting to the USA and Europe as a means of making money, they will be disappointed. Present trends *cannot* continue. As just mentioned, the West must move to increase its savings, decrease its spending and reduce its debts over the next decade. If the largest engines in the world economy are misfiring, Asia must learn to increase its own consumer spending, invest in its own infrastructure and compensate for the fall in western markets if global recession is to be curtailed. But restructuring and re-engineering the world economy will take time. Slack global demand is likely for the foreseeable future, therefore, and several crises may yet develop to impede a smooth increase of economic power and influence among the emerging nations.

The next crash

Do not underestimate the ability of large, interconnected and 'superspreading' financial corporations and their profit-seeking operatives to drive us into yet another financial crisis. Bankers who are accustomed to making a great deal of money will not be well disposed to making less. They will use their economic and political influence to reduce any attempt to break them up or seriously harness their power. In the foreseeable future, in their own interests, they will increase their capital to loans ratios and play along with world political concerns to 'reform' international finance, but ten and twenty years from now the same large, money-making institutions will still be there and still innovating, expanding credit and taking risks. Next time will be no different.

The IMF, the G20 and the Financial Stability Board should work together to insist on international financial standards: to restrict the overexpansion of short-term credit, to curtail off-balance-sheet deals and to establish a transparent early-warning system of where hot money is flowing and the risks accumulating. Will it happen? Probably not, if we continue not to learn that we do not learn. As the western world struggles with recession, then just as before in the 1980s, the focus of international finance will turn towards the more dynamic emerging nations. Brazil, Russia, India and China (the BRIC nations) emerged relatively unscathed from the last financial crash. We can predict that increasing funds, innovative deals and new forms of creating paper that we haven't heard of yet will revolve around these markets and, especially if their opaque political structures obstruct transparency and confuse responsibilities, risks will be taken, things will go wrong and debts will default. An emerging markets financial crisis is in the making.

Inequities bite

The global liberalisation of markets, and the booming growth this has brought to some, has simultaneously led to widening inequalities in a number of different dimensions.

Firstly, just as average income per head in the BRIC nations has increased and closed the gap somewhat between them and with the developed world, so *within* each developed and developing country the gap has recently widened between winners and losers. In China, for example, although on many economic indicators – average incomes, rates of growth, participation in education, life expectancy, etc. – the data show steady improvement, the picture beyond averages is less complimentary. The World Bank reports that since 1988, inequalities have widened faster there than in any other country, and its present Gini coefficient

(41.5) is now higher than that of the UK (36) and the USA (41). Chinese wealth is concentrated in its coastal enterprise zones, yet incomes in its vast agricultural hinterland, where 40 per cent of the population are still employed in farming, have been left behind. China had 271 dollar billionaires in 2011, up from 189 in 2010 – yet if its *average* income per head is only US$3,000, clearly there are many at the other extreme of the spectrum.

Inequalities meanwhile persist in nations irrespective of their ability, or not, to achieve rapid economic growth. Terrorism is typically a reaction to political grievance of one form or another, but the persistence of unemployment, regional differences and simmering discontent at an inequitable distribution of economic power and influence makes for a fertile recruiting ground for disaffected parties who opt for a violent means to achieve social and economic change. In Western Europe, the Middle East, the poorer nations of Asia, Africa and America, the experience of social exclusion allied with unemployment has fostered terrorist activity which only serves to exacerbate social break-up and impede political and economic progress.

Unemployment is thus socially destructive as well as economically wasteful. One of the impacts of Asian economic growth has been on the global demand for comparatively low-skilled manufacturing labour – booming in China and India, slumping elsewhere. The excessive growth of earnings in finance in the UK and the USA is contrasted with no or slow growth in the incomes of blue-collar workers in these countries as world demand shifts away from higher-cost manufacturers. Unemployment rose with the Great Recession and concerns have since increased about a jobless recovery – it will take some time for the West to exploit its comparative advantage and engage *all* its labour force in higher skill employments. In the meantime, a growing concentration of power amongst economic, financial and political elites has sparked an equally growing disquiet amongst those left behind by shifting global forces. Protests like 'Occupy Wall Street', the London riots and Chilean student demonstrations are spontaneous expressions of the unacceptability of increasing inequality.

Such outcries are well publicised and relatively easy to express on the streets of democracies. But popular discontent is now difficult to contain and censor in our digitally connected age, so we can predict that if inequalities continue to increase, then even the most secretive and repressive regimes must ultimately take account of them. The 'Arab Spring' – a dictator-toppling revolt inspired by the self-immolation of a desperate individual denied work and the political expression of his despair – may yet spread beyond North Africa and the Middle East. (Chinese authority efforts to manipulate the internet have intensified as a result.)

As demonstrated in earlier chapters, market systems are successful because they are flexible – but this also means they are volatile, they overreact, are liable to boom and bust, and inevitably reward those resources that move fastest. Without regulation, this can lead to a 'winner takes all' result. And winners are hardly likely to want to change this system. However, Nouriel Roubini, US economist and one of the few to foresee the 2008 crash, has since gone public with another warning to western market economies: 'Any economic model that doesn't properly address inequality will eventually face a crisis of legitimacy, as today's global protests are now demonstrating. Unless the relative economic roles of the market and the state are rebalanced, the protests of 2011 will become more severe, eventually harming long-term economic growth and welfare' (*Economy Watch*, 19 October 2011).

Where is Europe heading?

The sovereign debt crisis in Europe has exposed a number of serious fault lines in the European Union. Economists warned well before the establishment of the euro that the member countries involved did not form an optimum currency area, but European leaders smothered all criticism, the risks involved were never seriously made public and electorates were led blind into an uncertain future.

The fact is that Europe is a collection of nation-states with hundreds (in some cases, thousands) of years of independent evolution leading to very different cultures, languages, polities and norms of conduct. Germany's history has turned it away from military to economic expansion, and it has now built an economy that is dependent on export sales. Its incomes have risen as a result, but within a fixed exchange rate system and now a common currency, such an emphasis on exports can only succeed if others endure trade deficits and a loss of income as a result. Germany must open its markets to its neighbours and increase its imports: mercantilism is not a sustainable economic strategy within Europe.

Democracy – rule by the people – is a word with Greek roots. So is the word 'economy'. Greek civilisation underpins the European ideal, but Greece's modern economy has been forced into a severe contraction by the leaders of the EU who are insisting it cuts its public spending and repays the debts it owes. Whatever mistakes were made and by whom in running up enormous sovereign debts, the reality now is that, so long as the Greek economy is being forced by outsiders into negative growth, the country's debt-to-income ratio is unlikely to fall. People on the streets of Athens and elsewhere across the country are protesting, but in Brussels and Berlin they are not listening. The European Commission and the European Central Bank, in negotiation with euro finance ministers and with the support of the IMF, have regularly brokered deals to release funds to the Greek government so that it can pay off the next round of debts that fall due, but this is always subject to stringent conditions for cutbacks and does nothing to foment longer-term growth. How long must the torment of rising unemployment (20 per cent) and falling incomes (–7 per cent in 2011) continue? The reality is that democracy is dead in Greece. They are no longer in control of their own economic policies: they are being told what to do by European leaders behind closed doors who are fearful of the consequences of letting Greeks off the debt hook.

The ultimate objective of creating a more flexible market economy throughout Europe is the only way for a common currency to survive. But the eurozone is currently made up of economies pulling in different directions with insufficient mobility of capital and labour, no common market for services, no facility for fiscal transfers and a central bank that cannot act as a lender of last resort to governments. The objective of reducing state handouts, restructuring industry and increasing competition and productivity – this has an economic rationale. But this cannot be achieved in the short term. Europe is composed of different sovereign states. There is no acceptance that common sacrifices must be made, that winners must help losers to overcome a common crisis. How far can people in the south of the continent accept contractionary policies framed by northerners whom they have not elected, who are unmoved by their suffering and who are unwilling to generate any expansion in aggregate demand?

Europe is tied down with a currency straitjacket that doesn't fit and aloof physicians who can only recommend shock treatment. There is a real danger that the patient's reactions will become increasingly violent.

Environmental limits

If one continent is struggling to cope with unsustainable policies and practices, how about the whole world? The present rate of environmental degradation cannot continue into the long term without the planet exacting retribution. Despite the original *Limits to Growth* projection that warned we are running out of vital resources, there are sufficient oil, coal and other fossil fuels to power the industrial growth of all nations desperate to raise their incomes for the next half-century or more – but unless less-polluting practices of harnessing energy are employed, the climate change this provokes will put a brake on all our endeavours.

Human ingenuity in plundering the planet is unlimited, but our communal vision is short-sighted. All sorts of innovative means to drill deeper, build higher, travel faster and burn more can be expected. The waste this generates will spread wider and reach out further through the atmosphere and into outer space (increasing amounts of junk will orbit the Earth). Those fixated on increasing material wealth today heavily discount the future costs this incurs. Unless prices are adjusted to include all private, social and environmental costs, and thus the rate of time preference takes into account the cost of planetary warming, market liberalisation that has widened inequalities between people of the same country today will widen inequalities between generations over time.

Global warming has raised average temperatures by just less than 1°C to date since the pre-industrial era, a rate of growth that has accelerated over the period. The level of greenhouse gases in the atmosphere was 280 parts per million (ppm) of CO_2 equivalent (CO_2e) before the industrial revolution; in 2006 it was 430 ppm CO_2e, and it is projected to pass 550ppm by 2050 (that target might even be reached by 2035) if we continue with 'business as usual'. This would secure a rise in average temperatures of probably 2°C and possibly well above that by the next century.

Stoke the fires now and it takes time for our planet to warm. That is part of the problem: since we cannot see the immediate effect of our actions there is little incentive to change. But once put out into the atmosphere, the impact of carbon emissions is to start slowly warming our environment and it cannot be stopped.

Warming of 2°C could lead to 15–40 per cent species extinction; 3–4°C will seriously impede global food production, lead to millions being displaced by rising sea levels, and provoke droughts and famines in some areas, tempests, landslides and flooding in others. Stern reports that unless preventative action is taken, 'the stock of greenhouse gases could more than treble by the end of the century, giving at least a 50 per cent risk of exceeding 5°C global average temperature change during the following decades. This would take humans into unknown territory. An illustration of the scale of such an increase is that we are now 5°C warmer than in the last ice age.'

Some critics have argued that such doomsday scenarios are overdoing it. Maybe: we have seen that before. But even so, the costs of adjustments that need to be taken by us to change our ways and obviate such future scenarios rise over time the longer we delay: serious and irreversible impacts significantly increase as greenhouse gas concentrations accumulate.

So present processes and rates of economic growth cannot continue unchallenged. Natural disasters are nature's way of telling us to slow down and find more harmonious ways for humankind to live on the planet. Our life-support system is flashing danger signs.

The role of government and political leadership

The political and economic philosophy that has driven us to where we are today has been that of the supremacy of markets and of the need to reduce government intervention, spending, taxation and ownership, and to liberate private enterprise. That can be understood as a necessary corrective to repressive command regimes that dominated much of Asia and Eastern Europe in the twentieth century and to sclerotic, mature market systems that were unable to react to oil price shocks and a rapidly changing geographical distribution of economic influence. But that is all history and the challenges today have changed. The danger is now in going too far in reducing the role of government, in failing to accept sufficient responsibility for countering recession, for reducing inequalities, for rectifying market failure, for protecting our environment and all our futures.

In the absence of global government, but in the face of global challenges that no one nation can address on its own, the world economy needs political leadership at an international level to agree on the way forward. Having thrown off the yoke of central planning and excessive controls, having enjoyed the rewards of freeing up private enterprise, former communist and emerging nations are hardly likely to agree to rein back their dynamic growth. There is no denying the power of self-interest in fuelling the free market engine, but equally there is no excuse for our elected (or appointed) pilots to abdicate responsibility for where this motor is projecting spaceship Earth.

There is much that governments can, and must, do. If private markets display high discount rates and blinkered vision, then no one else other than public servants can moderate recurring cyclical instability and promote the long-run development of human resources, conservation strategies and community support.

All the undoubted, and accelerating, scientific progress achieved over the past hundred years, and the sophisticated technological wizardry which this has brought us, only serves to emphasise how limited is humankind's understanding of our own nature. 'Animal spirits' still seem to drive us from boom into bust. Human memories remain as short as ever, and our ability to hang together as a community – to make individual sacrifice for the common good – seems more elusive now than ever before. There is therefore no evidence to suggest that world markets can escape periodic cycles of growth and recession in incomes and employment, or plan for the long term, unless forced to confront such failures.

Unemployed people on their own are limited in their ability to move with the market. They cannot acquire new skills without help, and there will be few private businesses that will take on this long-term investment since they cannot guarantee the workers so trained will stay with them long enough to pay back a market rate of return. Additionally, highly productive human resources are far more complicated and costly to identify and develop than undersea oil reserves. How do you spot a potential genius amongst the children of Calcutta's teeming millions or in the unemployed of Moscow? Yet we all benefit if our neighbours are educated. This must remain a responsibility of public authority since no profit-maximiser will undertake it.

The private market imposes no prohibitive costs on chopping down trees to provide wood fuel, on dumping toxic wastes in the seas or on the killing of rhinoceros to smuggle out their profitable horns. The fallacy of composition ensures, however, that our spaceship will become impoverished – if not poisoned – unless we are persuaded to change our individually destructive habits. It would be monumentally myopic of the dominant species on this transport between the stars if we greedily exhausted all our supplies in the mere minute or two of the geological timescale we have been aboard.

By exactly the same argument, lack of awareness or concern about what we are doing to *human* environments can even more quickly bring about cumulative and irreversible decline. I refer here not so much to obvious communal insanities like drug wars, arms races and nuclear sabre-rattling which are fed by unscrupulous sellers of cocaine and military hardware, but to the far subtler, free market necessity for mobile labour that rewards private interest but places a negligible, if not negative, return earned on constructing family and community stability.

Stability is important in all human affairs. Humans are social animals and economic philosophies must recognise this. For example, the development of human relationships in business can bring long-term profit. The decision whether to cut one's losses and sell out in a failing business project, or to put more money, time and effort into turning it around, is extremely difficult, but building up trust between management and workforces and promoting goodwill with customers has proved to be a sound investment, particularly when the external economic environment turns nasty. This is particularly true of businesses engaged producing in higher-quality goods and services. Wherever private rates of return fail to recognise this, however, and buying and selling paper attracts more profit, then the market will opt to maximise short-term gain by selling out, liquidating capital and moving resources elsewhere.

Given the private losses endured since the 2008 crash, there is just a chance that the potential rewards of promoting trust and goodwill in business relationships will eventually cause management in both manufacturing and financial enterprises to raise their noses above the immediate short-term and take aboard this idea, but, if not, political leaders must put into place taxes and regulations to inhibit get-rich-quick financial speculation.

If private business takes little heed of developing long-term relationships, then an equal and even more pressing question is: where is the private profit in promoting stable family life, deepening friendships and supportive communities? The emphasis on individual mobility and reward leads indirectly to the fracturing of social ties, and with it increasing social costs such as a growing sense of isolation, inequality and disaffection; rising stress, heart disease and mental illness; more crime and terrorism; increasing divorces; neglect of the weak, unfortunate and elderly. There are enormous external benefits to be earned in societies that are stable and healthy, but the hand of government is necessary to guide markets to this end. Public programmes are needed to cope with the problems of social breakdown and growing disaffection, and to identify policies to avoid them.

Finally, it is the greatest injustice that we carry on into the new millennium with passengers on our starship that experience vastly different standards of living. Those in the first-class cabins enjoy a society that promotes growth and development, and seem to be totally unaware of the deprivation that exists for three-quarters of the passengers locked away down below. Simple rules of conduct separate the two communities. In the rich world, people have evolved sophisticated rules that reinforce property rights and commitment to contracts – such that consumers can pick up a phone or computer, order what they want and pay for it all in the safe knowledge that their transaction will be honoured. But in the poor world you can't trust anyone outside your immediate friends and family. How can the market place expand and the specialisation of skills and technologies develop if there is no central authority that can be trusted to uphold the law and insist that promises must be kept?

The conventional wisdom that government is the enemy of the market is a false dichotomy. Markets assume underlying social and power relationships as given and so, with free rein, they may do little to help the disadvantaged. Protestors outside Wall Street have spoken for many inside and outside their country. Liberating the supply-side resources of a country requires microeconomic intervention to dismantle barriers, provide equal opportunities, promote competitive enterprise, penalise those who would subvert trade and protect those (including the environment) who have little consumer influence. Markets *need* government.

We can no longer continue living in an *Alice in Wonderland* world, enjoying individual liberty, discounting the future or hoping that some magic potion will miraculously put things right. A new political economy is required which is devoted to examining the relationship between individuals, markets and the state and to intervening where necessary to remove rigidities and to empower all to participate to the fullest. It should be operative at three levels: supra-nationally, nationally and locally.

International debt crises are a product of an unregulated world market system. Supra-national guidance is required to push creditor nations to open up their markets, to limit financial malpractice and to lead those in debt out of a spiral of decline.

The major trading nations should be entreated to follow economic policies that, collectively, do not lead to overexpansionary growth or to beggar-my-neighbour mercantilism. There is always the tendency for the powerful to bully the weak. If the European dream is to mean anything, *all* Europeans need to contribute to it; if the world economy is to grow sustainably, then developing countries need trading rules and institutions that do not discriminate against them.

Similarly the environmental impact on the planet of localised consumption and production decisions – such as to cut down forests, or to pump out toxic exhaust gases – not to mention the global reach of multinational corporations and certain politically ambitious governments, requires a world forum for discussion, regulation and enforcement.

Wherever the single nation-state is too small to tackle problems on its own, international agencies such as the G20, the Financial Stability Board, the IMF and the World Trade Organization need to be strengthened and constitutionally charged to take the long view and safeguard world interests.

At a national level, the policing of competition, privatisation schemes, land reforms and the restructuring of taxes are necessary to engage all in the ownership and control of resources. A commitment to reduce unemployment and inflation requires analysis of their respective causes, plus demand- and supply-side intervention where appropriate.

Some nations have made a notable success of the strategic direction of their economies. This requires, however, a social structure that recognises the importance of state/industry partnerships, open government, rule-abiding businesspeople and civil servants, and a general willingness of all to contribute to the proper functioning of the market place.

The effective operation of essential public services such as the police, health, education and the caring professions is best managed at local levels where providers are in direct contact with their customers. Supply-side investment in human capital operates at this level. Identifying education and training needs, providing job information, promotion of native enterprise, all start with the individual – so too does the analysis of community and family dynamics, offering counselling services and recommending action to stabilise relationships, reduce exclusion, enrich lives and deepen human resources.

More than two hundred years ago Adam Smith wrote approvingly of the social benefits of the free market system where, by an 'invisible hand', self-interested agents brought about the greater good for all. This was in a tightly homogenous culture where all shared the same value system and the state operated effectively to protect individual rights. In a fast-changing, chronically uncertain world, where our economic and technological power to create or destroy embraces vastly disparate peoples, and indeed the entire planet, it must be concluded that some rather more visible hands would be very welcome to guide the wealth of nations throughout the twenty-first century and beyond.

Notes

2 Market failure and the great debate

1 Alan Greenspan, chairman of the US Federal Reserve until 2006, confessed to being in a state of shocked disbelief at the global financial crisis and 'very distressed' at his mistaken belief that the private sector was best capable of protecting its own interests (*Newsdesk*, 24 October 2008).

3 Unemployment and inflation

1 In the year 2000, the then UK Chancellor of the Exchequer, Gordon Brown, famously promised 'no return to boom and bust' on his watch. So during the good times he increased government spending on health and education services and ran an increasing budget deficit. This left him with little alternative but to eat his words and to widen the deficit when he subsequently became prime minister and was surprised by the biggest economic bust in his lifetime. (To his credit, he moved faster than any other world leader to put into effect monetary and fiscal policies to limit the slump.)

9 Financial crises, sovereign debt and future reform

1 When I asked my final honours class of economics students at a top UK university which career they were intending to follow, the great majority wished to apply to the City. *None* wanted to enter manufacturing.

10 Economic development, growth and inequality

1 GNP and GDP are both measures of national income, but GNP differs from GDP in that the latter does not include a country's net income from abroad (a significant difference for relatively small countries which have a high proportion of investments overseas, or have large foreign debt-service payments).

11 The economics of terrorism

1 This passage relies heavily on E. Berman and D. Laitin, 'Religion, terrorism and public goods: testing the club model', *NBER Working Paper 13725* (January 2008).

Index